ROOTS OF WESTERN CIVILIZATION

FROM ANCIENT TIMES TO 1715

ROOTS OF WESTERN CIVILIZATION

VOLUME I

FROM ANCIENT TIMES TO 1715

Edited by

WESLEY D. CAMP

Adelphi University

Translations, unless otherwise indicated, are by the editor.

McGraw-Hill, Inc.

New York St. Louis San Francisco Auckland Bogotá
Caracas Lisbon London Madrid Mexico City Milan
Montreal New Delhi San Juan Singapore
Sydney Tokyo Toronto

ROOTS OF WESTERN CIVILIZATION
VOLUME I: FROM ANCIENT TIMES TO 1715

First Edition

Library of Congress Cataloging in Publication Data:

Main entry under title:

Roots of Western civilization.

Bibliography: p.
Includes index.
Contents: v. 1. From ancient times to 1715—v. 2. From the Enlightenment to the 1980's
1. Civilization, Occidental—History—Sources.
1. Camp, Wesley Douglass, 1915—
CB245.R63 1983 909'.09821 82-13576
ISBN 0-07-554669-8
ISBN 0-07-554670-1

Printed in the United States of America

11 12 13 14 15 MAL MAL 0 9 8 7 6 5 4 3

for Matthew Douglass

PREFACE

Man has no nature; what he has is history.

—*Ortega y Gasset*

Historical sources provide entree into the past that only a visit to places like Athens or Rome might rival. Students learn to discover and explore history as a foreign country. The raw materials of the past—rather than being simple, neat, and orderly, like a textbook—are rarely above dispute and always subject to interpretation. Whereas the smooth flow of a narrative may give the impression that history is somehow predetermined, the documents themselves offer students the kind of situation confronting an archaeologist at a dig, filled with bits and pieces of the past that seldom fit together. Once students begin to see how history is "made"—out of whole cloth, so to speak—they may come to question not only the textbook but even the polished lectures of the instructor. *Caveat magister!* Gertrude Stein, asked for her solution to the "German problem" after World War II, recommended that children speak back to their parents and contradict their teachers at least once a day.

To do so with authority, however, the child would need reliable sources, and, as the Renaissance humanist Lorenzo Valla demonstrated, even the best of them are not above suspicion. But they do provide a basis for rational argument and criticism, which are central activities in the intellectual process. Also, the student who learns to see history as a series of problems to be explored may find that many of today's controversial questions can be illuminated by similar issues from the past. Such a student will be well on the way to becoming a mature and useful citizen.

"History, to be above dispute or evasion," said Lord Acton, "must stand on documents, not on opinion." Novice historians should learn this lesson early on. If they read Hammurabi's code, the Epic of Gilgamesh, and the book of Genesis all in the first week of class, they may change their minds about the meaning of "history."

Some students may be impressed with the literary quality of many of the sources: for example, Erasmus's "Julius II Excluded from Heaven" or Mary Wollstonecraft's "Rights of Woman." Or the conflict between Antigone and Creon in Sophocles' play, giving an immediacy to Greek civilization that few modern sources can convey. Once students find that history involves issues and ideas as well as names and dates, when they discover that even its heroes make mistakes, then their enthusiasm is sufficient reward for the teacher.

We in the History Department of Adelphi University have long followed the above philosophy in teaching the "Introduction to Western Civilization" course. But when we found various source books inadequate for one reason or another, I offered to compile a new anthology following certain principles now incorporated in the present work:

¶ Organize documents and sources by themes into chapters corresponding to standard textbook divisions.

¶ Keep excerpts as short as feasible, in order to focus on central issues and hold the student's interest.

¶ Where possible, choose the more familiar source over the less familiar, capitalizing on the student's shock of recognition: for example, the Bible, Aristotle, Galileo, Marx, Freud, Hitler.

¶ Make each chapter short enough to be covered in one assignment.

¶ Offer as wide a range of viewpoints as possible; the 250-odd documents in these volumes also provide some latitude of choice on the part of instructors and students.

¶ Write brief, provocative headnotes and introductions in order to arouse the student's curiosity while at the same time providing the necessary background information.

¶ Choose documents covering a broad spectrum of cultural phenomena: religion, art, literature, science, philosophy, mythology, as well as records of social, political, and economic life.

¶ Select a diversity of sources: monuments, chronicles, and biographies; satires, poems, and plays; letters, diaries, and speeches; essays and tracts, laws and decrees, architecture and sculpture, painting and photography.

¶ Carefully edit all sources, using ellipses and brackets [. . .] to eliminate extraneous material, for example, unkeyed names, parenthetical remarks.

¶ Revise or retranslate inadequate versions; the editor doubles as professional translator. For translations from the Russian, I thank my colleague Professor Devlin, who also compiled and edited the chapter "Lenin and the Russian Revolution."

Similarly, I thank my other colleagues in the Adelphi History Department who graciously adopted these readings in preliminary form for use in their classes and gave me the benefit of their own and their students' criticisms. I am also deeply indebted to Professor Frank L. Kidner of San Francisco State University and to Professor Howard R. Holtzer of California State University, Dominguez Hills, both of whom read an earlier version of this anthology and made many excellent criticisms and suggestions, from which I have greatly profited. The errors and shortcomings that remain are, of course, entirely my own.

Wesley D. Camp
Garden City, New York

NOTE TO THE TEACHER

Our experience in the use of sources has convinced us that, rather than their being merely "supplemental," they can be an integral or central feature of the course. First, however, it is necessary to insure that students *read* the sources, so we require them to submit brief "reaction papers"—one or two pages—before any topic is discussed. Volunteers are then asked to tell the class frankly what they thought of the various documents—what they liked, disliked, understood, or did not understand; also what they discovered that was not in the textbook or was at variance with it. Since not all students have the same reactions, arguments and discussions often ensue, leaving the instructor little to do except to act as moderator and make the final summation.

Later, the papers are read by the instructor or the graduate assistant or, preferably, both. Except for a check mark (✓) to indicate "assignment completed," papers are not usually graded, although some instructors may wish to reward brevity-cum-insight with *two* checks. Overly ambitious students should be informed that lengthy papers gain nothing, since only the first two pages will be read, in any case.

For the instructor, reaction papers often provide valuable feedback, indicating where students may have missed the point or become confused. For the students, there are several advantages: In addition to their improved "stage presence" from giving reactions in class, the mere act of writing a paper a week helps to improve their English composition, even when grades are not assigned. Some teachers provide guidance in the form of marginal notations, for example, "Verbiage?" "Logic?" or even, "What is your source here?"

Students also report that their reading speed and comprehension increase as they learn to look for ideas to record in their reaction papers, rather than getting bogged down in details. Some students, of course, may need to be warned that mere summaries are not acceptable.

Finally, when students once discover that historical documents are not sacred but may be evaluated and criticized like any other, they are well along toward proving Carl Becker's dictum: Every person his, or her, own historian.

W.D.C.

NOTE TO THE STUDENT

You are about to discover History! Like Columbus, who thought he was bound for India, you too may discover a whole new world. By the time you have finished reading the documents in this book, you should have acquired a new discipline as well. Does the word "discipline" scare you? It shouldn't. Almost everything we do, except sleep, involves some kind of control, coordination, and concentration: for example, sports. And thinking may also be a sport; it requires training, practice, coaching, and testing under pressure. One way to begin real thinking is to ask some hard questions: How do I know what I know? What evidence do I have for my opinions? Are my sources reliable? How may I test them? Many questions are similar to those a good lawyer would use in the courtroom: Is this witness reliable? Does the witness have a bias? Does other evidence rebut this witness's testimony?

Why should you read *original* sources? Why isn't the textbook enough? Some of the advantages of a textbook, in fact, supply arguments for the reading of source documents. Textbooks are usually well written, noncontroversial, factual, and biased—biased, that is, in favor of our own contemporary, Western culture whose values we always have to question, as John Stuart Mill says, in order to keep from holding them as mere prejudices. When we read history directly from the sources, without a textbook or a historian to smooth out the rough spots, we discover some new insights into human behavior, such as the Crusaders' killing 10,000 men, women, and children in Solomon's Temple after the fall of Jerusalem in 1099; or Susan B. Anthony's crusade for women's rights supported by such men as J. S. Mill and J. B. Shaw.

But probably the chief advantage of reading original sources is for the better understanding and interpretation of the past—how its story is written and how it relates to life in the present. Historians themselves have to work from documents like these and also, of course, from such physical remains as monuments, buildings, art, and artifacts.

Not all documents are easy to read, but some can be very exciting. For instance, when you read Socrates's own defense at his trial, you will get a heightened sense not only of an original folk hero but also of the life of Athens four centuries before the birth of Christ. Or when you read Cellini's story of his difficulties in creating a masterpiece, you will understand more about the meaning of art and the function of the artist. Finally, when you study the documents in English history from the king's charters to the Bill of Rights, you will see how far "we" had come before Washington and Jefferson were born.

W.D.C.

CONTENTS

CHAPTER 1

THE ANCIENT NEAR EAST: GOD, MORALITY, LAW

From Europe, the roots of Western Civilization extend south and east hundreds of miles into the region known as the Ancient Near East or, today, the Middle East. Three or four millenia before the birth of Christ, many tribes of nomadic peoples changed their old ways of life and settled down in the great river valleys of the Tigris, the Euphrates, and the Nile. There, instead of following herds of livestock, as in the past, they learned (or invented) agriculture. And they produced so much food that they created a surplus, which increased their total population and enabled many of their people to devote themselves to nonagricultural functions such as art, religion, and politics.

In the short space of a thousand years they invented written languages, complicated systems of government, art forms that are as vibrant as any that came later, and legal procedures and codes that are still followed in some parts of the world today. A dozen major civilizations rose and fell in the twenty-one centuries between the age of the pyramids in Egypt and the Classical Age of Athens (2600 to 500 B.C.). All of these civilizations contributed something to the greatness of Greece and the glory of Rome, though it would be well-nigh impossible to untangle the threads of these relationships.

Since we cannot deal with all the civilizations of the Ancient Near East, we have chosen documents from four—Egyptian, Sumerian, Babylonian, and Hebrew—as being particularly important, as well as interesting and exciting in their own right. Which of these documents impresses you as being the most humanitarian? Is ethnocentrism equally apparent in all four cultures? What do you learn about the daily lives of the people from each document?

Egyptian royal vizier *supervising the shipment of cattle on the Nile. Models found in the tomb (c. 2000 B.C.) of Mekitre, a nobleman of the Middle Kingdom. Brian Brake/Photo Researchers Inc.)*

EGYPT: INSTRUCTIONS OF THE VIZIER PTAH-HOTEP TO HIS SON

A. Erman, *Die Literatur der Aegypter* (Leipzig, 1923), pp. 86–99.

Egypt achieved political stability as early as the fourth millenium B.C. The environment of a steady climate and the remarkable regularity of the Nile helped to produce a society characterized by permanence, self-confidence, and optimism. Its authoritarian governments needed an army of civil servants and bureaucrats, most of whom were guided in their careers by detailed instructions such as the following. Such lists would be comparable to today's "How to succeed in business." This particular one was found in a papyrus dating from about 2400 B.C.

Do not be puffed up because of your knowledge nor overconfident because you are a learned person. Take counsel with the ignorant as well as with the wise, for the limits of proficiency cannot be reached and no person is ever fully skilled. Good speech is rarer than the emerald, yet it may be found among maidservants at the grindstones. . . .

If you are a leader commanding the multitude, strive to do every good thing, until there is no fault in your nature. Justice is great and its worth is lasting. It has been undisturbed since the time of him who made it, whereas he that neglects its laws is punished. It lies as the right path before him who knows nothing. Wrongdoing has never brought its venture to port. Evil may indeed gain wealth, but the power of justice is that it endures. . . .

If you are sitting at the table of one greater than yourself, take what he gives when it is set before you. Gaze not at that which lies before him, but only at what lies before you. Do not pierce him with many glances, for that is an abhorrence to the *ka*.* Keep your eyes cast down until he addresses you and speak only when he speaks to you. Laugh when he laughs; that will be pleasing to his heart and what you do will be acceptable. No one can know what is in the heart. . . .

Follow your heart so long as you live and do not more than is said. Do not diminish the time in which you follow the heart, for it is an abhorrence to the ka if its time is diminished. . . .

If you beget a son who pleases God and he does right and inclines to your will and hearkens to your instructions and he has regard for your substance as is fitting, seek out for him all that is good. . . . But if he does wrong and sins against your designs and does not follow your instructions and his designs are worthless in your house and he defies all that you say, . . . then drive him away, for he is not your son, he is not born to you. . . .

If you are one to whom a petition is made, be attentive to the petitioner's speech. Do not rebuff him before he has swept out his body and said what he came to say. A petitioner likes attention to his words even more than the fulfillment of that for which he came. . . . A favorable audience gladdens the heart. But whoever acts churlish towards petitioners, then men say: Now why is he doing that?

If you want to prolong friendship in a house to which you have admittance, as master or brother or friend, into whatever place you enter, beware of approaching the women. . . . On that account a thousand go to perdition. . . .

If you desire your conduct to be good, to free yourself from all that is evil, then beware of covetousness, which is a malady . . . incurable. Intimacy with it is impossible; it makes the sweet friend bitter, it alienates the trusted one from the master, it makes bad both father and mother, together with the brothers of the mother, and it divorces a man's wife. It is a bundle of every kind of evil and a bag of everything that is

*Ka: the protecting and guiding force of a man; particular care must be taken to avoid what is unpleasant to another's ka.

blameworthy. Long lived is the man whose rule of conduct is right, . . . he wins wealth thereby, but the covetous hath no tomb. . . .

If you are a man of standing, you should found a household and love your wife at home as is fitting. Fill her belly, clothe her back. Ointment is the prescription for her body. Gladden her heart as long as she lives. . . .

Satisfy your clients with what has accrued to you, what accrues to one favored of God. To do so is prudent, for there is none who knows his condition, if he thinks of the morrow. If therefore misfortune befall the favored ones, it is the intimates who still say: Welcome! . . . Thus retain for yourself their attachment against the time of trouble. . . .

Instruct a great one in that which is profitable to him. That will also be of advantage to you, for your sustenance depends upon his ka and your back will be clothed thereby. . . .

If you now are grown great after having been of small account, and now have substance after having been needy in the town which you know, do not be miserly with your wealth, which has accrued to you as the gift of God. You are not any better than another that is your equal, to whom the same has happened.

Bow your back to your superior in the king's administration. Then your house will endure with its substance and your pay will be duly awarded. Opposition to him that is in authority is evil, for one lives so long as he is indulgent. . . .

If you are seeking to know the nature of a friend, . . . draw near to him and deal with him alone until you are no longer troubled about him. Reason with him, test his heart with some conversation. If what he may have seen should come out or he should do something with which you are displeased, behold, he is still a friend. . . . Do not reply in a troubled state, do not remove yourself from him, do not trample on him. . . .

If you heed this that I have spoken to you, your every project will be better than those of the ancestors.

SUMERIA: THE EPIC OF GILGAMESH (ca. 2000 B.C.)

From M. Jastrow, *Religion of Babylonia and Assyria* (Boston, 1898), pp. 495–503 passim.

Gilgamesh was the hero of a series of tales from ancient Sumeria. The Epic is probably the first major work of literature in the world, antedating both Homer and the Hebrew Old Testament by 500 to 1000 years. Although most of the surviving tablets date from the seventh century B.C., the story comes down from at least the beginning of the second millenium B.C. For historians, the epic is a mine of information on early attitudes, customs, and ideas. The existing fragments deal with such issues as the nature of love, friendship, religion, and the afterlife. In the following section, on the Great Flood, note the parallel with the Biblical story of Noah.

Parnapishtim spoke to Gilgamesh:
I will tell thee, Gilgamesh, the marvellous story,

And the decision of the gods I will tell three,
Shurippak is a city which, as thou knowest,
Lies on the Euphrates.
That city was corrupt, so that the gods thereof
Decided to bring a rainstorm upon it,
All of the great gods, Anu, their father,
Their counsellor, the warrior Bel,
The bearer of destruction Ninib,
Their leader En-nugi,
The lord of unsearchable wisdom, Ea, was with them,
To proclaim their resolve to the reed-huts.
"Reed-hut, reed-hut, clay structure, clay structure,
Reed-hut, hear! Clay structure, give ear!"
O man of Shurripak, son of Kidin-Marduk!
Erect a structure, build a ship!
Abandon your goods, look after the souls,
Throw aside your possessions, and save your life,
Load the ship with all kinds of living things.

. . . . . .

But what shall I answer the city, the people, and the elders?
[Ea replies:] Thus answer and speak to them:
Bel has cast me out in his hatred,
So that I can no longer dwell in your city.
On Bel's territory I dare no longer show my face;
Therefore, I go to the deep to dwell with Ea, my lord.
Over you a rainstorm will come,
Men, birds, and beasts will perish.
When Shamash will bring on the time, those the lord of the whirlstorm
Will cause destruction to reign upon you in the evening.

. . . . . .

Then I built a structure of six stories [decks]
So that the whole consisted of seven apartments.
The interior I divided into nine parts.
I provided a pole, and all that was necessary.
Six [measures] of bitumen I smeared on the outside,
Three of pitch I smeared on the inside.

. . . . . .

All that I had I loaded on the ship.
With all the silver that I had, I loaded it,
With all the gold I had, I loaded it,
With living creatures of all kinds I loaded it.
I brought on board my whole family and household,
Cattle of the field, beasts of the field, workmen—all this I took on board.

. . . . . .

When the time came
For the lord of the whirlstorm to rain down destruction,
I gazed at the earth,
I was terrified at its sight,
I entered the ship and closed the door.
To the captain of the ship, to Puzur-Shadurabi, the sailor,
I entrusted the great structure with all its contents.
Upon the first appearance of dawn,
There arose from the horizon dark clouds,
Within which Ramman caused his thunder to resound.
Nabu and Sharru marched to the front,
The destroyers passed across mountains and land,
Dibbarra lets loose the [mischievous forces].
Ninib advances in furious hostility,
The Annunaki raise torches,
Whose sheen illumines the universe,
As Ramman's whirlwind sweeps across the heavens,
And all light is changed to darkness.

. . . . . .

Even the gods are terrified at the storm.
They take refuge in the heaven of Anu.
The gods cower like dogs at the edge of the heavens.
Ishtar groans like a woman in throes,
The lofty goddess cries with loud voice,
The world of old has become a mass of clay.
[Ishtar says:] That I should have assented to this evil among the gods!
That when I assented to this evil,
It was for the destruction of my own creatures [mankind]!
What I created, where is it?
Like so many fish, it fills the sea.
The gods together with the Annunaki wept with her,
The gods in their depression sat down to weep.

. . . . . .

For six days and nights
Wind, rainstorm, hurricane swept along;
When the seventh day arrived, the storm began to moderate,
Which had waged a contest like a great host.
The sea quieted down, wind and rainstorm ceased.
Bitterly weeping, I looked at the sea,
For all mankind had been turned to clay.
In place of dams, everything had become a marsh.
I opened a hatch so as to let the light fall upon my face.

Dumbfounded, I sat down and wept.
Tears flowed down my face.
I looked in all directions—naught but sea.
After twelve double hours an island appeared,
The ship approached the mountain Nisir.
At this mountain, Mount Nisir, the boat stuck fast.

. . . . . .

When the seventh day approached,
I sent forth a dove.
The dove flew about,
But finding no resting place, returned;
Then I sent forth a swallow.
The swallow flew about,
But finding no resting place, returned;
Then I sent forth a raven.
The raven flew off, and seeing that the waters had decreased,
[Cautiously] waded in the mud, but did not return.

BABYLONIA: HAMMURABI'S LAW CODE (ca. 1700 B.C.)

C.H.W. Johns, *Babylonian and Assyrian Laws, Contracts, and Letters* (New York, 1904), pp. 44–66, revised.

Built on the foundations of earlier Sumerian civilizations, the Babylonian Empire of Hammurabi stretched from the Persian Gulf to the Mediterranean Sea. Besides his famous code of laws, he is also thought to have begun the building of the Tower of Babel (Genesis 11:4).

Early in the present century Hammurabi's code was found near the Iranian city of Susa. It is carved on a diorite column which also depicts the king himself issuing his laws under the aegis of the sun god. The column contains more than 3600 lines of cuneiform characters and is now in the Louvre in Paris. Although not the oldest code in existence, it is the longest and most detailed of all that have been discovered.

Prologue

When the mighty Anu, King of the Anunnaki, and Enlil, Lord of heaven and earth, who determines the people's destinies, gave the rule of all mankind to Marduk, first-born son of Ea; . . . when they pronounced the lofty name of Babylon, made it great in all quarters of the world, and established in it an everlasting kingdom for him with foundations as firm as heaven and earth—then Anu and Enlil named me, Hammurabi, exalted prince and worshiper of the gods, to cause righteousness to

***Hammurabi and his code**. The stele contains the code in cuneiform, above which is a bas-relief of Hammurabi receiving the laws from the god of justice. Paris: Clichés des Musées Nationaux.)*

prevail in the land, to destroy the wicked, to prevent the strong from plundering the weak, . . . and to further the people's welfare . . .

The Laws

3. If a man has borne false witness in a trial, or has not established the statement that he made, if the case be a capital trial, he shall be put to death.

8. If a patrician has stolen an ox, sheep, ass, pig, or boat, whether from a temple or a house, he shall pay thirtyfold; if he is a plebian, he shall pay tenfold. If the thief cannot pay, he shall be put to death.

22. If a man has committed highway robbery and been caught, he shall be put to death.

23. If he has not been caught, the man he robbed shall state under oath what he has lost and the city or district governor . . . shall restore to him what he has lost.

53. If a man has neglected to strengthen his dike, . . . and the waters have flooded the farmland, he shall make good the grain he has damaged from neglect.

54. If he cannot make good the grain, he and his goods shall be sold and the farmers whose grain was carried away shall divide the proceeds.

108. If a barmaid not take grain in payment for drink, or has demanded silver in an excessive amount, or has made the measure of drink smaller than the measure of grain, she shall be prosecuted and thrown in the river.

109. If the mistress of a wineshop has assembled seditious slanderers in her house and not have them captured and brought to the palace, she shall be put to death.

128. If a man has taken a wife and not drawn up a marriage contract, that woman is not a wife.

129. If a man's wife be caught lying with another, they shall be bound and thrown into the water. If the woman's husband spares her life, the king shall save his servant.

130. If a man bind another's betrothed, and she had had no sexual intercourse and was still living in her father's house; if he lie in her bosom and they catch him, he shall be put to death and the woman shall go free.

132. If a man's wife has the finger pointed at her because of another, but has not been caught lying with him, for her husband's sake she shall throw herself in the sacred river.

138. If a man divorce his wife who has not borne him children, he shall pay her whatever was given for her bride-price and so shall divorce her.

139. If there was no bride-price, he shall give her one mina of silver.

140. If he is a plebian, he shall give her one-third mina of silver.

141. If a wife, living in her husband's house, has persisted in going out, has acted the fool, has wasted her house, has belittled her husband, he shall prosecute her. If her husband has said, I divorce her, she shall go her way; he shall give her nothing as her price of divorce. If he has said, I will not divorce her, he may take another woman to wife, and the [first] wife shall live as a slave in her husband's house.

142. If a woman hate her husband and say, Thou shalt not possess me, her past shall be inquired into for any deficiency of hers; if she has been discreet, without past sin, and her husband has gone out and greatly belittled her, that woman has no blame; she shall take her marriage portion and go off to her father's house.

143. [But] if she has not been discreet, has gone out, ruined her house, belittled her husband, she shall be thrown into the water.

153. If a wife for the sake of another has caused her husband to be killed, she shall be impaled.

154. If a man have sexual intercourse with his daughter, he shall be expelled from this city.

195. If a son shall strike his father, his hands shall be cut off.

196. If a man has put out the eye of a patrician, his eye shall be put out.

198. If he has put out the eye of a plebian, . . . he shall pay one mina of silver.

202. If a man strike the cheek of a man who is his superior, he shall publicly receive 60 strokes of an oxtail whip.

215. If a physician perform an operation on a patrician, using a bronze lancet and save his life, . . . he shall receive ten shekels of silver.

216. If it were a plebian, he shall receive five shekels.

217. If it were a man's slave, the slave owner shall give two silver shekels to the physician.

218. If a surgeon has operated . . . on a patrician for a serious injury and has caused his death, . . . his hands shall be cut off.

229. If a builder has built a house for a man and has not made it sound and the house has fallen, causing the death of its owner, the builder shall be put to death.

230. If it cause the death of the owner's son, a son of the builder shall be put to death.

232. If it destroyed goods, he shall replace them; and because he did not make it sound he shall rebuild the house at his own expense.

237. If a man has hired a boat and boatman, and loaded it with grain, wool, oil, or dates, or whatever it be, and the boatman has been careless and sunk the boat or lost what was in it, the boatman shall make good the boat and whatever he lost that was in it.

250. If a bull has gone wild and gored a man and caused his death, there can be no suit against the owner.

251. If a man's ox be a gorer and has shown its evil tendency and he has not blunted its horns or shut it up; and then that ox has gored a free man and caused his death, the owner shall pay half a mina of silver.

282. If a male slave say to his master, Thou art not my master, his master shall prove him to be his slave and cut off his ear.

THE ANCIENT HEBREWS: THE OLD TESTAMENT

The number and quality of recent translations of the Bible, as well as the controversies surrounding them, attest to the vitality and significance of the Great Book. But instead of pursuing that question, let us read the Old Testament as cosmology, history, and social thought. Beginning as early as 1000 B.C., sources were collected, handed down from generation to generation as a sacred trust, and finally put into writing around 500 B.C. However you read the Bible, it is compelling, but the King James version (used here), written by some of the leading scholars of the Elizabethan Age, evinces remarkable style and elegance of expression.

The first twelve books, from Genesis to Second Kings, recount the history of the Jews in their quest for the Promised Land; then come the major and minor prophets, followed by books of such varied form and content as Job, Esther, Psalms, and the Song of Solomon—for a total of thirty-nine books in the Old Testament, although the number varies according to the translation and definitions of the apochrypha.

We begin, then, with the story of creation, followed by the Ten Commandments and the prophet Isaiah.

CREATION AND THE FALL OF MAN (Genesis 1–3)

In the beginning God created the heaven and the earth. And the earth was without form, and void; and darkness was upon the face of the deep. And the Spirit of God moved upon the face of the waters. And God said, Let there be light: and there was light. And God saw the light, that it was good and God divided the light from the darkness. And God called the light Day, and the darkness he called Night. And the evening and the morning were the first day.

***Fragments of the Old Testament**, discovered in caves near the Dead Sea in 1947. Fragment of the Qumran manuscripts dating back to 200 B.C. (The Shrine of the Book, The Israeli Museum, Jerusalem: D. Samuel and Jeane H. Gottesman Center for Biblical Manuscripts.)*

And God said, Let there be a firmament in the midst of the waters, and let it divide the waters from the waters. And God made the firmament, and divided the waters which were under the firmament from the waters which were above the firmament; and so it was. And God called the firmament Heaven. And the evening and the morning were the second day.

And God said, Let the waters under heaven be gathered together unto one place, and let the dry land appear; and it was so. And God called the dry land earth; and the gathering together of the waters called he seas. And God saw that it was good. And God said, Let the earth bring forth grass, the herb yielding seed, and the fruit tree yielding fruit after his kind, whose seed is itself, upon the earth; and it was so. . . . And the evening and the morning were the third day.

And God said, Let there be lights in the firmament of the heaven to divide the day from the night; and let them be for signs, and for seasons, and for days and years; and let them be for lights in the firmament of the heaven to give light upon the earth, and it was so. . . . And the evening and the morning were the fourth day.

And God said, Let the waters bring forth abundantly the moving creature that hath life, and fowl that may fly above the earth in the open firmament of heaven. And God created great whales, and every living creature that moveth, which the waters brought forth abundantly, after their kind, and every winged fowl after his kind; and God saw that it was good. And God blessed them, saying, Be fruitful and multiply, and fill the waters in the seas, and let fowl multiply in the earth. And the evening and the morning were the fifth day. . . .

And God said, Let us make man in our image, after our likeness; and let them have dominion over the fish of the sea, and over the fowl of the air, and over the cattle, and over all the earth, and over every creeping thing that creepeth upon the earth. So God created man in his own image, in the image of God created he him; male and female created he them. And God blessed them, and God said unto them, Be fruitful, and multiply, and replenish the earth, and subdue it; and have dominion over the fish of the sea, and over the fowl of the air, and over every living thing that moveth upon the earth. . . .

Thus the heavens and the earth were finished, and all the host of them. And on the seventh day God ended his work which he had made; and he rested on the seventh day from all his work which he had made. And God blessed the seventh day, and sanctified it: because that in it he had rested from all his work which God created and made. . . .

And the Lord God planted a garden eastward in Eden; and there he put the man whom he had formed. And out of the ground made the Lord God to grow every tree that is pleasant to the sight, and good for food; the tree of life also in the midst of the garden, and the tree of knowledge of good and evil. . . . And the Lord God took the man, and put him into the garden of Eden to dress it and to keep it. And the Lord God commanded the man, saying, Of every tree of the garden thou mayest freely eat; but of the tree of knowledge of good and evil, thou shalt not eat of it; for in the day that thou eatest thereof thou shalt surely die.

And the Lord God said, It is not good that the man should be alone; I will make an helpmeet for him. And out of the ground the Lord God formed every beast of the field, and every fowl of the air; and brought them unto Adam to see what he would call them; and whatsoever Adam called every living creature, that was the name thereof. . . . And the Lord God caused a deep sleep to fall upon Adam, and he slept. And he took one of his ribs, and closed up the flesh instead thereof. And the rib, which the Lord God had taken from man, made he a woman, and brought her unto the man. And Adam said, This is now bone of my bones, and flesh of my flesh; she shall be called Woman, because she was taken out of Man. Therefore shall a man leave his father and mother, and shall cleave unto his wife; and they shall be one flesh. And they were both naked, the man and his wife, and were not ashamed.

Now the serpent was more subtil than any beast of the field which the Lord God had made. And he said unto the woman, Yea, hath God said, Ye shall not eat of every tree of the garden? And the woman said unto the serpent, We may eat of the fruit of the trees of the garden; but of the fruit of the tree which is in the midst of the garden God hath said, Ye shall not eat of it, neither shall ye touch it, lest ye die.

And the serpent said unto the woman, Ye shall not surely die; for God doth know that in the day ye eat thereof, then your eyes shall be opened, and ye shall be as gods, knowing good and evil. And when the woman saw that the tree was good for food, and that it was pleasant to the eyes, and a tree to be desired to make one wise, she took of the fruit thereof, and did eat, and gave also unto her husband with her and he did eat. And the eyes of them both were opened, and they knew that they were naked; and they sewed fig leaves together, and made themselves aprons. . . .

And the Lord said unto the woman, What is this that thou hast done?

And the woman said, The serpent beguiled me, and I did eat.

And the Lord God said unto the serpent, Because thou hast done this, thou art cursed above all cattle, and above every beast of the field; upon thy belly shalt thou go, and dust shalt thou eat all the days of thy life. . . .

And unto the woman he said, I will greatly multiply thy sorrow and thy conception; in sorrow thou shalt bring forth children; and thy desire shall be to thy husband, and he shall rule over thee.

And unto Adam he said, Because thou has hearkened unto the voice of thy wife, and has eaten of the tree, of which I commanded thee, saying, Thou shalt not eat of it: cursed is the ground for thy sake; in sorrow shalt thou eat of it all the days of thy life. . . . In the sweat of thy face shalt thou eat bread, till thou return unto the ground; for out of it wast thou taken: for dust thou art, and unto dust shalt thou return. . . .

Therefore the Lord God sent him forth from the garden of Eden, to till the ground from whence he was taken. . . .

THE TEN COMMANDMENTS AND JEWISH LAW (Deut. 5–7)

And Moses called all Israel, and said unto them, Hear, O Israel, the statutes and judgments which I speak in your ears this day, that ye may learn them and keep them, and do them. The Lord our God made a covenant with us in Horeb. The lord made not this covenant with our fathers, but with us, even us, who are all of us here alive this day. The Lord talked with you face to face in the mount out of the midst of the fire; I stood between the Lord and you at that time, to shew you the word of the Lord; for ye were afraid by reason of the fire, and were not up into the mount. [The Lord] saith,

I am the Lord thy God, which brought thee out of the land of Egypt, from the house of bondage. Thou shalt have none other gods before me.

Thou shalt not make thee any graven image, or any likeness of any thing that is in heaven above, or that is in the earth beneath, or that is in the waters beneath the earth: thou shalt not bow down thyself unto them, nor serve them: for I the Lord thy God am a jealous God, visiting the iniquity of the fathers upon the children unto the third and fourth generation of them that hate me, and showing mercy unto thousands of them that love me and keep my commandments.

Thou shalt not take the name of the Lord thy God in vain, for the Lord will not hold him guiltless that taketh his name in vain.

Keep the sabbath day to sanctify it, as the Lord thy God hath commanded thee. Six days thou shalt labour and do all thy work: but the seventh day is the sabbath of the Lord thy God: in it thou shalt not do any work, thou, nor thy son, nor thy daughter, nor thy manservant, nor thy maidservant, nor thine ox nor thine ass, nor any of thy cattle, nor thy stranger that is within thy gates; that thy manservant and thy maidservant may rest as well as thou. And remember that thou wast a servant in the land of Egypt, and that the Lord thy God brought thee out thence through a mighty hand and by a stretched out arm: therefore the Lord thy God commanded thee to keep the sabbath day.

Honour thy father and thy mother, as the Lord thy God hath commanded thee; that thy days may be prolonged, and that it may be well with thee, in the land which the Lord thy God giveth thee.

Thou shalt not kill.

Neither shalt thou commit adultery.

Neither shalt thou steal.

Neither shalt thou bear false witness against thy neighbour.

Neither shalt thou desire thy neighbour's wife, neither shalt thou covet thy neighbour's house, his field, or his manservant, or his maidservant, his ox, or his ass, or any thing that is thy neighbour's.

These words the Lord spake unto all your assembly in the mount out of the midst of the fire, of the cloud, and of the thick darkness, with a great voice: and he added no more. And he wrote them in two tables of stone, and delivered them unto me. And it came to pass, when ye heard the voice out of the darkness, (for the mountain did burn with fire,) that ye came near unto me, even all the heads of your tribes, and your elders; and ye said, Behold, the Lord our God hath showed us his glory and his greatness, and we have heard his voice out of the midst of the fire: we have seen this day that God doth talk with man, and he liveth. Now therefore why should we die? for this great fire will consume us: if we hear the voice of the Lord our God any more, we shall die. For who is there of all flesh, that hath heard the voice of the living God speaking out of the midst of the fire as we have and lived? Go thou near, and hear all that the Lord our God shall say: and speak thou unto us all that the Lord our God shall speak unto thee and we will hear it, and do it.

And the Lord heard the voice of your words, when ye spake unto me; and the Lord said unto me, I have heard the voice of the words of this people, which they have spoken unto thee: they have well said all that they have spoken. O that there were such an heart in them, that they would fear me, and keep all my commandments always, that it might be well with them, and with their children forever!

Go say to them, Get you into your tents again. But as for thee [Moses], stand thou here by me, and I will speak unto thee all the commandments, and the statutes, and the judgments, which thou shalt teach them, that they may do them in the land which I give them to possess it. . . .

Hear therefore, O Israel, and observe to do it, that it may be well with thee, and that ye may increase mightily, as the Lord God of thy fathers hath promised thee, in the land that flows with milk and honey.

Hear, O Israel: the Lord our God is one Lord; and thou shalt love the Lord thy God with all thine heart, and with all thy soul, and with all thy might. And these words which I command thee this day, shall be in thine heart; and thou shalt teach them diligently unto thy children, and shalt talk of them when thou sittest in thine house, and when thou walkest by the way, . . . And thou shalt write them upon the posts of thy house, and on thy gates.

And it shall be, when the Lord thy God shall have brought thee into the land which he sware unto thy fathers, to Abraham, to Isaac, and to Jacob, to give thee great and goodly cities, which thou buildest not, and houses full of all good things, which thou filledst not, and wells digged, which thou diggedst not, vineyards and olive trees, which thou plantedst not; when thou shalt have eaten and be full; then beware lest thou forget the Lord, which brought thee forth out of the land of Egypt, from the house of bondage. . . .

THE PROPHET ISAIAH (Is. 65)

The greatest and most influential of the Hebrew prophets, Isaiah predicted the fall of Judah to the Chaldeans in 568 B.C., sought to comfort the Jews in their Babylonian Captivity, and presented the concept of a fully developed monotheism—the God who made heaven and earth and ruled over the destinies of men and nations—as well as the idea of a Messiah, the expected king and deliverer of the Hebrews. The following selection, from the so-called deutero-Isaiah, indicates God's displeasure with His people for breaking His commandments.

I am sought of those that asked not for me; I am found of them that sought me not. I said, Behold me, behold me, unto a nation that was not called by my name. I have spread out my hands all the day unto a rebellious people, which walketh in a way that was not good, after their own thoughts. A people that provoketh me to anger continually to my face; that sacrificeth in gardens, and burneth incense upon altars of brick; which remain among the graves, and lodge in the monuments, which eat swine's flesh, and broth of abominable things is in their vessels; which say, Stand by thyself, come not near to me; for I am holier than thou. These are a smoke in my nose, a fire that burneth all the day. Behold, it is written before me: I will not keep silence, but will recompense, even recompense into their bosom, your iniquities, and the iniquities of your fathers together, saith the Lord, which have burned incense upon the mountains, and blasphemed me upon the hills. Therefore, will I measure their former work into their bosom.

Thus saith the Lord, As the new wine is found in the cluster, and one saith, Destroy it not, for a blessing is in it; so will I do for my servants' sakes, that I may not destroy them all. And I will bring forth a seed out of Jacob, and out of Judah an inheritor of my mountains; and mine elect shall inherit it, and my servants shall dwell there. And Sharon shall be a fold of flocks, and the valley of Achor a place for the herds to lie down in, for my people that have sought me.

But ye are they that forsake the Lord, that forget my holy mountain, that prepare a table for that troop, and that furnish the drink offering unto that number. Therefore will I number you to the sword, and ye shall all bow down to the slaughter, because when I called, ye did not answer; when I spake, ye did not hear; but did evil before mine eyes, and did choose that wherein I delighted not. Therefore thus saith the Lord God, Behold, my servants shall eat, but ye shall be hungry. Behold, my servants shall drink, but ye shall be thirsty. Behold, my servants shall rejoice, but ye shall be ashamed. Behold, my servants shall sing for joy of heart, but ye shall cry for sorrow of heart, and shall howl for vexation of spirit. And ye shall leave your name for a curse unto my chosen, for the Lord God shall slay thee, and call his servants by another name. That he who blesseth himself in the earth shall bless himself in the God of truth; and he that sweareth in the earth shall swear by the God of truth; because the former troubles are forgotten, and because they are hid from mine eyes.

For, behold, I create new heavens and a new earth; and the former shall not be remembered nor come into mind. But be ye glad and rejoice forever in that which I create. For, behold, I create Jerusalem a rejoicing, and her people a joy. And I will rejoice in Jerusalem, and my joy in my people; and the voice of weeping shall be no more heard in her, nor the voice of crying. There shall be no more thence an infant of days, nor an old man that hath not filled his days; for the child shall die an hundred years old. But the sinner being an hundred years old shall be accursed. And they shall build houses and inhabit them; and they shall plant vineyards, and eat the fruit of them. They shall not build, and another inhabit; they shall not plant, and another eat. For as the days of a tree are the days of my people, and mine elect shall long enjoy the work of their hands. They shall not labour in vain, nor bring forth for trouble; for they are the seed of the blessed of the Lord, and their offspring with them. And it shall come to pass, that before they call, I will answer; and while they are yet speaking, I will hear. The wolf and the lamb shall feed together, and the lion shall eat straw like the bullock; and dust shall be the serpent's meat. They shall not hurt nor destroy in all my holy mountain, saith the Lord.

CHAPTER 2

THE CLASSICAL AGE OF GREECE

The fifth century B.C. in Athens, like the Augustan Age in Rome or the Renaissance in Florence, was a breeding ground for great ideas and achievements. Aeschylus and Sophocles perfected classical drama; Socrates and Plato developed philosophical analysis; Aristotle examined such concepts as government and ethics in universal terms; while Herodotus and Thucydides made the writing of history a high art. One reason that later ages have been preoccupied with Classical Greece is that her thinkers dealt with timeless problems: What does it mean to be human? What is the Good Life? What is man's relationship to the State?

The following selections represent several varieties of Greek thought: Sophocles's play *Antigone;* Thucydides's reconstruction of a patriotic speech by Pericles; Socrates's trial as recreated by Plato, followed by one of Plato's philosophical dialogues; and an excerpt from Aristotle's *Politics,* analyzing governmental forms and their perversions. Then, for a contrasting type of *polis* from Athens, we turn to ancient Sparta, about 600 B.C., as described by the historian Plutarch.

There are also certain questions that might come to mind as you read these works. For instance, why is this called the Classical Age? How adequate is our impression of daily living in ancient Greece from these readings? Did Socrates have a fair trial? Is a jury of five hundred apt to be fairer than one of twelve members? What are the advantages and disadvantages of Aristotle's concept of government? What is the Good Life, according to the Athenians? According to the Spartans?

SOPHOCLES: ANTIGONE

From Sophocles, *Tragedies,* trans. Jebb, ed. E. Coleridge (London, 1905), pp. 151–169 passim, revised.

To the Greeks, drama was more than mere entertainment: it was religion, morality, art—Life itself. If Aeschylus (d. 456 B.C.) may be said to be the father of Greek tragedy, then Sophocles (d. 406 B.C.) was its mother, giving it lessons in morality and character building. His *Antigone,* like classical drama ever since, presents an internal conflict, in this case between Antigone's religious convictions and her obligations to the State, as well as other conflicts in the personages of Ismene and Creon.

Creon, King of Thebes, has decreed that one of Antigone's brothers, who has died fighting for the State, shall have a hero's funeral, while the other brother, who has fought against Thebes, shall not be buried but his body left where it fell, his soul denied eternal rest. These four siblings, Antigone, Ismene, and their brothers Eteocles and Polyneices, are the unfortunate offspring of the marriage between King Oedipus and his mother Jocasta, an incestuous union that is the subject of another of Sophocles's plays, *Oedipus Rex.*

Antigone and Ismene before the palace gates.

ANTIGONE. Ismene, dear sister, of all the ills brought on by the weird of Oedipus, is there any Zeus will not fulfill in thee and me? Have you heard the latest? Creon's proclamation?

ISMENE. No news, Antigone, either of joy or sorrow, has come to me since we lost both our brothers, slain the self-same day by double stroke. I know the enemy has fled this night, but nothing further.

ANTIGONE. I thought as much, and that is why I summoned thee outside the gates that thou alone might hear.

ISMENE. Hear what? What dark secret troubles thy breast?

ANTIGONE. Aye, truly. 'Tis our brothers' burial. Doth Creon not honor one and disgrace the other? Eteocles, they say, is to be buried with due reverence for right and custom. But for Polyneices, who fought as bravely, a decree forbids anyone to bury him or mourn him. Unwept, without a tomb, he is to be left a prize for carrion birds to swoop upon and gorge their fill. This, I hear, is what our worthy Creon hath proclaimed for thee and me, and he is coming here to say it publicly. Whoever transgresses that decree shall be stoned to death. So now thou knowest, and soon mayst show if thou art true sister or poor scion of a gallant breed.

ISMENE. If this be so, O rash-hearted sister, what could I do?

ANTIGONE. Decide: Wilt help me do the deed?

ISMENE. I don't understand. Help you do what?

ANTIGONE. Bury our brother. Will you lend a hand?

ISMENE. What! bury him?—the thing our city has forbidden?

ANTIGONE. Of course. He is my brother—and thine as well.

ISMENE. Rash girl! When Creon has forbidden it?

ANTIGONE. He has no right to keep me from my own.

ISMENE. Oh, sister mine! Think how our father died, scorned and hated, an outcast, driven by the sins he had himself detected to blind himself with his own hand. Then, she that was his mother and his wife as well took her own life with twisted noose. Thirdly, our brothers, in one day, brought about their mutual doom at one another's hands. And now us: we two are left alone; think how pitiably we shall die if we defy the law and violate what kings decree. We, weak women that we are, are not meant to fight with men. We are the subjects of a stronger power and must obey—if not in this, then something worse. I yield obedience to the powers that be and crave forgiveness of the dead. Meddling overmuch shows lack of reason.

ANTIGONE. I urge thee no more. Even if you later changed your mind, I would not welcome your assistance. Do as you think best. But I shall bury him. How sweet to die in doing that: I shall be laid to rest with him, my loving heart with his, my sin a saintly act. It is the dead rather than the living that we must please the longer: with them we shall abide forever. As for thee, show thy contempt for the laws of the gods, if thou wilt.

ISMENE. No, never. Not I. But defy the State I cannot; 'tis not my nature.

ANTIGONE. Make that your excuse, then, but I will go at once to heap a tomb above a brother very dear to me.

[They leave.]

* * * *

CREON *(addressing his councillors):* . . . To really know the soul, the thoughts, the judgment of a ruler is impossible until he has proved himself in office and in law-giving. To my mind a governor who would not seek the best advice when the *polis* is in his control, but through some fear remain tongue-tied—that person, I say, is the basest of knaves; or whoever would put a friend's welfare ahead of his country's—for him I have no use, either. As Zeus is my witness, I should not hesitate to speak out plainly if I saw my country headed for ruin. Need I remind you that I would have no truck with an enemy of the people. No one values friendship more than I, but friends at the expense of the State are no friends at all.

These are my principles, and that is why I have made the decision respecting the sons of Oedipus: Bury Eteocles, I say, and o'er his grave observe those holy rites which go down to heroes after death. But as for his brother, Polyneices, let no one honor him with a grave nor mourn for him, but leave him unburied, his corpse a prey to dogs and kites, outraged thus for all to see.

* * * *

Antigone, charged with having buried her brother's corpse, is brought before King Creon.

CREON. You there, with your head hanging and your eyes downcast, dost thou plead guilty? or dost deny the deed?

ANTIGONE. Guilty. I did it, I do not deny it.

CREON. Didst thou know there was a proclamation against doing this thing?

ANTIGONE. I knew it. Of course, I knew it. It was known to all.

CREON. And yet thou wast bold enough to break the law?

ANTIGONE. Yes. For I never heard that Zeus made such a proclamation; neither did Justice, who dwells among us here below, ordain such laws for mankind. Nor did I think that those decrees of thine were of sufficient power to override the unwritten rules of Heaven; for these, I trow, are not today's or yesterday's decrees. No! They live on from everlasting, and no man knoweth the date of their appearing. I was not about to answer at Heaven's bar for their transgression, from fear of any *man's* proud will. That I was doomed to death I knew full well—how should I not? e'en though thou hadst issued no decree; and if I am to die before the appointed time, I count that gain. For whoso liveth in the thick of ills, as I do, doth surely gain by death. And so for me to meet this doom is grief of no account; but if dogs had mangled the corpse of my own mother's son, as it lay unburied, that indeed had caused me grief, but for this I grieve not now. And if perchance I seem to thee to be acting foolishly herein, it may well be a fool who charges me with folly.

[Exit.]

CHORUS. Untamed, the maiden shows she is the offspring of an untamed sire; she hath not learned to bend to suffering.

CREON. Know this, that wills, which are too stubborn, are abased the most; and thou wilt see the stiffest iron, tempered by fire to utmost stubbornness, most often snapped in pieces; and I have known of restive steeds tamed by a tiny curb; for he may not have high thoughts who is his neighbor's slave. This girl, e'en then, had learnt the whole art of insolence, when she o'erstepped the laws set forth by me; and, after doing that, behold her second insult—boasting of it and laughing to have done it.

Of a truth, I am no man but this maid is, if this victory is to rest with her unchallenged . . . Now summon her; I saw her just now in the palace raving and out of her wits; for the mind of those, who are scheming nought but villainy in secret, is oft detected, ere the time, in its stealthy fraud. I hate such folks, 'tis true; but this I hate as well: when one being caught in crime, then seeks to gloss it over.

ANTIGONE. Wouldst thou do more than take and kill me?

CREON. For me, I want no more; that is enough.

ANTIGONE. Then why delay? I find no pleasure in thy words—God grant I never may!—and my words are probably just as distasteful to thee. Yet, how else could I have won a name so glorious as by burying a brother? All these men would say as much, were they not afraid to speak. A despot has this among his many blessings, that he is free to say and do as he pleases.

CREON. That is *thy* view, and thine alone among all these citizens.

ANTIGONE. 'Tis their view too, but they have fawning, cringing words for thee.

CREON. Art thou not ashamed of holding different views from them?

ANTIGONE. No, for there is no disgrace in reverencing one's kith and kin.

CREON. Was he not a brother too, who fell upon the other side?

ANTIGONE. My brother, yes; one mother ours, the self-same sire.

CREON. Then why insult his memory?

ANTIGONE. That will not be the verdict of the dead man.

CREON. Indeed it will, if you honor a traitor as much as him.

ANTIGONE. No, it was no slave of his, but his *brother* that fell.

CREON. He made war on his country; Eteocles defended it.

ANTIGONE. No matter; all the dead are due these rites.

CREON. But not the same for the wicked as for the good.

ANTIGONE. Who knows if, in Hades, this is not righteousness.

CREON. A foe is ne'er a friend, no! not even in death.

ANTIGONE. My nature is to share in love, but not in hate.

CREON. Die then. Go love the dead in Hades, if thou must, for while I live, no woman shall rule me.

THUCYDIDES: PERICLES'S FUNERAL ORATION

From *The Peloponnesian War,* trans. Jowett (1881), 2:35–43, revised.

A vivid imagination is important to the study of history. Perhaps no one understood this better than Thucydides, the historian of the Peloponnesian War, in which he himself was a participant. After several years as a general, however, he was sent into exile for having failed to prevent an Athenian city from surrendering to Sparta. Fortunately, this gave him the leisure to write his great history, covering the years 431 to 411 B.C., although he did not live to complete it, since the war was ended only in 399 with the defeat of Athens.

To return to the role of imagination, mentioned above, Thucydides was fond of inventing speeches for his leading characters, such as Pericles's funeral oration, excerpts from which follow. But it is probably just as valuable to know what was in the mind of the one as in the speech of the other; by using our imagination we can learn what an ancient Athenian (Thucydides/Pericles) thought about his polis and about poleis in general. Note that the polis is a whole way of life—a nation as well as a city—as different from all other poleis as England is from the United States, each sharing a common language, but having different ways.

I will speak first of our ancestors, for it is right and becoming that now, when we are lamenting the dead, a tribute should be paid to their memory. There has never been a time when they did not inhabit this land, which by their valor they have handed down from generation to generation, and we have received from them a free state. . . . Now before I praise the dead, I should like to point out by what principles of action we rose to power, and under what institutions and through what manner of life our empire became great. For I conceive that such thoughts are not unsuited to the occasion, and that this numerous assembly of citizens and strangers may profitably listen to them.

Our form of government does not enter into rivalry with the institutions of others.

We do not copy our neighbors, but are an example to them. It is true that we are called a democracy, for the administration is in the hands of the many and not of the few. But while the law secures equal justice to all alike in their private disputes, the claim of excellence is also recognized; and when a citizen is in any way distinguished, he is preferred to the public service, not as a matter of privilege, but as a reward of merit.

Neither is poverty a bar, but a man may benefit his country whatever be the obscurity of his condition. There is no exclusiveness in our public life, and in our private intercourse we are not suspicious of one another, nor angry with our neighbor if he does what he likes; we do not put on sour looks at him which, though harmless, are not pleasant. While we are thus constrained in our private intercourse, a spirit of reverence pervades our public acts; we are prevented from doing wrong by respect for authority and for the laws, having an especial regard to those which are ordained for the protection of the injured as well as to those unwritten laws which bring upon the transgressor the reprobation of the general sentiment.

And we have not forgotten to provide for our weary spirits many relaxations from toil. . . . And because of the greatness of our city, the fruits of the whole earth flow in upon us, so that we enjoy the goods of other countries as freely as our own.

Then, again, our military training is in many respects superior to that of our adversaries. Our city is open to the world, and we never expel a foreigner nor prevent his seeing or learning anything. . . . We rely not upon manipulation or trickery, but upon our own hearts and hands. In matters of education, whereas the [Spartans] from early youth are always undergoing laborious exercises to make them brave, we live a life of ease, and yet are equally ready to face the perils they face. . . .

If then we prefer to meet danger with a light heart but without laborious training and with courage gained from habit, not enforced by law, are we not greatly the gainers? Since we do not anticipate the pain, but when the hour comes can be as brave as those who never allow themselves to relax, our city is equally admirable in peace and war. For we are lovers of the beautiful, yet simple in our tastes; we cultivate the mind without loss of manliness. Wealth we employ not for talk and ostentation but for actual needs as they arise. To avow poverty with us is no disgrace: the true disgrace is in doing nothing to avoid it. An Athenian citizen does not neglect the state because he takes care of his own household, and even those engaged in business have a good idea of politics. A man who takes no interest in public affairs we regard not as a harmless but a useless character. If few of us are originators, we are all sound judges of policy. The great impediment to action, in our opinion, is not discussion but lack of knowledge gained by the exchange of ideas before action. . . .

To sum up, I say that Athens is the school of Hellas, and that the Athenian in his own person seems to have the power of adapting to the most varied forms of action with the utmost grace and versatility. . . .

Assuredly we shall not be without witnesses; there are mighty monuments of our power that will make us the wonder of this and succeeding ages. . . . Such is the city for whose sake these men nobly fought and died; they could not bear the thought that she should be taken from them. . . .

I have dwelt on the greatness of Athens because I want to show you that we are contending for a higher prize than those who enjoy none of these privileges, and to establish by manifest proof the merit of these men whom I now commemorate. Their loftiest praise has already been spoken. For in magnifying the city I have magnified them, and men like them whose virtues made her glorious. . . .

Fix your eyes day by day on the greatness of Athens, until you become filled with love of her; and when you are impressed by the spectacle of her glory, reflect that this empire has been acquired by men who knew their duty and had the courage to do it, who in the hour of conflict had the fear of dishonor always present, and who, if ever they failed in an enterprise, would not allow their virtues to be lost to their country, but freely gave their lives to her as the fairest offering they could present at her feast. The sacrifice they collectively made was individually repaid them, for they received, each for himself, a praise that does not age and the noblest of all sepulchres—not that in which their remains are laid but that in which their glory survives and is proclaimed on every fitting occasion. . . . For the whole earth is the sepulchre of famous men; not only are they commemorated by columns and inscriptions in their own country but in foreign lands also, where an unwritten memorial of them is graven in the hearts of men. Make them your example, and, esteeming courage to be freedom and freedom happiness, do not weigh too nicely the perils of war. . . .

PLATO: THE TRIAL OF SOCRATES (399 B.C.)

From "The Apology," in *Dialogues,* trans. Jowett (London, 1892), revised.

Socrates was probably one of the greatest teachers of all time. His pupil Plato tells the story of his trial on the charges of failing to honor the gods, introducing new divinities, and corrupting the young. In defending himself, Socrates relates how he became committed to a life of inquiry and how much hatred and enmity it earned him. After his conviction, friends urged him to flee the country, but he argued that to run away from the consequences of his own actions and the just operation of the laws would violate all he had ever stood for.

Socrates: How you may have been affected, O Athenians, by my accusers, I cannot tell, but I do know that they almost made me forget who I was—so persuasively did they speak. And yet they have uttered hardly one word of truth. . . . But some of you will ask: Well, Socrates, what about these accusations? There must be something strange about what you have been doing; all this talk about you would not have come up if you had been like other men. . . .

Now, that I regard as a fair challenge and I will try to explain why I am called wise and have such ill repute. . . . I refer you to a witness whose credibility is beyond doubt—the god of Delphi. He will tell you of my wisdom, if I have any, and of what sort it is. You must have known my late friend Chaerephon. . . . He was always impulsive. He went to Delphi and boldly asked the Oracle to tell him if anyone was wiser than Socrates, and the [answer] was that no one was wiser. Chaerephon's brother is here to confirm that.

When I heard the reply, I said to myself, What can the god mean? what is the answer to this riddle? for I know I have no wisdom, either great or small. Yet he is a god and cannot lie. Finally, I thought of a way to test the hypothesis: If I could find a man who was wiser, I could go to the God and say, Here is someone wiser than I am, yet you said I was the wisest.

Accordingly, I went to see a man reputed to be a sage; after having observed him, I spoke with him and could not help thinking that he was not really wise, despite his reputation and his own opinion of himself. As a consequence, he hated me, as did several who were present at the time. I went away saying to myself: Well, I don't suppose that either of us knows what is really beautiful or good, but I am better off than he is: he knows nothing but *thinks* he knows, whereas I neither know nor think I know. . . . Then I went to another who had still higher pretensions to wisdom, and my conclusion was just the same; whereupon I made another enemy, and after him many others.

This kind of questioning has caused me much hostility and calumny. Since my hearers imagine that I must have wisdom because I find it lacking in others, they call me wise, but the truth is, O men of Athens, that only God is wise: by his answer he intends to show that the wisdom of men is of little account. He uses me only as an example, as if to say, He only is wise who, like Socrates, knows his "wisdom" is worthless. So I go about searching and inquiring into the wisdom of one and all, vindicating the Oracle, which leaves me no time for any public or private matter, in utter poverty from my devotion to the God.

There is another thing: Young men of the richer classes, who have not much to do, come about me of their own accord; they like to hear the pretenders questioned, and they often imitate me, and proceed to question others. There are plenty of persons, as they quickly discover, who think they know something but who really know very little or nothing. Then those whom they question, instead of being angry with themselves, are angry with me: Curse that Socrates, they say, that villanous misleader of youth, and then, if somebody asks them, Why? what evil does he do or teach? they do not know and cannot tell. But in order not to appear at a loss, they repeat the ready-made charges that are used against all philosophers about things up in the clouds and under the earth, and having no gods and making the worse appear the better cause. . . .

[Next Socrates questioned Meletus, trying to show that the charge of corrupting the young is ridiculous and that of unorthodoxy, false. Finally, he returned to the main charge and his role as "gadfly."]

And now, Athenians, I am not going to argue for my own sake, as you may think, but for yours, that you may not sin against the god by condemning me, who am his gift to you. For if you kill me, you will not easily find a successor to me, who, if I may use such a ludicrous figure of speech, am a sort of gadfly, given to the State by God; and the State is a great and noble steed, which is dilatory in movement because of his very size, and has to be goaded into action. I am that gadfly, . . . and all day long, everywhere, I am always fastening upon you, arousing, persuading, reproaching you. You will not easily find another like me, so I therefore advise you to exonerate me. I dare say that you may feel out of sorts—like someone suddenly awakened from sleep—and you think you might easily strike me dead, as Anytus advises, so that you could go back to sleep for the rest of your lives, unless God, in his care for you, should send you another gadfly.

When I say that I am given to you by God, the proof of my mission is this: If I had been like other men, I should not have neglected all my own concerns. . . . all these years in order to be doing yours, coming to you personally, like a father or an elder brother, exhorting you to consider virtue; such conduct on my part, I say, is not typical. If I had made any money from it, if my services had been paid for, then my having done these things would have made sense; but now, as you perceive, not even my accusers in all their impudence dare say that I ever exacted or sought pay from anyone; of that they have no witnesses. And I myself have a sufficient witness to the truth of what I say—my poverty.

[Socrates was found guilty by a vote of 280 to 220.]

PLATO: THE PARABLE OF THE CAVE

The Republic (vii), trans. B. Jowett (London, 1888), pp. 209–212, revised.

Among the young men who followed Socrates around Athens, listening and learning, was the son of a noble and wealthy family. Named Aristocles, he is better known by his nickname, Plato ("broad-shouldered") and stood out from the crowd not only because of his good looks but also because of his great intellect. After the trial and execution of Socrates, Plato gave up a career in politics for one of teaching and writing. He founded "The Academy" on the outskirts of Athens, dedicated to the Socratic method of dialectics. Plato's most famous book is the Republic, representing a series of dialogues between Socrates and his friends; it offers Plato's plans for an ideal society ruled by philosophers. The following allegory defines and illustrates Plato's concept of reality—quite the opposite of what we understand by that word today. It was to have great influence on Christian thinkers from St. Augustine to Thomas Aquinas and beyond.

[Socrates addressing Glaucon] And now . . . let me show in a figure how far our nature is enlightened or unenlightened. Imagine human beings living in an underground cave, with a long entrance open towards the light and as wide as the interior of the cave. Here they have been from childhood, chained by their legs and necks so they cannot move and can see only what is in front of them. . . . Above and behind them at a distance is the light of a fire; between them and the fire is a raised way and a low wall along it, like the screen at a marionette show to hide the performers, who show their puppets over the top.

I see, he said.

And do you see men passing along the wall carrying all sorts of vessels, statues of men and animals, made of wood, stone, or other materials, which appear over the wall? Some talk, some are silent.

A strange image, he said, and they are very strange prisoners.

Very like ourselves, for in the first place do you think they would have seen anything of themselves or of one another, except the shadows which the fire throws on the opposite wall of the cave?

How could they, he asked, if they were never allowed to move their heads?

And of the objects being carried they would similarly see only the shadows?

Yes, he replied.

And if they could converse with one another, would they not suppose that the things they saw were the real thing?

Very true.

And suppose further that the prison had an echo which came from the other side, would they not imagine, when one of the passers-by spoke, that the voice came from one of the passing shadows?

No question, he replied.

To them the truth would be literally nothing but the shadows of the images.

That is certain.

And now consider if they could be released from their bonds and cured of their error, whether the process would be as follows. At first, when one of them is freed and compelled to stand up and turn his head around and walk or look towards the light, he will feel sharp pains, the glare will hurt him, and he will be unable to see the reality of which he had formerly seen only the shadows. Then imagine someone telling him that what he saw before was an illusion, but that now when he is coming closer to reality and his eye is turned towards more real existence, he has a clearer vision. What will be his reply? And you may further imagine that his instructor is pointing to the objects as they pass and asking him to name them. Will he not be perplexed? Will he not believe that the shadows which he formerly saw are truer than the objects which are now shown to him?

Yes, far truer.

And if he is compelled to look straight at the light, will he not have a pain in his eyes which will make him turn away to take refuge in the objects of vision which he can see and which he will conceive to be in reality clearer than the things which are now being shown to him?

True, he said.

And suppose moreover that he is reluctantly dragged up that steep and rugged ascent and held fast until he is forced into the presence of the sun itself, is he not likely to be pained and vexed? When he approaches the light, his eyes will be dazzled and he will not be able to see anything at all of what are now called realities.

Not all in a moment, he said.

He will need to grow accustomed to the sight of the upper world. And first he will see the shadows best, next the reflections of men and other objects in the water, and then the objects themselves; and when he turns to the heavenly bodies and the heaven itself, he will find it easier to gaze upon the light of the moon and the stars at night than to see the sun or the light of the sun by day?

Certainly.

Lastly, he will be able to see the sun, not turning aside to the illusory reflections of it in the water, but gazing directly at it in its own proper place and contemplating it as it is.

Certainly.

He will then proceed to argue that it is the sun that gives the seasons and the years and is the guardian of all that is in the visible world and that the sun is in a way the cause of all the things that he and his fellows have been accustomed to behold?

Clearly, he said, he would arrive at that conclusion after what he had seen.

And when he remembered his old habitation and the wisdom of the cave and his fellow prisoners, do you not suppose that he would congratulate himself on the change, and pity them?

Certainly, he would.

And if they were accustomed to confer honors among themselves on those who were quickest to observe the passing shadows and to remark which of them went before and which followed after and which were together, and who were best able to divine the future, . . . do you think he would be eager for such honors, or envy those who attained honor and sovereignty among men? Would he not agree with Homer, "Better to be the poor servant of a poor master," and endure anything rather than go back to his old beliefs and his old way of life.

Yes, he would prefer anything to such a life.

Imagine once more such a one coming down suddenly out of the sunlight and being replaced in his old seat. Would he not be certain to have his eyes full of darkness?

To be sure, he replied.

And if there were a contest and he had to compete in measuring the shadows with the prisoners who had never moved out of the cave, while his sight was still weak, and before his eyes had become steady, . . . would he not make himself ridiculous? Men would say of him that he had returned from the place above with his eyes ruined, and that it was better not even to think of ascending. And if anyone tried to free another and lead him up to the light, let them only catch the offender, and they would put him to death.

No question, he said.

[In] this allegory . . . the prison is the world of sight, the light of the fire is the power of the sun, and you may take the journey upwards to be the ascent of the soul into the intellectual world. Then you will be in possession of what I surmise. . . . Whether it is right or wrong, heaven knows. But whether true or false, my opinion is that in the world of knowledge the Idea of the Good appears last of all and is seen only with an effort. When seen, however, it is inferred to be the universal author of all things beautiful and right; it gives birth to light and to the lord of light in the visible world, and the immediate and supreme source of reason and truth in the intellectual. This is the power upon which he who would act rationally either in public or private life must have his eye fixed. . . .

ARISTOTLE: THE IDEA OF THE POLIS

From *The Politics of Aristotle*, trans. Jowett (2 vols., Oxford, 1885), 1:77–80, 203–213, revised.

Like his teacher Plato and his pupil Alexander, Aristotle is a towering figure in Western Civilization. He is a rich source of Greek history and his rational analysis of complex questions is a model for any age. At this point, however, we can deal with only one of his many pioneering works, his *Politics,* in which he describes over 150 city-states in the Greece of his day, analyzing the nature of government, its ideal forms, and its "perversions." Much of our political thinking, including our vocabulary, comes to us via Aristotle.

First let us consider the purpose of a *polis,* and how many forms of government by which human society is regulated. . . . Man is by nature a political animal. And therefore, even when they do not need one another's help, men desire to live together all the same, and are in fact brought together by their common interests in proportion as they severally attain to any measure of well-being.

This is certainly the chief end both of individuals and of states. And also for the sake of mere life (in which there is possibly some noble element) mankind meet together and maintain the political community, so long as the ills of existence do not greatly overbalance the good. And we see that men cling to life even in the midst of misfortune, seeming to find in it a natural sweetness and happiness. . . .

When the state is constituted on a principle of equality, the citizens think they should hold office by turns. In this system, every one takes his turn, while somebody else looks after his interests. . . . But nowadays, because of the advantage to be gained from office and the public treasury, men want to stay in office permanently. It is as if the officeholder were ailing and kept in health only by being in office. In any case, the conclusion is clear: governments that have a regard for the common interest are the *true* forms, being constituted in accordance with strict principles of justice, whereas those which consider only the interest of the rulers are defective and perverted forms, for they are despotic, whereas the polis is a community of free men.

Having determined these points, we next consider how many forms of government exist, and what they are. Once we have determined the true forms, the perversions will be apparent. The words *constitution* and *government* have the same meaning; and government, which is the supreme authority in states, must be in the hands of one, a few, or many. The true forms of government, therefore, are those in which the one, the few, or the many govern with a view to the common interest. Governments which rule with a view to the private interest, whether of the one, the few, or the many, are perversions.

Citizens who are truly citizens ought to participate in the advantages of a state. Of the forms of government in which one person rules, we call it *kingship* when it regards the common interest; that in which more than one but not the many rule, *aristocracy,* because the best men rule or because they have at heart the interests of the state and its citizens. When the citizens at large administer the state for the common interest, the government is called by the generic name *constitution*. There is a reason for this usage.

One man or a few may excel in virtue, but virtue is of many kinds; and as the numbers increase, it becomes more difficult for them to attain perfection in all; although they may excel in military virtue, which is found in the masses. Hence, in a constitutional government the fighting men have the supreme power, and those who possess arms are the citizens.

Of the above-mentioned forms, the perversions are as follows: Of royalty, *tyranny;* of aristocracy, *oligarchy;* of constitutional government, *democracy*. For tyranny is a kind of monarchy which has in view the interest of the monarch only; oligarchy has in view the interest of the wealthy; democracy, of the needy: and none of them, the common good. . . .

There remains the question, Whether the happiness of the individual is the same as that of the state? Here again there can be no doubt: No one denies that they are the same. For those who hold that the well-being of the individual consists in his wealth, also think that riches make the happiness of the whole state, and those who value most highly the life of a tyrant deem that city the happiest which rules over the greatest number; while those who approve an individual for his virtue say that the more virtuous a polis is, the happier it is.

Two questions arise: First, which is the more acceptable life, that of a citizen who is a member of a polis, or that of an alien who has no political ties? Secondly, which is the best form of constitution or the best condition of a state, either on the premise that political privileges are desirable for all, or for a majority only? Since the good of the state and not of the individual is the proper subject of political thought, . . . while the first of these two points has a secondary interest for us, the latter will be the main subject of our inquiry.

Now it is evident that that form of government is best in which every man, whoever he is, can act best and live happily. But even those who agree in thinking the life of virtue is the most acceptable raise a question, Whether the life of business and politics is more acceptable than one which is wholly independent of external goods, I mean a contemplative life, which some say is the only one worthy of a philosopher. For these two lives—the philosopher's and the statesman's—appear to have been preferred by those who have been keenest in pursuit of virtue, both in our day and formerly. Which is better is a question of no small moment; for the wise man, like the wise state, will necessarily regulate his life after the best end. There are some who think that while a despotic rule over others is the greatest injustice, to exercise a constitutional rule over them, even though not unjust, is a great impediment to an individual's well-being. Others take an opposite view: they maintain that the true life of man is the practical and political, and that every virtue admits of being practiced, quite as much by statesmen as by individuals; others, again, are of the opinion that arbitrary and tyrannical rule is alone consistent with happiness; in some states, indeed, the entire aim both of laws and constitution is to give men a despotic power over their neighbors.

Therefore, although the laws of most poleis may be said to be in a chaotic state, still if they aim at anything they aim at the maintenance of power; thus in Crete and Sparta the system of education and most of the laws are framed with a view to war, and in all nations able to gratify their ambition, military power is esteemed. . . . [But] warlike pursuits, although generally deemed honorable, are not the supreme or final end; they are only means. The good lawgiver should inquire how states, races, and communities may participate in the good life. . . . [If] happiness is virtuous activity, then the active life will be the best, both for the polis and for the individual.

PLUTARCH: LIFE OF LYCURGUS—SPARTA (ca. 600 B.C.)

From *Ideal Commonwealths*, ed. H. Morley (London, 1889), pp. 19–43 passim, revised.

Contrasted with the Athenian way of life was the Spartan. In the following extract Plutarch, who lived in the first century A.D., offers his version of Spartan culture. Since he was interested in history as a source of moral lessons, he may have exaggerated some elements of the story, but no one has seriously disputed his overall picture. Lycurgus was the Spartan leader who was supposed to have given Spartans their constitution.

Lycurgus . . . found a prodigious inequality, the city overcharged with many indigent persons who had no land, and the wealth centered in the hands of a few. Determined to root out the evils of insolence, envy, avarice, and luxury, and those distempers of a state still more inveterate and fatal—I mean poverty and riches—he persuaded them to cancel all former divisions of land and make new ones, in such manner that they might be perfectly equal in their possessions and manner of living. Hence, if they were ambitious of distinction they might seek it in virtue, as no other difference was left between them but that which arises from the dishonor of base actions and the praise of good ones. His proposal was adopted: he made 9,000 lots for the territory of Sparta, which he distributed among so many citizens, and 30,000 for the inhabitants of the rest of Laconia. . . . Each lot could produce 70 bushels of grain for each man, and 12 for each woman, besides a proportionate quantity of wine and oil. Such a provision was thought sufficient for health and good habit of body, and they wanted nothing more. . . .

He commanded that all gold and silver coin should be called in, and that only a sort of money made of iron should be current, a great weight and quantity of which was worth very little, so that to lay up 20 or 30 pounds required a pretty large closet and, to remove it, nothing less than a yoke of oxen. With the spread of this money, a number of vices were at once banished, for who would rob another of such coin?

Next, he excluded unprofitable and superfluous arts; indeed, if he had not done so, most of them would have fallen of themselves when the new money took place, as manufactures could not be disposed of. Their iron coin would not pass in the rest of Greece, but was ridiculed and despised; so that Sparta had no means of buying any foreign or curious wares, nor did any merchant ships unload in their harbors. In all their country were found no sophists, wandering fortune-tellers, keepers of infamous houses, or dealers in gold and silver trinkets, because there was no money. Thus luxury, losing by degrees the means that supported it, died away; even those who had great possessions had no advantage from them, since they could not be displayed in public. . . .

Then he introduced a third institution, which was wisely and ingeniously contrived. This was the use of public tables where all were to eat in common of the same meat, and such kinds of it as were decided by law. At the same time they were forbidden to eat at home, upon expensive tables and couches, to call in the assistance of butchers and cooks, or to fatten like voracious animals in private. For so not only their manners would be corrupted, but their bodies disordered; abandoned to all manner of sensuality and dissoluteness, they would require long sleep, warm baths, and the same indulgence as in perpetual sickness. . . .

It was left to the father to rear what children he pleased, but he was obliged to take the child to a place called Lesche, to be examined by the most ancient men of the tribe. If it was strong and well proportioned, they gave orders for its education and assigned it one of the 9,000 shares of land; but if it was weakly or deformed, they ordered it to be thrown into the place called Apothetae, which is a deep cavern near Mount Taygetus; concluding that its life could be of no use either to itself or to the public, since nature had not given it any strength or fitness to begin with. . . .

As the nurses never swathed the infants, their limbs had a freer turn and their countenances a more liberal air; in addition, they accustomed them to all kinds of food to have no fear of the dark or of being alone, and to abandon all ill-humor and unmanly crying. . . . As soon as they were seven years old, Lycurgus ordered them to be enrolled in companies, where they were all kept under the same order and discipline and had common exercises and recreations. He who showed the best conduct and the most courage was made captain of the company. The others kept their eyes on him, obeyed his orders, and bore up under the punishments he inflicted; so that their whole education was an exercise of obedience. . . .

As for learning, they had only what was absolutely necessary. It was all calculated to make them subject to command, to endure labor, and to fight and conquer. As they advanced in age, their discipline was increased, their hair was cut short, they were made to go barefoot and to play, for the most part, quite naked. At 12 years of age, their under garment was taken away, and only one upper a year allowed them. Hence, they were necessarily dirty and not indulged the luxury of baths and oils, except on some particular days of the year. They slept in companies, on beds made of reed tops which they gathered themselves. . . . In winter, they were allowed to add a little thistle-down, as that seemed to give some warmth. . . .

The Spartan discipline continued after they had reached maturity. For no man was free to live as he pleased. The city being like one great camp, where all had their stated allowance and knew their public charge, each man concluded that he was born not for himself but for his country. Hence, if they had no particular orders, they employed themselves in inspecting the boys and teaching them something useful, or in learning from those who were older than themselves. One of the greatest privileges that Lycurgus provided was the enjoyment of leisure, the consequence of his forbidding them to exercise any mechanic trade. It was not worth their while to work to raise a fortune, since riches were of no account, and the Helots, who tilled the soil, were answerable to the produce. . . .

[Lycurgus] did not allow everybody to go abroad and see other countries, lest they contract foreign manners, see lives with little discipline and different forms of government. He forbid foreigners to come to Sparta, if they could not give a good reason for coming, . . . lest they teach his own people some evil. For along with foreigners come new subjects of discourse; new discourse produces new opinions, from which there necessarily spring new passions and desires which, like discords in music, would disturb the establishsd government. He therefore thought it even more necessary to keep corrupt customs and manners out of the city than to prevent the introduction of a pestilence.

CHAPTER 3

ROME: THE AUGUSTAN AGE

Caesar Augustus, adopted son and heir of Julius Caesar, took over the Roman Republic in 31 B.C. He instituted an imperial administration that lasted two hundred years, enforcing "peace"—*Pax Romana*—at home and abroad. Calling himself *Princeps,* meaning "First Citizen of the State," he rejected all grandiose titles because he wanted the people to think they still enjoyed a republic. Some, like Cicero, were not fooled and paid with their lives. But Augustus kept up a republican façade of old forms and institutions, such as the Senate, so the citizens could go through the motions of governing while he himself held all the real power.

Arresting the plague of civil wars that had beset the Republic for over a century, the *Principate,* as it was called, produced a Golden Age of the arts that lasted until the death of Marcus Aurelius in A.D. 180. Although literature was the chief product of that age, other arts flourished as well: architecture, in such works as the Colosseum and the Pantheon; sculpture, in equestrian statues and realistic busts of famous people; and engineering feats, such as the famous Roman roads and aqueducts.

The Roman Empire, extending from the Straits of Gibraltar to the Persian Gulf, and from the North Sea to the Sahara, offered great opportunities for political ambition, at the same time that it produced a leisure class that could devote its energies to "higher" forms of art. Or some combined both politics and art, as did Seneca, Nero's tutor.

Rome also profited from earlier civilizations, notably the Hellenic and the Hellenistic Ages of Pericles and Alexander the Great, respectively. Those were hard acts to follow, of course, and much of Roman culture is derivative. But the point should not be overemphasized. Rome preserved Greek ideas and forms for later ages and did so conscientiously, in many faithful copies of art and literature. Equally important, however, is the fact that Rome also gave us many original concepts: in government, law, language, military science, and religion, to mention a few. Note, for instance, how much Western religions owe to Rome: Saint Paul himself was a Roman citizen who, because of the Pax Romana and Roman communications, was able to travel and write to Christian communities throughout the Empire, thus helping to insure the propagation of the faith.

Several questions that might be raised here are: If Rome was a republic for five hundred years before Augustus, if the Augustan Age lasted two hundred years, and if the barbarian invasions did not occur for another two hundred years, then what is meant by the "Fall of Rome"? Secondly, was Augustus a "good" ruler? If your answer is yes, then do you favor dictatorship over a republic? or is there another solution to the dilemma? Remember, he ruled for forty-four years (31 B.C. to A.D. 14) and was succeeded by people such as Tiberius Caesar and Nero. How does the Augustan Age compare with the Classical Age of Greece?

CICERO: THE REPUBLIC AND THE LAWS

The Treatises of Cicero, trans. C.D. Yonge (London, 1853), pp. 411–421, 430–435, revised.

Marcus Tullius Cicero (d.43 B.C.) was one of those rare people able to combine the roles of politician and writer. Dedicated to the Roman Republic, Cicero fought all attempts to make it a dictatorship. He lost. Under the Second Triumvirate (Octavian & Co.), Cicero was executed as an enemy of the State. But his works endure. As a prose writer, Cicero was unexcelled; later, he would be a model for the Italian Renaissance. Besides political works, he wrote on such subjects as rhetoric, oratory, and philosophy, plus many letters that are a mine of information about the period.

. . . When the sublime philosopher Xenocrates was asked what his students had learned, he replied, "To do of their own will what they might be compelled to do by law." But the citizen who obliges everybody to behave properly by the authority of laws . . . is certainly preferable to the wisest of philosophers, who spend their lives in such discussions in order to convince a few. Which of their fine orations . . . is to be favored over a well-constituted government, public justice, and good customs? . . .

A commonwealth is a constitution of the entire people. Now, the people is not any and every association, however congregated, but the association of the whole, bound together by the compact of justice and the exchange of utility. The chief cause of this association is not so much the weakness of the individual as it is a certain spirit of congregation inherent in mankind. For the human race is not composed of isolated individuals, wandering and alone; even in abundance and without the need of mutual aid, it seeks company spontaneously. . . .

Every people which consists of an association of the entire multitude, . . . every city which consists of an assemblage of the people, and every commonwealth which embraces the members of these associations, must be regulated by a certain authority in order to be permanent.

Such an intelligent authority should always refer to that first grand principle which established the commonwealth. It must be in the hands of one supreme person, or entrusted to the administration of certain delegated rulers, or undertaken by the whole people. When the direction depends on one individual, he is called a king; . . . when it is in the power of privileged delegates, the state is said to be ruled by an aristocracy;

and when the people are all in all, it is a democracy of popular constitution. If the bond of social affection which originally united the people in political association for the sake of the public interest maintains its force, each of these forms is not perfect, in my opinion, nor necessarily good, but tolerable and such that one may be accidentally better than another: either a just and wise king, or a selection of the most eminent citizens, or even the populace itself (though this is the least commendable) may, if there is no interference from crime and cupidity, form a constitution that is sufficiently secure. . . .

The worst state of affairs results from those factious tyrannies into which kings, aristocrats, and democrats sometimes degenerate. From these diverse elements there occasionally arises . . . a new kind of government. Then the revolutions and upheavals, the changes and vicissitudes, are amazing indeed; in such cases, the wise politician must weigh his actions carefully. To calculate his approach, to apply the skills that moderate the course of events, to keep a steady hand on the reins of authority, and to lead the people safely through the dangers to which they are exposed—that is the work of a most illustrious citizen and almost divine genius.

There is a fourth kind of government preferable, in my opinion, to all of the above: that is a mixed and moderate government composed of the three basic forms I have mentioned.

The Laws

Of all the questions argued among learned men, none is more important to understand than this: that man is born for justice and that laws and equity are based not on opinion but on nature. This truth will become apparent if we investigate the quality of human association and society.

Nothing is so like or so equal as one person is to another. If the corruption of customs and false opinions did not mislead weaker minds and turn them aside from the course of nature, no one would more nearly resemble himself than all men resemble all others. Therefore, whatever definition we give of man will be applicable to the whole human race. This is a good indication that there is no difference in kind among men; if there were, one definition would not apply to all.

In fact, reason, which alone gives us our superiority over the animals—by enabling us to conjecture, argue, prove, disprove, and reach conclusions—is assuredly common to us all, for the ability to learn and acquire knowledge is invariable in all human minds, although the knowledge itself may be endlessly diverse. We all perceive the same objects with the same senses and those things which stimulate the senses stimulate them in the same way in all men. And those first rudimentary elements of intelligence . . . which are imprinted on the mind are imprinted similarly on all; speech, which is the interpreter of the mind, though differing in its choice of words, agrees in the ideas expressed. Therefore, if he adopt nature for his guide, any person in any nation may attain to virtue.

This similarity among humans is found not only in those things that are good but also in evil. For all men are alike captivated by pleasure, which, though it is an enticement to vice, yet bears some likeness to what is naturally good. For it delights us by its delicacy and sweetness, and for this reason, through an error of the mind, it is embraced as something wholesome.

By an error scarcely less universal we shun death as if it were a dissolution of nature, and cling to life because it keeps us in that condition to which we were born. Likewise we look upon pain as one of the greatest of evils, not only because of its cruelty but also because it seems to lead to the destruction of nature. Again, because of the resemblance between renown and honor, those who are publicly honored are considered happy, while those who do not attain fame are thought to be miserable. Troubles, joys, desires, and fears permeate all minds without distinction; nor if different people have different beliefs does it follow that those who worship dogs and cats do not labor under superstitions equally with other nations, though they may differ from them in their manifestations.

Again, what nation does not love courtesy, kindliness, gratitude, and remembrance of past favors? What people does not hate and despise arrogance, malice, cruelty, and ungratefulness? While this uniformity of opinion proves that the human race is united, the last point is that a system of living properly makes us better. . . .

It follows then that nature made us just, so that we might share our goods with each other and supply each other's wants. You will note that when I speak of nature I mean nature in its pure form, but there is in fact such corruption, engendered by evil ways, that the sparks, as it were, of virtue given by nature are extinguished and vices arise and thrive around it.

But if men were to follow nature and . . . "hold nothing alien that concerns mankind," then justice would be cultivated equally by all. For to those whom nature has given reason she has also given right reason, enjoining the good and forbidding evil. If nature has given us law, she has also given us right; she has bestowed reason on all and therefore right has been bestowed on all. . . .

There is no expiation for crimes against men or sacrilege against the gods. The guilty, therefore, must pay the penalty and bear the punishment; not so much punishments inflicted by the courts—which were not always there, do not exist today in many places, and where they do exist, they are often biased and partial—but the guilty are tormented and pursued by the furies, not with blazing torches, as in the tragedies, but with the anguish of remorse and the torture of a guilty conscience.

But if it were the fear of punishment and not nature that ought to keep men from wickedness, what anxiety would there be to trouble the wicked when the danger of punishment was removed? There has never been a villain so brazen as not to deny that he was guilty, or invent some story of justifiable anger to excuse his crime and seek justification in some natural principle of right. Now, if even the wicked dare appeal to such principles, how jealously should they be guarded by the good! But if it is the penalty and the fear of punishment, and not the wickedness itself, that is to keep men from a life of crime, then none could be called unjust and the greatest offender ought to be called inprudent rather than wicked.

Furthermore, those who are determined to practice goodness, not for its own sake but for the sake of some private advantage, are merely shrewd rather than good. For what will that person not do in the dark who fears nothing but a witness and a judge? What will such a one do if, in some desolate spot, he meets a solitary individual, who can be robbed of a fortune? The virtuous man, who is just and good by nature, will talk with such a person, help him, and guide him on his way. But the other, who does nothing for anyone else's sake, measuring every act by the standard of his own advantage—it is obvious, I think, how he will act. But if he does deny that he would kill the person and rob him, it will not be because he sees the wickedness in it but only because he is afraid of being discovered and that that will have bad consequences. . . .

It is an absurdity to state, as some do, that everything is just which is found in the customs and laws of nations. Are the laws of tyrants just simply because they are laws? . . . In my opinion, such laws deserve no more consideration than that passed during our own interregnum empowering the dictator to put to death any citizen he pleased, even without a trial.

For there is only one basic justice which cements society and one law which establishes this justice: that law is right reason, the true rule of all commands and prohibitions. Whoever neglects this law, whether it has been recorded in writing or not, is unjust and wicked.

If justice, however, consists in submission to written laws and national customs, and if, as some affirm, everything is to be measured by this standard of utility, then anyone who thinks it will be profitable will break the laws, if he is able. It follows that justice does not exist at all if it does not exist in nature, and that which was established by utility may be overturned by some other utility.

If nature is not the foundation of justice, then all the virtues may lose their sway. For what becomes of generosity, patriotism, loyalty? Where will the desire to help one's neighbor or the gratitude for favors received be able to exist? For these virtues come from our natural inclination to love our fellowmen, and this is the foundation of justice. Otherwise, not only consideration for people but also rites and religious services of the gods would be at an end. For I think that these ought to be maintained, not through fear, but because of the close relationship that exists between mankind and the Divinity.

If the principles of justice were founded on the will of the people, the edicts of princes, or the decisions of judges, then it could become right to rob, commit adultery, or forge wills, if these acts were approved by the votes or decrees of the populace. But if such power belongs to the decisions and decrees of fools and the laws of nature can be changed by their votes, then why do they not ordain that what is bad and pernicious shall henceforth pass for good and salutary? Why, if a law can make justice out of injustice, should it not be able to change evil into good?

We have no other standard of distinguishing between a good and a bad law than the standard given us by nature. Nor is it only right and wrong that are distinguished by nature, but also and without exception things which are honorable and dishonorable. For since an intelligence common to us all makes things known to us and formulates them in our mind, honorable actions are seen as virtue, and dishonorable as vice, and only an insane person would conclude that these judgments are matters of opinion and not fixed by nature.

AUGUSTUS EVALUATED

AUGUSTUS: MEMORIAL TO HIMSELF (A.D. 13)

From *Res gestae divi Augusti*, ed. Th. Mommsen (Berlin, 1883), pp. 144–155.

The following inscription, from a Roman temple in Ankara, Turkey, was devised by Augustus a year before he died. Tablets bearing the inscription were placed before his mausoleum, while others were sent abroad.

In my sixth and seventh consulships, after I had put out the fires of civil war and after I had received complete control of public matters by common consent, I then removed the control of the republic from my own hands to the will of the Senate and the Roman people. For this service to the State I was honored with the title of AUGUSTUS by decree of the Senate; the entranceway to my house was covered with laurels by the people and a civic crown was set over my door. A golden shield was placed in the Curia Julia with an inscription testifying that the Senate and the Roman people had given me this recognition of my valor, my justice, my clemency, and my piety. After that, I took precedence in rank above all, but of power I possessed no more than those who were my colleagues in the magistracy.

TACITUS: ON AUGUSTUS

Annals, 1:2-10, trans. Church and Brodribb (London, 1877).

Tacitus, a Roman Consul and major historian, survived Domitian's Reign of Terror, when leading citizens were judicially murdered simply to allay the Emperor's fears of plots and subversion. Tacitus longed for the "good old days" of the Roman Republic, when life, he felt, was more virtuous. Despite this bias, however, his works present a profound picture of Roman life in the first century A.D. His *Annals* (those that survive) are especially complete for the reign of Tiberius, whom he particularly blamed for the moral decline under the Empire.

Augustus won over the soldiers with gifts, the populace with cheap food, and all men with the sweets of repose, and so grew by degrees, while he concentrated in himself the functions of the Senate, the magistracy, and the laws. He was wholly unopposed, for the bravest spirits had fallen in battle or in the proscription, while the remaining nobles, the readier to be his slaves, were raised the higher by wealth and promotion, so that, aggrandized by revolution, they preferred the safety of the present to the dangerous past. Nor did the provinces dislike that state of affairs, for they distrusted the government of the Senate and the people, because of the rivalries between the leading men and the rapacity of the officials, while the protection of the laws was unavailing, as they were continually deranged by violence, intrigue, and finally corruption. . . .

The State had been revolutionized and there was not a vestige of that old sound morality. Stripped of equality, all looked up to the commands of a sovereign without the least apprehension for the present, while Augustus in the vigor of life could maintain his own position, that of his house, and the general tranquillity. When in advanced age, he was worn out with a sickly constitution and the end was near and new prospects opened, a few spoke in vain of the blessings of freedom, but most dreaded and some longed for war. . . .

[On the occasion of his death,] there was much talk of Augustus himself. . . . People extolled the number of his consulships, . . . the continuance of the tribunitian power for 37 years, and the title *Imperator* [Emperor] earned 21 times, as well as his other honors, some of which had been frequently repeated and others were entirely new. Thoughtful men, however, spoke variously of his life, either to praise or to censure it. Some said that dutiful feelings toward his father [Julius Caesar] and the necessities of State, in which laws then had no place, drove him into civil war—which can never be planned nor conducted on any moral principles. . . . The only rule for his distracted country, said these critics, was that of a single man. But the State was organized under the name of neither a kingdom nor a dictatorship, but a *Princeps*. The oceans and distant rivers were the boundaries of the empire; the legions, provinces, fleets, everything was linked together. There was law for the citizens; there was respect shown to the allies. The capital was embellished on a grand scale. Only in a few instances did he resort to force, and then simply to secure general tranquillity.

It was said, on the other hand, that filial duty and State necessity were merely assumed as a mask. It was really from a lust for power that he had excited the veterans by bribery; had, when a young man and a subject, raised an army, tampered with the Consul's legions, and feigned an attachment to the faction of Pompey. . . . Then, when Hirtius and Pansa were slain, . . . he at once took possession of both their armies, wrested the consulate from a reluctant Senate, and turned against the State the arms with which he had been entrusted against Antony. Citizens were proscribed, lands divided, without so much as the approval of those who executed the deeds. Even granting that the deaths of Cassius and Brutus were sacrifices to a hereditary enmity (though duty calls for us to waive private feuds for the sake of the public weal), still Sextus Pompey had been deluded by the phantom of peace, and Lepidus by the mask of friendship. Subsequently, Antony had been lured on by . . . his marriage with the sister, and paid with his death the penalty of a treacherous alliance. No doubt there was peace after all this, but it was a peace stained with blood.

SUETONIUS: ON AUGUSTUS

History of the Twelve Caesars, trans. P. Holland (London, 1899), 1:103-4, 128-31, revised.

Suetonius, in the second century, wrote lively biographies of the early Roman emperors. Uncritical and anecdotal, they are still informative and useful, as this one on Augustus.

Twice Augustus thought of giving up his absolute rule: once, just after the overthrow of Antony, when he was stung by the latter's charge that it was his (Augustus's) fault that the republic had not been restored; and again, during his long, lingering sickness, when he summoned the magistrates and the senate to his house and submitted an account of the condition of the empire. Realizing, however, that once he was a private citizen he could not live without danger, and also aware that it would imperil the republic to put it into the hands of the many, he continued to keep control of it himself. It is hard to say whether his decision and the results of it were better. He not only expressed his good intentions orally from time to time, but he also issued them in the form of an edict:

> May it be my privilege to establish the State on a firm and secure basis and thereby reap the benefits that I seek: i.e., to be the author of an excellent government and to carry with me when I die the hope that the basis I have laid for the State shall endure.

And he achieved his wish by doing all in his power to prevent any dissatisfaction with the new regime. . . .

When the people tried to force the Dictatorship upon him, he knelt down, threw off his toga, and with bared breast begged them not to insist. He always shrank from the title of *Lord* [*Dominus*] as a reproach and an insult [because it was used by slaves towards their masters]. When the phrase *O just and gracious Lord* was spoken in a play at which he was a spectator, the people sprang to their feet with applause. . . . Not only did he check them by look and gesture, but next day he reproved them in an edict. . . .

If he could avoid it, he would not enter or leave a town except in the evening or at night, in order to avoid disturbing anyone by obligations of ceremony. During his consulship he usually went through the streets on foot, and when he was not a consul, in a closed litter. His morning receptions were open to all, even commoners, and he answered the requests of those who approached with great affability. . . .

As he was delivering a speech in the Senate, someone said, "I did not understand you," and another: "I would contradict you if I had the chance." Several times when he was rushing from the Senate in anger at the excessive bickering, someone shouted, "Senators ought to have the right to speak their minds on public questions. . . ." Still, no one suffered for their freedom of speech or insolence. Even when some infamous libels were scattered in the Senate house, he was not disturbed nor did he trouble to refute them. Without trying to discover the authors, he merely proposed that in the future those who published anonymous defamatory notes or verses about anyone should be called to account. . . .

When he appeared as a witness in court, he willingly submitted to questions and even to contradiction. . . . He never recommended his sons for office without adding: If they deserve it. . . . He wanted his friends to be influential in the State but to be bound by the same laws and judgments as the rest.

How well he was loved for his conduct in all these respects it is easy to judge. . . . The whole body of the citizens with a sudden accord presented him with the title of *Pater Patriae*, Father of the Country: first the commons sent a deputation to Antium, where he refused it, and then again at Rome as he entered the theatre. . . . Soon afterwards not by decree or acclamation, but through Valerius Messala, who was commissioned to speak for the whole body, saying:

Good fortune and divine favor attend thee and thy house, O Caesar Augustus; for thus we feel that we are praying for lasting prosperity for our country and happiness for our city. The Senate in accord with the people of Rome hails thee *Pater Patriae*.

PLINY: PANEGYRIC OF TRAJAN (A.D. 100)

From *Correspondence with Trajan*, ed. E. G. Hardy (London, 1889).

In the Roman Republic the office of Consul was one of the highest. Although its prestige declined under the Principate, it was still held in awe. Pliny, newly elevated to the consulship, addressed the following eulogy to Emperor Trajan. Since he was one of the Five Good Emperors, and since Pliny certainly remembered some of the bad ones, his praise is credible.

It is not a tyrant of whom we speak, but a fellow-citizen—not a master but a father. His excellence and preeminence are all the greater because he considers himself one of us and remembers that he is no less a man for being a ruler of men. Let us therefore appreciate our good fortune and prove ourselves worthy of him. Let us always ask ourselves whether we owe greater obedience to a princeps who finds satisfaction in the servitude of his people or to one who delights in their freedom. . . .

We are ruled by you, [Sire,] and subject to you, just as we are subject to the laws. The laws curb our impulses and our desires, yet they exist with us and dwell with us. You are preeminent among us, you excel us, just as honor and power, though above men, nevertheless belong to them. Because of scorn for us and apparent fear of equality, your predecessors forgot how to proceed. Where they were raised above us on the backs of slaves, you are raised by glory, by love of your fellow citizens, and by freedom. . . .

Your statues are like those that used to be dedicated to private citizens for outstanding public services; statues of Caesar are made of the same material as those of a Brutus or a Camillus, and for the same reason. They drove kings and a conquering enemy from our walls; but he [Trajan] wards off and prevents kingship itself and other evils coupled with defeat; he occupies the seat of the Princeps so there will be no room for a master. . . .

I turn now to your consulship. . . . When the usual formalities of election had been completed, . . . you, to everyone's amazement, advanced to the presiding consul and offered yourself to be bound by the oath [of obedience to the laws]—hitherto unknown for a prince. . . . Fellow Senators, I am amazed and I keep asking myself if I really saw and heard what I thought I did. The Commander, Caesar, Augustus, Pontifex Maximus, stood before the seated consul, [who] dictated the oath, without getting up, and the Princeps swore, spoke, and proclaimed aloud the words that bound himself and his lineage to the wrath of the gods if he knowingly lied. . . . You, Caesar, made yourself subject to the laws, laws that were never written for a princeps. Now, for the first time, I hear not princeps above the laws, but *laws above Princeps*.

STOICS AND EPICUREANS

LUCRETIUS: ON THE NATURE OF THINGS

Trans. H. Munro (Cambridge, 1891), Bk. II, pp. 28–29 revised.

The Greek philosophies of Epicureanism and Stoicism were widely followed in Rome. Lucretius, in his *De rerum natura* put into verse in the first century B.C. the philosophy of the Greek Epicurus (d. 270 B.C.) Although our translation is in prose, you may still sense something of the Latin hexameter through the English.

'Tis sweet, when on the mighty sea the winds stir up its waters, to watch from land another's deep distress. Not that we take pleasure and delight in anyone's affliction, but because 'tis sweet to see what evils we ourselves are spared. 'Tis sweet also to observe the mighty struggles of armies arrayed along the plains without sharing ourselves in the danger. But nothing is as sweet as holding the high serene plateaus well fortified by the learning of the wise, looking down upon others wandering all about and searching blindly for the path of life: to see their rivalry in intellect, their status-seeking, their striving night and day towards the summit of power and the mastery of the world.

O miserable minds of men! O blinded hearts! in what darkness of living and in what dangers you pass this term of existence, whatever its duration! O not to see that nature for herself craves nothing save that pain hold off from the body and that the mind experience pleasure free from care and fear? We see moreover that for the body's nature few things are needed, and only such as take away the pain, although there may be many choice delights, besides, that come from time to time. . . .

If there are no golden images of youths along the halls holding in their right hands flaming lamps to light the nightly banquet, if the house shines not with silver nor glitters with gold nor do the panelled and gilded ceilings resound—still, though these things be wanting, to lounge with others in the soft grass beside a stream and under the boughs of a lofty tree and at no great expense pleasantly refresh our bodies, especially if the weather is smiling and the season sprinkles the green of the grass with flowers. Hot fevers do not sooner leave the body because you toss and turn on pictured tapestry or blushing purple, than if you lie upon a poor man's pallet.

Wherefore, since treasures nor status, nor princely glory avail us nothing in respect of our body, you must also hold that they are of no service to the mind either; unless perhaps, if you see your legions swarming over the battleground waging mock warfare, strengthened flank and rear by powerful reserves and great force of cavalry, and you marshall them equipped in arms and animated with one spirit, thereupon you find that religious scruples, scared by these things, fly panic-stricken from the mind; and that the fears of death leave the breast untrammeled and free from care, when you see your fleet swarm forth and deploy itself on every side.

But if we see that these things are fit for nothing but laughter and ridicule, and that, in truth, men's fears and dogging cares are not the clash of arms and cruel weapons; if unabashed we mingle with kings and emperors and are not overawed by the glitter of gold nor the sheen of the purple robe, how then can you doubt that this is entirely the power of reason, since the whole of life is but a struggle in the dark? Even as children are flurried and dread all things in the darkness, so we in the daylight sometimes fear things not one whit more to be dreaded than those at which children shudder in the dark, thinking them real. This terror therefore and darkness of mind must be dispelled not by the sun's rays and glittering shafts of day, but by the aspect and law of nature.

EPICTETUS: DISCOURSES

From James Harvey Robinson, *Readings in European History* (New York, 1904), 1:15–16, revised.

A slave in Nero's household, Epictetus (d. 139 A.D.) managed somehow to obtain a good education and eventually became a teacher of philosophy in Rome. Although he wrote nothing himself, his faithful pupil Arrian has left us detailed reports of his thinking and teaching, which is an advanced form of Stoicism. It makes an interesting comparison with Christianity or with Epicureanism.

When you are going in to see any great personage, remember that another also sees what is going on, from above, and that you ought to please him before all others. He who sees you from above, therefore, asks you: What did you used to say in school about exile, about bondage, about death, and about disgrace?

I used to say that they are neutral, neither good nor bad. And what do you say of them now? Are they changed, different? No. Are you changed, then? No. Then tell me what things are neutral? Things that are independent of the will. Tell me also what follows from this? The things that are independent of the will are nothing to me.

Tell me also about the Good; what did you hold it to be? A will such as we ought to have and also a right use of things about us. And our aim, what is it? To follow thee. Do you say this now also? I say the same now also.

Then go in to the great personage boldly and remember these things; and you will see what a youth is who has studied these things when he is among men who have not studied them. . . .

If the things are true which are said by philosophers about the kinship between God and man, what else remains for men to do than what Socrates did? Never say, in reply to the question, To what country do you belong? that you are an Athenian, or a Corinthian, but that you are a citizen of the world. . . . He who has observed with intelligence the administration of the world, and has learned that the greatest, supreme, and most comprehensive community is that which is composed of men and God. . . . Why should not such a man call himself a citizen of the world, why not a son of God, and why should he be afraid of anything which happens among men? Is kinship with the emperor or with any other powerful men in Rome sufficient to enable us to live in safety, and above contempt, and without any fear at all? But to have God for our maker, and father, and guardian, shall not this release us from our sorrows and fears?

MARCUS AURELIUS: MEDITATIONS

Trans. G. Long (New York, 1900), pp. 4–5, 85–86, 124–125, revised.

Not only was Marcus Aurelius a leading stoic philosopher of the second century A.D., but he was also one of the Five Good Roman Emperors. Although he spent a major portion of his time putting down revolts in Germany, Britain, and Parthia, he did good things for the Roman people, such as lowering taxes on the poor, limiting the brutality of gladiatorial combats, and reducing the harshness of criminal penalties. True, he is noted for his persecution of the Christians, but always reluctantly, with the hope that they would mend their ways, which he saw as an attack on the Empire. His *Meditations* provide a rare insight into the mind and heart of a major political figure.

In my father [Emperor Antoninus Pius] I saw mildness of temper and steady resolution in the things he had decided upon after due deliberation; no vain glory in those things which men call honors; a love of labor and perseverance; a readiness to listen to those who had anything to propose for the common weal; undeviating firmness in giving to every man according to his deserts; and a knowledge gained from experience of the times for vigorous action or for slacking off. I observed that he had overcome all passion for boys. He considered himself no more than any other citizen. He released his friends from all obligation to sup with him or attend him of necessity when he went abroad. . . .

I observed too his habit of careful inquiry in all matters of deliberation . . . and that he never stopped his investigation by being satisfied with appearances. . . . He was ever watchful over the things which were necessary for the administration of the empire. . . . He was neither superstitious with respect to the gods, nor did he court men by gifts or by trying to please them or by flattering the populace; but he showed sobreity and firmness in all things and never any mean thought or action, nor love of novelty. And the things which conduce in any way to the comfort of life, and of which fortune gives an abundant supply, he used without arrogance and without excusing himself; so that when he had them he enjoyed them without affectation, and when he had them not, he did not want them. . . .

He took a reasonable care of his body, not as one who was greatly attached to life, nor out of regard to personal appearance, nor yet in a careless way, but so that, through his own attention, he very seldom stood in need of the physician's art or of medicine or external applications. . . .

He was not fond of change nor was he unsteady; he loved to stay in the same places and apply himself to the same things; and after his paroxysms of headache he came immediately fresh and vigorous to his usual occupations. His secrets were not many, . . . and those only about public matters. . . . There was nothing harsh in him, nor implacable, nor violent, nor, as one might say, anything carried to the sweating point. . . . And that might be said of him which is recorded of Socrates, that he was able both to abstain from and to enjoy those things which many are too weak to abstain from and cannot enjoy without excess. But to be strong enough both to bear the one and to be sober in the other is the mark of a man who has a perfect and invincible soul. . . .

Do not despise death, but be well content with it, since this too is one of those things that nature wills. For such as it is to be young and grow old, to increase and to reach maturity, to have teeth and beard and gray hairs, to beget and be pregnant and bring forth, and all the other natural operations which the seasons of thy life bring, such also is dissolution. This, then, is consistent with the character of a reflecting man, to be neither careless nor impatient nor contemptuous with respect to death but to wait for it as one of the operations of nature. As thou now waitest for the time when the child shall come out of thy wife's womb, so be ready for the time when thy soul shall fall out of this envelope.

But if thou requirest also a vulgar kind of comfort, thou wilt be made best reconciled to death by observing the objects from which thou art going to be removed, and the morals of those with whom thy soul will no longer be mingled. . . . Remember that thy departure will not be from men who have the same principles as thyself. For this is the only thing, if there be any, which could . . . attach us to life, to be permitted to live with those who have the same principles as ourselves. . . .

Wipe out imagination; check desire; extinguish appetite; keep the ruling faculty in power. . . .

What dost thou wish? To continue existing? Well, dost thou wish to have feeling? movement? growth? and then cessation of growth? to use thy speech? to think? . . . If it is easy to set little store by all these things, then turn to what remains—following reason and god. But it is inconsistent with reason and god to be troubled that man by death will be deprived of those other things. . . .

Man, thou hast been a citizen in this great State [the world]. What matters it to thee whether for five years [or only three]? for whatever conforms to law is fair for all. Where is the hardship if—no tyrant nor unfair judge—but Nature, who brought thee into the world, also sends thee away from it? just as if a praetor employed an actor and then sent him off the stage—"But I have not finished all five acts, only three!" Well thou sayest, but in life three acts are the whole play; what makes a play complete is decided by Him who caused its composition, and now its dissolution; and thou art the cause of neither. Depart satisfied, then, for He who releases thee is also satisfied.

CHAPTER 4

ROME: THE CHALLENGE OF CHRISTIANITY

How explain the rise of Christianity? From an obscure Jewish sect, whose leader left no writings and did not travel outside his native Judaea, Christianity rose from persecution under Nero and others to become the religion of the emperor Constantine (in 312) and the official religion of the whole Roman Empire in 395. Neither was there any absence of competitors: Stoicism and Epicureanism from Greece; Isis and Osiris from Egypt; Manichaeism, Mithraism, and other mystery cults from the Orient. Then, of course, there was the most formidable competitor of all, the official Roman religion of Emperor-worship, which accounted for so many Christian deaths that it is a wonder any survived at all. Except for the fact that Christians, to the astonishment of the blasé Romans, met their deaths in the arena gloriously, singing hymns, praising God, and seeing Heaven itself open its gates.

Furthermore, the Empire offered many advantages to the spread of the new faith: the Pax Romana, Roman roads and shipping lanes, and toleration for everything—except treason, of course. So Paul could travel to and keep in touch with the Christian communities in such faraway places as Ephesus, Corinth, Galatia, Philippi, and others, besides Rome and Jerusalem.

Questions for thought:

What is the significance of John the Baptist?

G. B. Shaw once said that Christianity might be a fine thing, but it had never been tried. Do you agree? Is it really so difficult to love one's enemies?

Is there a difference between the teachings of Paul and of Jesus?

Do you think the persecution of Christians had anything to do with the propagation of the faith among the Romans?

What is Augustine's concept of man's role on earth? What might be the environmental impact of such a philosophy?

JOHN THE BAPTIST

The King James Version, Luke 3.

In the following excerpt, John the Baptist preaches repentance of sins and the coming of Jesus. His vehemence offended the aristocracy, especially Herod's wife; she and her daughter demanded John's head—and got it!

Now in the fifteenth year of the reign of Tiberius Caesar, Pontius Pilate being governor of Judea, and Herod being tetrarch of Galilee, . . . the word of God came unto John the son of Zacharias in the wilderness. And he came into all the country about Jordan, preaching the baptism of repentance for the remission of sins, as it is written in the book of Isaiah the prophet, saying, The voice of one crying in the wilderness. Prepare ye the way of the Lord, make his paths straight. Every valley shall be filled, and every mountain and hill shall be brought low; and the crooked shall be made straight, and the rough ways shall be made smooth; and all flesh shall see the salvation of God. Then he said to the multitude that came forth to be baptised of him:

O generation of vipers, who hath warned you to flee from the wrath to come? Bring forth therefore fruits worthy of repentance, and begin not to say within yourselves, We have Abraham to our father: for I say unto you, That God is able of these stones to raise up children unto Abraham. And now also the ax is laid unto the root of the trees: every tree therefore which bringeth not forth good fruit is hewn down and cast into the fire.

And the people asked him, saying, What shall we do then?

He answereth and saith unto them, He that hath two coats let him impart to him that hath none; and he that hath meat, let him do likewise.

Then came also publicans to be baptized, and said unto him, Master, what shall we do?

He said unto them, Exact no more than that which is appointed you.

And soldiers likewise demanded of him, saying, and What shall we do? And he said unto them, Do violence to no man, neither accuse any falsely; and be content with your wages.

And as the people were in expectation and all men mused in their hearts about John, whether he were Christ or not, John answered, saying unto them all, I indeed baptize you with water, but one mightier than I cometh, the latchet of whose shoes I am not worthy to unloose; He shall baptize you with the Holy Ghost and with fire.

JESUS BEGINS HIS MINISTRY: THE SERMON ON THE MOUNT (LUKE 5–6)

As the people pressed upon him to hear the word of God, he stood by the lake of Gennesaret and saw two boats standing by the lake; the fishermen were gone out of them and were washing their nets. And he entered one of the boats, which was Simon's, and [asked] him to push out a little from the land. And he sat down and taught the people out of the boat. Now when he had finished speaking, he said to Simon, Launch out into the deep and let down your nets for a draught.

And Simon answered, Master, we have toiled all night and have taken nothing; nevertheless at thy word I will let down the net. And when they had done this, they inclosed a great multitude of fishes, and their nets broke. And they beckoned to their partners . . . in the other boat that they should come and help them. And they came and filled both boats so that they began to sink.

When Simon Peter saw it, he fell down at Jesus's knees, saying, Depart from me, for I am a sinful man, O Lord. For he was astonished, and all that were with him, at the draught of fishes which they had taken. . . .

And Jesus said unto Simon, Fear not; from henceforth thou shalt catch men. And when they had brought their boats to land, they forsook all and followed him. . . .

One day, as he was teaching, there were Pharisees and doctors of the law sitting by, which were come from every town of Galilee and Judaea and Jerusalem; and the power of the Lord was there to heal them. And . . . men brought in a bed a man with a palsy, and they tried to bring him in and lay him before Jesus; and when they could not find [a way] because of the multitude, they went up on the house top and let him down through the tiling with his couch into the midst before Jesus. And when he saw their faith, he said unto him, Man, thy sins are forgiven thee.

And the scribes and the Pharisees began to reason, saying, Who is this which speaketh blasphemies? Who can forgive sins but God alone?

But Jesus [said] unto them, What reason ye in your hearts? [Which] is easier, to say, Thy sins be forgiven thee; or to say, Rise up and walk? But that ye may know that the Son of man hath power upon earth to forgive sins, (he said unto the sick of the palsy,) I say unto thee, Arise, and take up thy couch and go into thine house.

And immediately he rose up before them and took up that whereon he lay and departed to his own house, glorifying God. And they were all amazed and they glorified God. . . .

And it came to pass in those days that he went out into a mountain to pray, and continued all night in prayer to God. And when it was day he called unto him his disciples; and of them he chose twelve, whom also he named apostles: Simon, whom he named Peter, and Andrew his brother, James and John, Philip and Bartholomew, Matthew and Thomas, James the son of Alphaeus, and Simon called the Zealot, and Judas the brother of James, and Judas Iscariot, which was also the traitor.

And he came down with them and stood in the plain [with] his disciples and a great multitude of people out of all Judaea and Jerusalem and from the sea coast of Tyre and Sidon, which came to hear him and to be healed of their diseases; and they that were vexed with unclean spirits, and they were healed. And the whole multitude sought to touch him, for there went virtue out of him and healed them all. And he lifted up his eyes on his disciples and said:

Blessed are the poor, for yours is the kingdom of God.

Blessed are ye that hunger now, for ye shall be filled.

Blessed are ye that weep now, for ye shall laugh.

Blessed are ye when men shall hate ye and separate you from their company and reproach you and cast out your name as evil, for the Son of man's sake. Rejoice ye in that day and leap for joy, for behold, your reward is great in heaven, for in like manner did their fathers unto the prophets.

But woe unto you that are rich, for ye have received your consolation.

Woe unto you that are full, for ye shall hunger.

Woe unto you that laugh now, for ye shall mourn and weep.

Woe unto you when all men shall speak well of you, for so did their fathers to the false prophets.

But I say unto you which hear, Love your enemies, do good to them which hate you, bless them that curse you, and pray for them which despitefully use you. And unto him that smiteth thee on the one cheek offer also the other; and him that taketh away thy cloke forbid not to take thy coat also. Give to every man that asketh of thee; and of him that taketh away thy goods, ask them not [back] again. And as ye would that men should do to you, do ye also to them likewise.

For if ye love them which love you, what thank have ye? for sinners also love those that love them. And if ye do good to them which do good to you, what thank have ye? for sinners also do even the same. . .

But love your enemies and do good and lend, hoping for nothing again: and your reward shall be great and ye shall be the children of the Highest; for he is kind [even] to the unthankful and the wicked.

Be ye therefore merciful, as your Father also is merciful.

Judge not, and ye shall not be judged; condemn not, and ye shall not be condemned; forgive, and ye shall be forgiven.

Give, and it shall be given unto you. . . .

And he spake a parable unto them: Can the blind lead the blind? shall they not both fall into the ditch? The disciple is not above his master, but every one that is perfect shall be as his master. And why beholdest thou the mote that is in thy brother's eye, but perceivest not the beam that is in thine own eye? How canst thou say to thy brother, Brother, let me pull out the mote that is in thine eye, when thou thyself beholdest not the beam that is in thine own eye? Thou hypocrite, cast out first the beam of thine own eye, and then shalt thou see clearly to pull out the mote that is in thy brother's eye. . . .

For a good tree bringeth not forth corrupt fruit; neither doth a corrupt tree bring forth good fruit. For every tree is known by its fruit. For of thorns men do not gather figs, nor of a bramble bush gather they grapes.

A good man out of the treasure of his heart bringeth forth that which is good; and an evil man out of the evil treasure of his heart bringeth forth that which is evil: for of the abundance of the heart his mouth speaketh.

And why call ye me, Lord, Lord, and do not the things which I say? Whosoever cometh to me and heareth my sayings and doeth them, I will shew you to whom he is like: He is like a man which built a house, and digged deep and laid the foundation on a rock. And when the flood arose, the stream beat vehemently upon that house, and could not shake it, for it was founded upon a rock.

But he that heareth and doeth not is like a man that without a foundation built a house upon the earth; against which the stream did beat vehemently, and immediately it fell, and the ruin of that house was great.

THE PASSION OF JESUS

Mark 15; 16:1–6.

Pontius Pilate, Roman governor of Judaea, tried to avoid responsibility when Jesus was brought before him. Assigned to keep the peace in Palestine, Pilate was afraid of the power of the high priests.

And straightway in the morning the chief priests held a consultation with the elders and scribes and the whole council, and bound Jesus, and carried him away and delivered him to Pilate.

And Pilate asked him, Art thou the King of the Jews?

And he answering said unto him, Thou sayest it.

And the chief priests accused him of many things; but he answered nothing.

And Pilate asked him again, saying, Answerest thou nothing? behold how many things they witness against thee.

But Jesus yet answered nothing; so that Pilate marveled. Now at that feast he released unto them one prisoner, whomsoever they desired. And there was one named Barabbas, which lay bound with them that had made insurrection with him, who had committed murder in the insurrection. And the multitude crying aloud began to desire him to do as he had ever done unto them. But Pilate answered them, saying, Will ye that I release unto you the King of the Jews? For he knew that the chief priests had delivered him for envy. But the chief priests moved the people, that he should rather release Barabbas unto them.

And Pilate answered and said unto them, What will ye then that I shall do unto him whom ye call the King of the Jews?

And they cried out again, Crucify him.

Then Pilate said unto them, Why, what evil has he done?

And they cried out the more exceedingly, Crucify him.

And so Pilate, willing to content the people, released Barabbas unto them, and delivered Jesus, when he had scourged him, to be crucified. And the soldiers led him away into the hall, called Praetorium; and they call together the whole band. And they clothed him with purple, and platted a crown of thorns, and put it about his head, and began to salute him, Hail, King of the Jews!

And they smote him on the head with a reed, and did spit upon him, and bowing their knees worshipped him. And when they had mocked him, they took off the purple from him, and put his own clothes on him, and led him out to crucify him. And they compel one Simon, a Cyrenian, who passed by, . . . to bear his cross.

And they bring him unto the place Golgotha, which is, being interpreted, The place of a skull. And they gave him to drink wine mingled with myrrh; but he received it not. And when they had crucified him, they parted his garments, casting lots upon them, what every man should take. And it was the third hour and they crucified him. And the superscription of his accusation was written over:

THE KING OF THE JEWS

And with him they crucified two thieves; the one on his right hand, and the other on his left. And the scripture was fulfilled, which saith, And he was numbered with the transgressors. And they that passed by railed on him, wagging their heads, and saying, Ah, thou that destroyest the temple, and buildest it in three days, save thyself, and come down from the cross.

Likewise also the chief priests mocking said among themselves with the scribes, He saved others; himself he cannot save. Let Christ the King of Israel descend now from the cross, that we may see and believe.

And they that were crucified with him reviled him. And when the sixth hour was come, there was darkness over the whole land until the ninth hour. And at the ninth hour Jesus cried with a loud voice, saying, Eloi, Eloi, lama sabachthani? which is, being interpreted, My God, my God, why hast thou forsaken me?

And some of them that stood by, when they heard it, said, Behold, he calleth Elias.

And one ran and filled a spunge full of vinegar, and put it on a reed, and gave him to drink, saying, Let alone; let us see whether Elias will come to take him down. And Jesus cried with a loud voice, and gave up the ghost. And the vail of the temple was rent in twain from the top to the bottom.

And when the centurion, which stood over against him, saw that he so cried out, and gave up the ghost, he said, Truly this man was the Son of God. There were also women looking on afar off, among whom was Mary Magdalene and Mary the mother of James the less and of Joses and Salome (who also when he was in Galilee, followed him, and ministered unto him) and many other women which came up with him unto Jerusalem.

And now when the even was come, because it was the preparation, that is, the day before the sabbath, Joseph of Arimathaea, an honourable counsellor, which also waited for the kingdom of God, came and went in boldly unto Pilate, and craved the body of Jesus. And Pilate marvelled if he were already dead; and calling unto him the centurion, he asked him whether he had been any while dead. And when he knew it of the centurion, he gave the body to Joseph. And he bought fine linen, and laid him in a sepulchre which was hewn out of a rock, and rolled a stone unto the door of the sepulchre. And Mary Magdalene and Mary the mother of Joses beheld where he was laid.

And when the sabbath was past, Mary Magdalene and Mary the mother of James, and Salome, had bought sweet spices, that they might come and anoint him. And very early in the morning the first day of the week, they came unto the sepulchre at the rising of the sun. And they said among themselves, Who shall roll us away the stone from the door of the sepulchre? And when they looked, they saw that the stone was rolled away; for it was very great. And entering into the sepulchre, they saw a young man sitting on the right side, clothed in a long white garment; and they were affrighted. And he saith unto them, Be not affrighted. Ye seek Jesus of Nazareth, which was crucified. He is risen; he is not here. Behold the place where they laid him. . . .

SAUL OF TARSUS BECOMES THE APOSTLE PAUL

Acts of the Apostles 7–9.

Born in the Near East, Saul of Tarsus was a Roman citizen and a Jew. After having been educated in Jerusalem, he became an ardent nationalist and persecutor of Christians. Sometime around 33 A.D., the Sanhedrin commissioned him to help suppress Christianity in Damascus. But as he was on his way there, he had a shattering experience, converted to Christianity, and changed his name from Saul to Paul. Henceforth he devoted himself to studying the words of the Master, preaching, traveling, and working with Christian communities throughout the Empire. In the process he wrote them many letters explaining theology and giving his own interpretation of Christ's message—which letters (epistles) now form a major portion of the New Testament. One of Paul's essential convictions was that a person could become a Christian without having to be a practicing Jew. On this he disagreed with the Jewish community of Christians in Jerusalem. And so, on his last visit to the city, he was arrested, spent two years in jail, had several hearings, and was finally sent to Rome because of his citizenship in the Empire. There he was again imprisoned and eventually executed about 62 A.D., probably under Nero. Luke tells the story, beginning with the martyrdom of St. Stephen.

Stephen, . . . being full of the Holy Ghost, looked up steadfastly into heaven and saw the glory of God . . . and said, Behold, I see the heavens opened and the Son of man standing on the right hand of God. Then they . . . ran upon him with one accord and cast him out of the city and stoned him; and witnesses laid down their clothes at a young man's feet, whose name was Saul. And they stoned Stephen, [who called] upon God, saying, Lord Jesus, receive my spirit. . . .

And Saul was consenting unto his death. At that time there was a great persecution against the church at Jerusalem; and they were all scattered abroad throughout the regions of Judea and Samaria, except the apostles. And devout men carried Stephen to his burial and made great lamentation over him. As for Saul, he made havoc of the church, entering every house, and haling men and women, committed them to prison. . . .

Saul, yet breathing out threatenings and slaughter against the disciples of the Lord, went unto the high priest and desired of him letters to Damascus to the synagogues, that if they found any of this [Christian] Way, men or women, he might bring them bound unto Jerusalem. And as he journeyed, [nearing] Damascus, suddenly there shined round about him a light from heaven; he fell to the earth and heard a voice saying unto him, Saul, Saul, why persecutest thou me?

And he said, Who art thou, Lord?

And the Lord said, I am Jesus whom thou persecutest. . . . And he trembled and astonished said, Lord, what wilt thou have me to do?

And the Lord said unto him, Arise, and go into the city and it shall be told thee what thou must do. And the men which journeyed with him stood speechless, hearing a voice, but seeing no man. And Saul arose from the earth and [although] his eyes were open, he saw no man. But they led him by the hand and brought him into Damascus. And he was three days without sight, and neither did he eat nor drink.

[Now] there was a certain disciple at Damascus named Ananias, and to him said the Lord, in a vision: Ananias!

And he said, Behold, I am here, Lord.

And the Lord said unto him, Arise, and go into the street which is called Straight and inquire in the house of Judas for one called Saul of Tarsus. For, behold, he prayeth and hath seen in a vision a man named Ananias coming and putting his hand on him, that he might receive his sight.

Then Ananias answered, Lord, I have heard by many [people] of this man, how much evil he hath done to thy saints at Jerusalem, and here he hath authority from the chief priests to bind all that call on thy name.

But the Lord said unto him, Go thy way, for he is a chosen vessel unto me, to bear my name before the Gentiles, and kings, and children of Israel. For I will shew him how many great things he must suffer for my name's sake.

And Ananias went his way and entered into the house; and putting his hands on him, said, Brother Saul, the Lord, even Jesus, that appeared unto thee in the way as thou camest, hath sent me that thou mightest receive thy sight and be filled with the Holy Ghost. And immediately there fell from his eyes as it had been scales, and he received sight forthwith, and arose, and was baptized.

PAUL TO THE ROMANS

Chap. 3–13 passim.

Paul's letters illustrate the scope of his thinking. To the Christians at Rome, after explaining that Jews and Gentiles are all children of God, Paul offers some lessons in Christian theology. To his friend Timothy, by contrast, Paul gives advice on running the churches at Ephesus and warns him of the heresies besetting Christianity in those days.

All [men] have sinned and come short of the glory of God; [but] all are justified freely by his grace through the redemption that is in Christ Jesus, whom God hath set forth as a propitiation through faith; . . . for remission of sins, . . . through the forbearance of God; to declare . . . his righteousness: that he might be just, and the justifier of him that believeth in Jesus. . . . Therefore, we conclude that a man is justified by faith without the deeds of the law. Is he the God of the Jews only? Is he not also of the Gentiles? . . .

Let love be without dissimulation. . . . Be kindly affectioned to one another with brotherly love, . . . rejoicing in hope, patient in tribulation. . . Bless them which persecute you; bless and not curse them. Rejoice with them that rejoice, and weep with them that weep. . . . Repay no man evil for evil. . . . If possible, live peaceably with all men. . . . Avenge not yourselves, . . . Vengeance is mine, saith the Lord, I will repay. Therefore, if thine enemy hunger, feed him; if he thirst, give him drink, for in so doing thou shalt heap coals of fire on his head. Be not overcome of evil, but overcome evil with good. . . .

Render therefore to all men their due: tribute to whom tribute is due, custom to whom custom, fear to whom fear, honor to whom honor. Owe no man anything but to love one another; for he that loveth hath fulfilled the law. . . . For all . . . the commandments are [summed up] in one: Thou shalt love thy neighbor as thyself. Love worketh no ill to his neighbor; therefore love is the fulfilling of the law. . . .

God commended his love toward us, in that, while we were yet sinners, Christ died for us. . . . If, when we were enemies, we were reconciled to God by the death of his Son, much more, being reconciled, we shall be saved by his life. And not only so, but we also joy in God through our Lord Jesus Christ, by whom we have now received the atonement. Wherefore, as by one man sin entered into the world, and death by sin; and so death passed upon all men, for all have sinned. . . . Death reigned from Adam to Moses, even over them that had not sinned after the similitude of Adam's transgression, who is the figure of him that was to come. . . . If by one man's offense death reigned by one; much more they which receive abundance of grace and of the gift of righteousness shall reign in life by one, Jesus Christ. . . .

PAUL TO TIMOTHY

I, 1–6 passim.

Paul, an apostle of Jesus Christ by the commandment of God our Saviour, and Lord Jesus Christ, which is our hope:

To Timothy, my own son in the faith: Grace, mercy, and peace, from God our Father and Jesus Christ our Lord. . . . I exhort that . . . supplications, prayers, intercessions, and giving of thanks, be made for all men; for [emperors] and all that are in authority; that we may lead a quiet and peaceful life in all godliness and honesty. For this is good and acceptable in the sight of God our Saviour. . . . I will therefore that men pray everywhere, lifting up holy hands, without wrath [or] doubt.

In like manner also, that women adorn themselves in modest apparel, with shamefacedness and sobriety; not with braided hair, or gold, or pearls, or costly array; but . . . with good works. Let the women learn in silence with all subjection. But I suffer not a woman to teach, nor to usurp authority over the man, but to be in silence. For Adam was first formed, then Eve. And Adam was not deceived, but the woman being deceived was in the transgression. Notwithstanding, they shall be saved in childbearing, if they continue in faith and charity and holiness with sobriety.

. . . If a man desireth the office of a bishop, he desireth a good work. A bishop then must be blameless, the husband of one wife, vigilant, sober, of good behavior, given to hospitality, apt to teach; not given to wine, not [pugnacious], not greedy of filthy lucre; . . . one that ruleth his own house, having his children in subjection. . . .

Rebuke not an elder, but entreat him as a father, and the younger men as brethren; the elder women as mothers, the younger as sisters, with all purity. Honor widows that are widows indeed, but if [they] have children or nephews, let them learn first to show piety at home, and to requite their parents, for that is good and acceptable before God. . . . Let not a widow be taken into the number under three-score years old, having been the wife of one man, well reported for good works: if she have brought up children, if she have lodged strangers, if she have washed the saints' feet, if she have relieved the afflicted, if she have diligently followed every good work.

But the younger [widows] refuse, for when they have begun to wax wanton against Christ, they will marry, having damnation because they have cast off their first faith. And withal they learn to be idle, wandering about from house to house, and not only idle, but tattlers also and busybodies, speaking things which they ought not to. . . .

Against an elder receive no accusation [without] two or three witnesses. Them that sin rebuke before all, that others may also fear. . . . Lay hands suddenly on no man, neither be partaker of other men's sins; keep thyself pure. Drink no longer water, but use a little wine for thy stomach's sake. . . .

Charge them that are rich in this world, that they be not highminded nor trust in uncertain riches, but in the living God, who giveth us richly all things to enjoy; that they do good, that they be rich in good works, ready to distribute, willing to communicate, laying up in store for themselves a good foundation against the time to come, that they may lay hold on eternal life.

O Timothy, keep that which is committed to thy trust, avoiding profane and vain babbling, and oppositions of science falsely so called, which some professing have erred concerning the faith. Grace be with thee. Amen.

TACITUS: PERSECUTION OF CHRISTIANS UNDER NERO

Annals, trans. Church and Brodribb, pp. 304–305.

Nero's persecutions are proverbial. Hence we are fortunate in having a reliable account by an historian, Tacitus, whom we have met before. Then follows an exchange of letters on the subject of the Christian martyrs between the Emperor Trajan and his faithful lieutenant Pliny the Younger, whom we also met in the last chapter. The rational approach of these Romans contrasts with the religious zeal of the Christians, many of whom welcomed martyrdom with hymns and praise for the Lord.

All human efforts, all the Emperor's lavish gifts, and all the propitiation of the gods, did not banish the belief that the burning [of Rome] was the result of an [imperial] order. Consequently, to dispel that rumor, Nero fixed the blame on a sect whom the people call Christians and who are hated for their abominations. On them Nero

Roman catacombs*. Underground burial vaults were frequently used as secret meeting places by the Christians of the first four centuries. They also covered the walls with paintings and symbols of Christian iconography. (Scala/Editorial Photocolor Archives.)*

inflicted the most exquisite tortures. Christus, from whom the name is derived, suffered the extreme penalty during the reign of Tiberius at the hands of one of our procurators, Pontius Pilate. This most mischievous superstition, thus checked for the moment, again broke out not only in Judea, the first source of the evil, but even in Rome, where all things hideous and shameful from every part of the world converge and become popular.

Accordingly, all those who admitted their guilt were arrested, and on their information, a vast multitude were [apprehended] and convicted, not so much of the crime of firing the city as of hatred for mankind. Ridicule of every kind accompanied their deaths. Clothed in the skins of animals, they were torn to pieces by dogs; or they were nailed to crosses; or they were set on fire to serve as illumination after dark. Nero offered his gardens for the spectacle, . . . while he mingled with the people in the dress of a charioteer or stood aloft in a chariot. Hence, even for criminals who deserved extreme and exemplary punishment people began to feel compassion, for it was not for the public good, apparently, but to glut one man's cruelty that they were being killed.

PLINY: PERSECUTION OF CHRISTIANS

Pliny the Younger, *Epistolae*, 10:96–97.

Pliny to the Emperor Trajan

. . . Not having been present at the trials of Christians, I do not know what crime is usually punished or investigated or to what extent. So I have no little uncertainty whether there is any distinction of age, or whether the weaker offenders fare in no respect otherwise than the stronger; whether pardon is granted on repentance, or whether when one has been a Christian there is no gain to him that he has ceased to be such; whether the mere name [Christian], if it is without crimes, or crimes connected with the name are punished.

Meanwhile, I have taken this course with those who were accused before me: I have asked them if they were Christians. To those who confessed I put the question a second and a third time, threatening punishment. If they persisted, I ordered them led away to execution. For I did not doubt that, whatever it was they admitted, obstinacy and unbending perversity certainly deserved to be punished. Others of like insanity who were Roman citizens I noted down to be sent to Rome for trial.

Soon after this, as often happens, because the matter was taken notice of, the crime became widespread and many cases arose. An anonymous paper presented the names of many people. But these denied that they were or had been Christians, and I thought it right to let them go, since at my bidding they prayed to the gods and made supplication with wine and incense to your statue, which I had ordered brought into the court for this purpose, together with the images of the gods; in addition, they cursed Christ; none of which things, it is said, can those who are really Christians be made to do. Others named by an informer said they were Christians and soon after denied it, saying that they had indeed once been but had ceased to be Christians, some three years ago, some several years, and one even 20 years ago. All these not only worshipped your statue and the images of the gods, but they also cursed Christ. They asserted that the extent of their fault—or delusion—was this: that they had been wont to assemble on a fixed day before dawn to sing hymns by turns [antiphonally] to Christ as a god; and that they bound themselves by oath, not for any crime, but resolving to commit neither theft, nor robbery, nor adultery, and not to break their word nor deny a deposit when demanded; after these things were done, it was their custom to depart and meet together again to take food, but ordinary, harmless food; and they said that even this had ceased after my edict by which, following your orders, I had forbidden the existence of clubs. On this account I deemed it the more necessary to find out, by torture, from two maidservants who were called deaconesses, what was the truth. I found out nothing but a perverse and excessive superstition.

I therefore adjourned the examination and hastened to consult you. The matter seemed to me worth deliberation, especially on account of the number of those in danger. For many of every age, rank, and even of both sexes, are put in jeopardy, and will be in the future. The contagion of this superstition has penetrated not only the cities but also the villages and rural areas. Still, it seems possible to stop it and set it right. . . .

Trajan to Pliny

You have followed the right procedure, my dear Secundus, in investigating the cases of those brought before you as Christians. For, indeed, nothing can be laid down as a general rule which contains anything like a definitive policy. They are not to be sought out. If they are informed against and convicted, they should be punished, but on condition that anyone who denies being a Christian and makes this evident by actions, such as worshiping our gods, even though suspected as to his past conduct, shall obtain pardon on his repentance. Anonymous information, however, ought not to be permitted in any accusation—a course that would not only form the worst kind of precedent but which is not in accord with the spirit of our times.

AUGUSTINE: THE CITY OF GOD (A.D. 412)

Trans. M. Dods (1872), in *Fathers of the Christian Church,* ed. P. Schaff and H. Wace (New York, 1888 ff.), 2:282–285.

Greatest of the Latin fathers of the Church, Augustine (354–430), bishop of Hippo, probably had more influence on Christianity than any other thinker after St. Paul. Also, many theologians, Protestant as well as Catholic, consider him to be the founder of the discipline of theology. Best known of his works are the *Confessions,* a classic of Christian mysticism, and *The City of God,* from which the following excerpts are taken. Augustine's defense of Christianity against pagan attacks after the sack of Rome by Alaric in 410 presents a uniquely Christian view of history as a conflict between two mystical cities, one the heavenly city of God, the other the earthly city of mammon, or the devil. The fall of the earthly city of Rome, therefore, should cause not weeping and wailing but rejoicing. This interpretation of life as a struggle against earthly values in the quest for eternal salvation was to dominate the thinking of the Middle Ages until the Italian Renaissance "rediscovered" classical antiquity.

Two cities have been formed by two loves: the earthly city by the love of self, even to the contempt of God, and the heavenly city by the love of God, even to the contempt of self. The former, in a word, glories in itself, the latter in the Lord. The one seeks glory from men, but the greatest glory of the other is God, the witness of conscience. The one lifts up its head in its own glory; the other says to its God, "Thou art my glory, and the lifter up of mine head" [Ps. 3:3]. In the one, the princes and the nations it subdues are ruled by the love of ruling; in the other, the princes and the subjects serve one another in love, the latter obeying while the former take thought for all. The one delights in its own strength, represented in the persons of its rulers; the other says to its God, "I will love thee, O Lord, my strength" [Ps. 18:1]. And therefore the wise men of the one city, living according to man, have sought for profit to their own bodies or souls, or both, and those who have known God "glorified him not as God, neither were thankful, but became vain in their imaginations, and their foolish heart was darkened; professing themselves to be wise"—that is, glorying in their own wisdom, and being possessed by pride—"they became fools, and changed the glory of the incorruptible God into an image made like to corruptible man, and to birds, and four-footed beasts, and creeping things." For they were either leaders or followers of the people in adoring images, "and worshipped and served the creature more than the Creator, who is blessed forever" [Rom. 1:21–25]. But in the other city there is no human wisdom but only godliness, which offers due worship to the true God, and looks for its reward in the society of the saints, of holy angels as well as holy men, "that God may be all in all" [I Cor. 15:28].

Of the bliss of Paradise, of Paradise itself, and of the life of our first parents there, and of their sin and punishment, many have thought much, spoken much, written much. We ourselves, too, have spoken of these things in the foregoing books, and have written either what we read in the Holy Scriptures, or what we could reasonably deduce from them. And were we to enter into a more detailed investigation of these matters, an endless number of endless questions would arise which would involve us in a larger work than the present occasion admits. . . . I trust we have already done justice to these great and difficult questions regarding the beginning of the world, or of the soul, or of the human race itself. This race we have distributed into two parts, the one consisting of those who live according to man, the other of those who live according to God. And these we also mystically call the two cities, or the two communities of men, of which the one is predestined to reign eternally with God, and the other to suffer eternal punishment with the devil. This, however, is their end, and of it we shall speak later. At present, as we have said enough about their origin, whether among the angels, whose numbers we know not, or in the two first human beings, it seems suitable to attempt an account of their career from the time when our two first parents began to propagate the race until all human generation shall cease. For this whole time or world-age, in which the dying give place and those who are born succeed, is the career of these two cities concerning which we treat.

Of these two first parents of the human race, then, Cain was the first born and he belonged to the city of men; after him was born Abel, who belonged to the city of God. For as in the individual the truth of the apostle's statement is discerned, "that is not first which is spiritual, but that which is natural, and afterward that which is spiritual" [I Cor. 15:46], whence it comes to pass that each man, being derived from a condemned stock, is first of all born of Adam evil and carnal, and becomes good and spiritual only afterwards, when he is grafted into Christ by regeneration; so was it in the human race as a whole. When these two cities began to run their course by a series of deaths and births, the citizen of this world was the first born, and after him the stranger in this world, the citizen of the city of God, predestined by grace, elected by grace, by grace a stranger below, and by grace a citizen above. By grace—for so far as regards himself he is sprung from the same mass, all of which is condemned in its origin: but God, like a potter (for this comparison is introduced by the apostle judiciously and not without thought) of the same lump made one vessel to honor, another to dishonor [Rom. 9:21]. But first the vessel to dishonor was made and after it another to honor. For in each individual . . . there is first of all that which is reprobate, that from which we must begin, but in which we need not necessarily remain; afterwards is that which is well approved, to which we may by advancing attain, and in which, when we have reached it, we may abide. Not, indeed, that every wicked man shall be good, but that no one will be good who was not first of all wicked; but the sooner anyone becomes a good man, the more speedily does he receive this title, and abolish the old name in the new. Accordingly, it is recorded of Cain that he built a city [Gen. 4:17], but Abel, being a sojourner, built none. For the city of the saints is above, although here below it begets citizens, in whom it sojourns till the time of its reign, when it shall gather together all in the day of the resurrection; and then shall the promised kingdom be given to them, in which they shall reign with their Prince, the King of the ages, time without end.

CHAPTER 5

EASTERN ROMAN EMPIRE: SOURCES OF BYZANTINE AND RUSSIAN HISTORY

In 330 A.D., Constantine I moved the capital of the Roman Empire to Constantinople. Built at the site of Byzantium, an ancient Greek settlement on the Bosporus, Constantine's "new Rome" soon became a thriving metropolis. And unlike the Western portion of the Empire, it did not fall to the barbarians until a thousand years later, in 1453.

The culture that developed in the Eastern half of the Empire was markedly different from and superior to that of the Medieval West. Although the Emperor Justinian tried to reunite the Empire in the sixth century and sough to maintain the Latin language in his law code, it was a losing battle: Greek had been and continued to be the language of Byzantium, and despite all of General Belisarius's military successes in North Africa and Italy, the West was lost to the Empire.

The form of Christianity—Greek Orthodox—that developed in the East was also different: more mystical, abstract, and pessimistic than Roman Catholicism. It was likewise prone to more doctrinal disputes and, perhaps most significantly, it was under the control of the Emperor, who ruled as the head of both church and state, a form of government called *caesaropapism*.

When Russian culture began to develop in the ninth and tenth centuries, it was heavily influenced by Constantinople. In 988 and 989 King Vladimir adopted the Greek Orthodox religion for himself and his people and married a Byzantine princess. And it is probably no accident that the Russian government from then on exhibited the same caesaropapism found in the Eastern Roman Empire. Russian art, language, and literature all show strong Byzantine influence.

Among the following documents are some concrete forms of evidence such as Justinian's law code and the regulation of trade in Constantinople, some eyewitness accounts by Procopius and Bishop Liudprand, some theological arguments by John of Damascus, and two legendary accounts of King Vladimir and his sons—all of which will test your skills in sifting fact from myth or in finding nuggets of truth in the reporting of biased observers.

Hagia Sophia, or "Church of Holy Wisdom." *Built by the Emperor Justinian in the sixth century, it is one of the architectural wonders of the world. The forty windows at the base of the dome—an engineering tour de force—not only flood the interior with light but also cast the dome in shadow, making it appear to be "suspended on the golden thread from heaven," as one Western visitor described it. (From Fossati,* Aya Sophia, Constantinople, as Recently Restored . . . *London, 1852. Art Reference Bureau.)*

JUSTINIAN: THE INSTITUTES (533)

The Institutes of Justinian, trans. T. Sandars (London, 1874), pp. 1–7.

Among the many achievements of Justinian I (527–565), the greatest and most enduring was the reformation, or "codification," of the enormous accumulation of Roman law over 1,000 years, from the Twelve Tablets of the Republic down to the time of Justinian. By this means he provided an accessible authority for the centralized state and influenced all subsequent legal history. With the help of his competent deputy, Tribonian, who directed most of the work, four great books were produced: the *Code,* the *Digest,* the *Institutes,* and the *Novels*. The *Institutes* was intended for the beginning law student and has continued as a guide for all those studying Roman law today.

Preamble

In the Name of Our Lord Jesus Christ.

The Emperor Caesar Flavius Justinianus, Vanquisher of the Alamani, Goths, Franks, Germans, . . . Triumphant Conqueror, Ever August, to the youth Desirous of Studying Law. Greetings.

The Imperial majesty should not only be made glorious by arms, but also strengthened by laws that, alike in time of peace and in time of war, the state may be well governed, and that the emperor may not only be victorious in the field of battle, but also may by every legal means repel the iniquities of men who abuse the laws, and may at once religiously uphold justice and triumph over his conquered enemies.

1. By our incessant labors and great care, with the blessing of God, we have attained this double end. The barbarian nations reduced under our yoke know our efforts in war; to which also [Tunis, Tripoli,] and very many other provinces bear witness, which, after so long an interval, have been restored to the dominion of Rome and our empire by our victories gained through the favor of heaven. All nations moreover are governed by laws which we have either promulgated or arranged.

2. When we had arranged and brought into perfect harmony the hithero confused mass of imperial constitutions, we then extended our care to the endless volumes of ancient law; and, sailing as it were across the mid-ocean, have now completed through the favor of heaven a work we once despaired of.

3. When by the blessing of God this task was accomplished, we summoned the most eminent Tribonian, master and ex-quaestor of our palace, together with the illustrious Theophilus and Dorotheus, professors of law, all of whom have on many occasions proved to us their ability, legal knowledge, and obedience to our orders; and we specially have charged them to compose, under our authority and advice, Institutes, so that you may no more learn the first elements of law from old and erroneous sources, but apprehend them by the clear light of imperial wisdom; and that your minds and ears may receive nothing that is useless or misplaced, but only what obtains in actual practice. So that whereas, formerly, the foremost among you could scarcely, after four years' study, read the imperial constitutions, you may now commence your studies by reading them, you who have been thought worthy of an honor and happiness so great as

that the first and last lessons in the knowledge of the law should issue forth from the mouth of the emperor.

4. When therefore, by the assistance of the same eminent person Tribonian and that of other illustrious and learned men, we had compiled the fifty books, called *Digests* or *Pandects,* in which is collected the whole ancient law, we directed that these *Institutes* should be divided into four books, which might serve as the first elements of the whole science of law.

5. In these books a brief exposition is given of the ancient laws, and of those also which, overshadowed by disuse, have been again brought to light by our imperial authority.

6. These four books of *Institutes* thus compiled, from all the Institutes left us by the ancients, and chiefly from the commentaries of our Gaius, both from his Institutes and his Journal, and also from many other commentaries, were presented to us by the three learned men we have mentioned. We have read and examined them, and accorded them all the force of our constitutions.

7. Receive therefore, with eagerness and study with cheerful diligence these our laws, and show yourselves persons of such learning that you may conceive the flattering hope of yourselves being able, when your course of legal study is completed, to govern our empire in the different portions that may be entrusted to your care.

Given at Constantinople on the eleventh day of the calends of December, in the third consulate of the Emperor Justinian, ever August.

Book One

Justice is the constant and perpetual wish to render everyone his due.

Jurisprudence is the knowledge of things divine and human, the science of the just and the unjust.

Having explained these general terms, we think we shall begin our exposition of the law of the Roman people most advantageously if we pursue first a plain and easy path and then proceed to explain particular details with the utmost care and exactness. For, if at the outset we overload the mind of the student, while yet new to the subject and unable to bear much, with a multitude and variety of topics, one of two things will happen—we shall either cause him wholly to abandon his studies or, after great toil and often after great distrust of himself (the most common stumbling block in the way of youth), we shall at last conduct him to the point to which, if he had been led by an easier road, he might, without great labor or distrust of his own powers, have been sooner conducted.

The maxims of law are these: to live honestly, to hurt no one, to give everyone his due.

The study of law is divided into two branches, that of public and that of private law. Public law regards the government of the Roman Empire, private law the interest of individuals. We are now to treat of the latter, which is composed of three elements, and consists of precepts belonging to natural law, the law of nations, and the civil law. . . .

PROCOPIUS: SECRET HISTORY OF JUSTINIAN

Ανεκδοτα, ou histoire secrète de Justinien, ed. M. Isambert (Paris, 1856, pp. 94–102, 178–186).

Lawyer and historian in the Eastern Roman Empire, Procopius (d. ca. 565) was secretary and legal adviser to General Belisarius in the wars against the Vandals and Ostrogoths in North Africa and Italy, respectively. In his eight volumes of histories, Procopius recorded many of the events of his time. He also described the public works of the Emperor Justinian in his *Buildings*, but the *Secret History* is an animated and vindictive attack on all those in power, especially Justinian and his wife the Empress Theodora, possibly because Procopius's hero, Belisarius, was accused of conspiracy and imprisoned.

Justinian was neither very tall nor very short, but of average height and weight. His face was round, not uncomely, and of a ruddy complection even after two days of fasting. To put it very succinctly, he was the perfect double of the Emperor Domitian, the son of Vespasian. Because of his evil deeds, Domitian provoked the hatred of the Romans to such an extent that after they had dismembered his body, the Senate decreed the obliteration of his name from all public documents and the destruction of all of his statues. . . .

Such was Justinian's portrait. But as to his character, I could never describe it with such accuracy. The man was an evildoer at the same time that he was everybody's dupe—both devil and fool, in other words. Dishonest in his dealings with all and sundry, his words and deeds were instinctively false, although nothing was easier than deceiving him if that was your intention. His original nature, totally devoid of principle, was corrupted by folly and maliciousness. As an ancient philosopher once said, the most contradictory faults are sometimes found in the same individual, just as colors are formed by mixtures.

Crafty, dissembling, and hypocritical, Justinian was implacable in his rages, always double-dealing; he was cruel, very adept at concealing his thoughts, easily brought to tears—but not from joy or sorrow, only on purpose, after the needs of the moment. He always played false. Not accidentally but rather by design did he multiply solemn promises and commitments, both in words and in deeds, even to his own subjects, only to renege on them later. . . .

Fickle friend and implacable enemy, he was addicted to the taking of property through robbery and murder. He was fond of all change and novelty, but always on the side of evil, never that of good and never did he accept or follow good advice, and he was known to ridicule all good deeds.

What person could ever adequately describe the instincts of this man? Some people are found to be better than their reputations in some ways, but in Justinian's case Nature seems to have accumulated in one soul all the vices that are usually dispersed among many. Ever ready to lend ear to slander, ever harsh in his punishments, he never bothered to check the facts. As soon as he heard the slanderer's charges, he gave his decision. Without the least hesitation he issued orders for the capture of towns, the burning of cities, the enslavement of whole peoples—for no reason whatever. So that, if one were to estimate all the calamities of this nature inflicted by the Romans from the earliest times to the present, Justinian would, I believe, be charged with more murders than any of his predecessors.

While he had no scruples against taking other men's wealth, paying no attention to the rules of justice, he was ever ready, on the other hand, to dispose of his own possessions with prodigality, throwing them to the barbarians for no reason at all. In effect, he owned nothing himself and did not want anyone else to own anything. He did not appear to be driven by avarice, but rather by a violent envy of those who possessed wealth. Thus, he abolished riches from the Roman world, while causing the general impoverishment of all. . . .

Justinian succeeded in managing all sorts of affairs, if not by his native intelligence, then by his little need for sleep and by his making himself available to everybody. This openness extended to the humblest and least-known persons; and the interviews were not limited to a mere admission into the tyrant's presence but included meetings and conferences that were quite confidential.

The Empress Theodora, on the other hand, was not accessible even to the chief magistrates without endless waiting and painful supplication. Always received as a group, they had to stay, like a troop of slaves, until the end of the entire audience, standing in a stuffy anteroom, terrified of falling out of favor. To be absent was to run the greatest risk. Constantly on tiptoe, each one straining to rise above his neighbors so that the eunuchs might see him when they came out. If one were summoned at last, after days of waiting, he would go into her presence in trepidation and depart quickly, after having lightly kissed each of her feet. There was no opportunity to speak or make a request unless she ordered it. Such was the servile state of society and politics, and Theodora was headmistress of the New Academy.

Thus was the Roman State being ruined by a tyrant who seemed too good-natured, on the one hand, and by Theodora, who was harsh and despotic, on the other. The good nature of the one was unreliable, while the harshness of the other was all too certain.

If the thinking and life habits of this pair were contrasting, they shared a common avarice, a lust for blood, and an aversion for truth. When anyone who had offended Theodora was reported to have committed a misdeed, no matter how trivial and unworthy of notice, accusations totally unfounded would immediately be brought against him, making the affair very serious indeed. This multiplication of charges would lead the court to the obvious finding and a sentence which was invariably the dispossession of the accused.

Theodora would bring together the appropriate judges and discuss the particular case with them in order to discover which jurists should be chosen so that the judgment would conform to her sense of appropriate cruelty. In this way, the accused immediately faced the confiscation of his life's savings to the benefit of the public treasury, and in addition, he might very well undergo the harshest kind of corporal punishment, even if he were a member of an old, established, and famous family. Neither did she hesitate to impose penalties of exile or death.

On the other hand, if one of her favorites were arrested and threatened with death by reason of premeditated murder or some similar offense, she would force his accusers, either by threats or by ridicule, to drop the charges and hush up the case. . . .

Among the innovations of Justinian and Theodora in the administration of the government was the following: In ancient times the Senate coming into the emperor's presence was accustomed to do obeisance. Any man of patrician rank would salute him on the right breast, and the emperor would kiss him on the head and then dismiss him, while all the others would first bend the right knee to the emperor and then withdraw. It was not at all the custom to salute the empress. But in the case of Justinian and Theodora, all the members of the Senate, of whatever rank, would prostrate themselves on the floor, flat on their faces, and while holding their hands and feet stretched far out, they would touch with their lips the foot of each [ruler] before rising. For even Theodora was not inclined to forgo this testimony to her dignity, she who acted as if the Roman Empire lay at her feet, but who was not at all averse to receiving even the ambassadors of the Persians and of the other barbarians and bestowing presents of money upon them, something that had never happened since the beginning of time.

Whereas in earlier days those who attended the emperor used to call him simply "Emperor" and his consort "Empress" and address each of the other magistrates in accordance with his standing at the moment, [now] if anyone who entered into conversation with either of these [rulers] should use the words "Emperor" or "Empress" and fail to call them "Master" or "Mistress," or undertake to use any word but "slave" in referring to any of the magistrates, such person would be accounted both stupid and too free of tongue, and would leave the imperial presence as though he had erred most grievously and treated with gross indignity those he should not have so treated.

And whereas in former times very few persons entered the palace, and even that with difficulty, yet since the time when these succeeded to the throne, both magistrates and all others together remained constantly in the palace. And the reason was that in the old days the magistrates were permitted to do what was just and lawful according to their own judgment. Hence, the magistrates, being occupied with their own administrative business, used to remain in their own lodgings; and the subjects of the emperor, since they neither saw nor heard of any act of violence, bothered him very little, as was to be expected. But these rulers, drawing all matters into their own hand to the ruin of their subjects, compelled everybody to dance attendance upon them in the most servile fashion. It was possible to see, almost every day, all the lawcourts for the most part empty, while at the Emperor's Court, by contrast, one would find crowds and much insolence and great shoving and pushing and withal nothing but servility. Those who were supposed to be intimate with the royal pair stood there continuously the entire day and often the greater portion of the night, without sleep or food at the usual hours, dead tired, with nothing but this to show for their apparent good fortune. And when at length they were set free, the poor chaps would quarrel among themselves over what had become of the money of the Romans.

THE BOOK OF THE PREFECT (Ninth and Tenth Centuries)

J. Nicole, *Le livre du préfet: traduction française du texte grec de Genève* (Paris, 1894).

Ranking among the top twenty dignitaries of the Eastern Empire, the prefect was the highest city official in Constantinople. Under him a host of subordinates—deputies, assessors, inspectors, etc.—enforced his regulations. Besides administrative control over all citizens, guilds, and foreign residents, the prefect enjoyed the judicial authority to enforce compliance with his orders, as shown in the following excerpts from a document discovered in Geneva by Professor Jules Nicole in 1892.

Preface

God, having created all things and given order and harmony to the universe, with his own finger engraved the Law on the tablets and published it openly so that men, being well directed thereby, should not shamelessly trample upon one another and the stronger do violence to the weaker, but that all things might be apportioned with just measure. Therefore it has seemed good for Our Serenity likewise to issue the following ordinances based on the statutes in order that the human race may be governed fittingly and no person injure his fellow.

The Notaries

Anyone wishing to be appointed a notary must be elected by vote and decision of both the head of the guild and by the notaries themselves, to ensure that the candidate has a knowledge and understanding of the laws, excels in handwriting, is neither garrulous nor insolent, and does not lead a dissolute life; but that, on the contrary, he is sober in his habits, straightforward in his thinking, eloquent, intelligent, an accomplished reader, and accurate in his diction, to obviate his giving false interpretations to what he writes or inserting deceptive clauses. If such notary is found to have contravened the law and the written regulations at some future time, those who acted as his witnesses shall be held responsible.

The candidate must know by heart the forty articles of the *Law Manual,* as well as the sixty books of the *Basilika* [law code]. He must have had a general education so that he will not make mistakes in formulating documents or in reading aloud. He shall have sufficient time to give proofs of his mental and physical ability. Let him prepare a handwritten document before the assembled guild, so that he will not make careless errors; but if he should later be detected in any, let him be expelled from the guild. . . .

The Silk-Garment Merchants

These merchants shall buy only silk garments and no other merchandise, except things for their personal use, which they may not sell to others. They shall not supply foreigners with any prohibited articles, such as red or purple silk goods of large size, so that these may not be transported to foreign countries. Whoever violates these regulations shall be flogged and suffer confiscation of goods.

Silk-garment merchants, whether slaves or free persons, when purchasing garments valued at 10 *nomismata* for persons of any sort whatever, even from princes or silk weavers, shall declare the same to the prefect so that he may know where they are to be sold. Those who fail to do so are liable to the aforementioned punishment. . . .

The Perfume Dealers

Each perfume dealer shall have his own station and not try to outdo his fellows. However, they shall watch one another to prevent any from lowering prices, selling unreasonably small quantities, or keeping in stock victualers' wares or any other sort of common goods, for an unpleasant odor does not harmonize with a pleasant one. They shall not sell pepper, nard, cinnamon, wood of aloes, ambergris, musk, incense, myrrh, balsam, wild beet, balm, assafoetida, thapsia, hyssop, or any other things of use in the trade of perfumers and dyers. They shall place their show tables with the containers in a line extending from the sacred image of Christ our Lord which is by the chalce [part of the imperial palace] up to the Milestone, so that these may send forth a savory aroma befitting the sacred image and perfume the porches of the palace. All who are caught disobeying these ordinances shall be scourged, shorn, and banished. . . .

The Victualers

The victualers shall open their shops in the squares and streets throughout the whole city so that the necessities of life may easily be found. They shall sell meat, pickled fish, meal, cheese, honey, olive oil, green vegetables of all sorts, butter, solid and liquid pitch, cedar resin, hemp, flax, plaster, pottery vessels, bottles, nails, and all the other things sold by a bar-balance and not by twin scales. They are forbidden to engage in the trades of the perfumers, soap-makers, linen merchants, tavernkeepers, or butchers even in the slightest degree. If anyone is found acting contrary to these regulations, he shall be scourged, shorn, and banished. . . . If a victualer is caught cheating another in a purchase and raising the price agreed upon, he shall be fined 10 nomismata. . . .

The Tavernkeepers

The chiefs of the tavernkeepers [guild] shall inform the prefect whenever wine is imported so that he may decide how it shall be sold, it being the assessor's duty to compel the tavernkeepers to make the measures and jars in which they sell the wine conform to the conditions of purchase. . . .

Any tavernkeeper found raising the rental of another's shop in order to acquire it for himself shall be flogged and shorn.

Tavernkeepers are forbidden to open their shops and sell wine or food before the second hour [7 A.M.] on the days of high festivals or on Sundays. At night they shall close their shops and put out the fires at the second hour [7 P.M.], in order to prevent habitual daytime patrons from having the opportunity to return at night, become intoxicated, and shamelessly engage in fights, acts of violence, or brawls. . . .

BISHOP LIUDPRAND'S MISSION TO CONSTANTINOPLE (968)

From *Die Werke Liudprands von Cremona*, ed. J. Becker (3rd ed., Leipzig and Hanover, 1915), pp. 175–180.

Already embittered by doctrinal disputes dating back to the fifth century, East-West relations worsened after Pope Leo III crowned Charlemagne Emperor and *Augustus* in 800, especially since there was already a reigning head of the Roman Empire in

Constantinople. One hundred sixty-two years later, the German King Otto I was also crowned Roman Emperor by another pope and then proposed to heal the breach by seeking the hand of a Byzantine princess for his son. Bishop Liudprand, who was Otto's special emissary for this mission, tells what happened.

On the fourth of June we arrived at Constantinople, and after a disreputable reception, meant as an insult to you (Otto), we were given the most miserable and disgusting quarters. The palace where we were confined was large and open enough, but it neither kept out the cold nor gave any shelter from the heat. Armed soldiers were set to guard us and to keep my people from going out or any others from coming in. This dwelling, accessible only to us who were shut inside it, was so far away from the emperor's residence that we were quite out of breath on having to walk there, since we could not ride. To add to our troubles, the Greek wine was quite undrinkable because of its being mixed with pitch, resin, and plaster. The house itself had no water and we could not even buy any to quench our thirst.

We . . . waited with our horses in heavy rain outside the Carian gate until five o'clock in the afternoon. Then Nicephorus ordered us to be admitted on foot, for he did not think us worthy to use the horses which your clemency had provided us, and we were escorted to the aforesaid hateful, waterless, draughty stone house. On the sixth of June, which was the Saturday before Pentecost, I was brought before the emperor's brother Leo, marshal of the court and chancellor; there we exhausted each other in a heated argument over your imperial title. He called you not emperor, which is *Basileus* in his language, but insultingly *Rex,* which is king in ours. He told me it meant the same thing even if the word was different, and said that I had come not to make peace but to stir up trouble. Finally he flew into a rage, and really wanting to insult us, did not accept your letter himself but had it read to him by an interpreter. He is a man commanding enough in person but feigning humility, though of such acuity that it could cut your flesh.

On the seventh of June, the sacred day of Pentecost, I was brought before Nicephorus himself in the palace called *Stephana,* that is, the Crown Palace. He is a human deformity, a dwarf, fat-headed with tiny mole-like eyes; disfigured by a short, broad, thick beard half going gray; deformed by a neck scarcely an inch high; porcine because of the big close bristles on his head; in color an Ethiopian and, as the poet says, "You would not care to meet him in the dark"; a big belly, lean posterior, very long in the hip considering his short stature, small legs, fair-sized heels and feet; dressed in a robe made of fine linen, but old, foul-smelling and discolored by age; wearing Greek sandals; bold of tongue, a fox by nature, in perjury and falsehood a Ulysses. He began as follows:

> It was our duty and desire to give you a courteous and magnificent reception. That, however, has been rendered impossible by the impiety of your master, who in the guise of a hostile invader has laid claim to Rome, robbed Berengar and Adalbert of their kingdom contrary to law and right, slain some of the Romans by the sword, some by hanging, while others he has either blinded or sent into exile. Furthermore, he has tried to subjugate, by massacre and conflagration, cities belonging to our empire. His wicked attempts have proved unsuccessful, so he has sent you, the instigator and promoter of this villainy, under pretense of peace, to act . . . as a spy on us.

To add to my calamities, on the day of the Assumption of the Virgin Mary the holy mother of God, an ill-starred embassy came from the apostolic and universal Pope John with a letter asking Nicephorus, "the Emperor of the Greeks," to conclude an alliance and firm friendship with "his beloved and spiritual son" Otto, "august Emperor of the Romans." If you ask me why these words and this mode of address—wicked impertinence to the Greeks—did not overwhelm the bearer and cost him his life even before they were read, I cannot answer. On other subjects I have shown a fine and abundant flow of words; on this I am dumb as a fish. The Greeks abused the sea, cursed the waves, and wondered greatly how they could have transported such an abomination, and why the deep did not open up and swallow the ship.

"The audacity of it!" they cried, "to call the universal Emperor of the Romans, the one and only Nicephorus, the great and august 'Emperor of the Greeks,' and then to style a poor barbaric creature 'Emperor of the Romans!' O earth! O sea! O sky! What shall we do with these scoundrels, these criminals? They are paupers, so if we kill them we pollute our hands with vile blood; they are ragged, they are slaves, they are peasants; if we beat them we disgrace not them but ourselves; they are not worthy of our gilded Roman scourge, or any such punishment. Would that one of them were a bishop and the other a marquis! Then we would sew them in a sack and, after beating them with rods and pulling out their beards and hair, we would throw them in the sea. As for these chaps, their lives may be spared, but we shall keep them in close custody until Nicephorus, the sacred Emperor of the Romans, be informed of these insults."

EASTERN ORTHODOX CHRISTIANITY

JOHN OF DAMASCUS: CONCERNING HOLY IMAGES (Eighth Century)

Exposition of the Orthodox Faith, trans. S. Salmond, in P. Schaff and H. Wace, eds., *A Select Library of Nicene and Post-Nicene Fathers of the Christian Church* (2d ser., 1899), 9:88, revised.

Although John "Damascene" (d. ca. 750) inherited his father's position as a caliph in Damascus, he gave it up to become a monk in Palestine and devoted his life to the fight for orthodoxy against iconoclasm. His works, which are models of the Greek language, became prime sources for the medieval scholastics and are widely used today as models of theology.

Some find fault with us for worshipping and honoring the image of our Savior and that of our Lady, as well as those of other saints and servants of Christ, [but] let them remember that in the beginning God created man after His own image. On what basis, then, do we respect each other unless because we are made after God's image? . . . Why was it that the Mosaic people honored on all hands the tabernacle which bore an image and type of heavenly things, or rather of the whole creation? God indeed said to Moses, Look that thou make them after their pattern which was shown thee in the mount. . . . What, further, is the celebrated temple at Jerusalem? Is it not hand-made and fashioned by the skill of men?

Moreover, the divine Scripture blames those who worship graven images, but also those who sacrifice to demons. The Greeks sacrificed and the Jews also sacrificed; but the Greeks to demons and the Jews to God. And the sacrifice of the Greeks was rejected and condemned, but the sacrifice of the just was wholly acceptable to God. . . .

Besides this, who can make an imitation of the invisible, incorporeal, uncircumscribed, formless God? Therefore to give form to the Deity is the height of folly and impiety. Hence, in the Old Testament the use of images was not uncommon. But after God in His bowels of pity became in truth man for our salvation, not as He was seen by Abaham in the semblance of a man, nor as He was seen by the prophets, but in being truly man, and after He lived upon the earth and dwelt among men, worked miracles, suffered, was crucified, rose again, and was taken back to Heaven. Since all those things actually took place and were seen by men, they were written for the remembrance and instruction of us who were not alive at that time, in order that though we saw not, we may still, hearing and believing, obtain the blessing of the Lord.

However, since not everyone has a knowledge of letters nor time for reading, the Fathers gave their sanction to depicting these events on images as being acts of great heroism, in order that they should form a concise memorial of them. Often, no doubt, when we are not thinking of the Lord's passion and see the image of Christ's crucifixon, His saving passion is brought back to us, and we fall down and worship not the material of which the Gospels are made, nor the material of the Cross, but that which these typify. For how does the cross that typifies the Lord differ from a cross that does not? It is the same in the case of the Mother of the Lord. . . . And similarly also the brave acts of holy men stir us up to be brave and to emulate their valor and glorify God.

THE COMING OF CHRISTIANITY TO RUSSIA (988ff)

From *The Russian Primary Chronicle,* ed. Samuel H. Cross, in *Harvard Studies and Notes in Philosophy and Literature,* Volume 12, copyright Harvard University Press, Cambridge, Mass., 1930. Reprinted by permission.

The Russian Primary Chronicle, or "Tale of Bygone Years," is the earliest known source of Russian history. Compiled by monks, it records events from 852 to 1120, with special attention to relations between Kiev and Constantinople.

[In 987, King] Vladimir summoned together his vassals and the city-elders, and said to them, "Behold, the Bulgars* came before me urging me to accept their religion. Then came the Germans and praised their own faith; and after them came the Jews. Finally the Greeks appeared, criticizing all other faiths but commending their own. . . . They preached the existence of another world. 'Whoever adopts our religion and then dies

*Bulgars: Inhabitants of a Turkic state on the Upper Volga; not to be confused with the Slavic Bulgars in the Balkans.—Ed.

shall arise and live forever. But whosoever embraces another faith, shall be consumed with fire in the next world.' What is your opinion on this subject, and what do you answer?" The vassals and the elders replied, "You know, oh Prince, that no man condemns his own possessions, but praises them instead. If you desire to make certain, you have servants at your disposal, send them to inquire about the ritual of each and how he worships God."

Their counsel pleased the Prince and all the people, so that they chose good and wise men to the number of ten, and directed them to go first among the Bulgars and inspect their faith, . . . then among the Germans, . . . and finally [among] the Greeks. . . .

Thus they returned to their own country, and the Prince called together his vassals and the elders. Vladimir then announced the return of the envoys who had been sent out, and suggested that their report be heard: . . . "When we journeyed among the Bulgars, we beheld how they worship in their temple, called a mosque, while they stand ungirt. The Bulgar bows, sits down, looks hither and thither like one possessed, and there is no happiness among them, but instead sorrow and a dreadful stench. Their religion is not good. Then we went among the Germans, and saw them performing many ceremonies in their temples; but we beheld no glory there. Then we went to Greece, and the Greeks led us to the edifices where they worship their God, and we knew not whether we were in heaven or on earth. . . . We only know that God dwells there among men, and their service is fairer than the ceremonies of other nations. . . ." Then the vassals spoke and said, "If the Greek faith were evil, it would not have been adopted by your grandmother Olga who was wiser than all other men."

After a year had passed, in [988], Vladimir proceeded with an armed force against Kherson, a Greek city [in the Crimea]. . . . [When] Vladimir and his retinue entered the city, he sent messages to the Emperors Basil and Constantine, saying, "Behold, I have captured your glorious city. I have also heard that you have an unwedded sister. Unless you give her to me to wife, I shall deal with your city as I have with Kherson." When the Emperors heard this message they were troubled, and replied, "It is not meet of Christians to give in marriage to pagans. If you are baptized, you shall have her to wife, inherit the kingdom of God, and be our boon companion in the faith. Unless you do, however, we cannot give you our sister in marriage." When Vladimir learned their response, he directed the envoys to report to their Emperors that he was willing to accept baptism, having already given some study to their religion, and that the Greek faith and ritual, as described by the emissaries sent to examine it, had pleased him well.

When the Emperors heard this report, they rejoiced, and persuaded their sister Anna to consent to the match. They then requested Vladimir to submit to baptism before they should send their sister to him, but Vladimir desired that the Princess should herself bring priests to baptize him. The Emperors complied with his request, and sent forth their sister, accompanied by some dignitaries and priests. . . .

By divine agency, Vladimir was at that time suffering from a disease of the eyes and could see nothing, being in great distress. The Princess declared to him that if he desired to be relieved of this disease, he should be baptized with all speed, otherwise it could not be cured. When Vladimir heard her message, he said, "If this proves true, then of a surety is the God of the Christians great," and gave order that he should be baptized. The Bishop of Kherson, together with the Princess's priests, after announcing the tidings, baptized Vladimir, and as the Bishop laid his hand upon him, he straightway received his sight. Upon experiencing this miraculous cure, Vladimir glorified God, saying, "I have now perceived the one true God." When his followers beheld this miracle, many of them were also baptized.

Vladimir was baptized in the Church of St. Basil, which stands at Kherson upon a square in the center of the city, where the Khersonians trade. The palace of Vladimir stands beside this church to this day, and the palace of the Princess is behind the altar. After his baptism, Vladimir took the Princess in marriage. . . .

He ordained that churches should be built and established where pagan idols had previously stood. He thus founded the Church of St. Basil [in Kiev] on the hill where the idol of Perun and the other images had been set, and where the Prince and the people had offered their sacrifices. He began to found churches and to assign priests throughout the cities, and to invite the people to accept baptism in all the cities and towns.

He took the children of the best families, and sent them to schools for instruction in book learning. The mothers of these children wept bitterly over them, for they were not yet strong in the faith, but mourned as for the dead. When these children were assigned for study, there was thus fulfilled in the Russian land the prophecy which says, "In those days, the deaf shall hear words of Scripture, and the voice of the stammerers shall be made plain" (Is. 29:18). For these persons had never before heard words of Scripture, and now heard them only by the act of God, for in his mercy the Lord took pity upon them, even as the prophet said, "I will be gracious to whom I will be gracious" (Ex. 33:19).

[After Vladimir's death in 1015, his eldest son Sviatopolk seized power and plotted to eliminate his three brothers, Boris, Gleb, and Yaroslav. In the passage below, the chronicler describes the treacherous murder of Boris and Gleb, whose humble acceptance of death, after the example of Christ, was to become a significant theme of Russian Christianity down to the twentieth century.]

Upon his father's death, Sviatopolk settled in Kiev and after calling together all the inhabitants of Kiev, he began to distribute largess among them. They accepted it, but their hearts were not with him, because their brethren were with Boris.

When Boris returned with the army, . . . he received the news that his father was dead. He mourned deeply for him, for he was beloved of his father before all the rest. When he came to the Alta, he halted. His father's retainers then urged him to take his place in Kiev on his father's throne, since he had at his disposal the latter's retainers and troops. But Boris protested: "Be it not for me to raise my hand against my elder brother. Now that my father has passed away, let him take the place of my father in my heart." When the soldiery heard these words, they departed from him, and Boris remained with his servants.

But Sviatopolk was filled with lawlessness. Adopting the device of Cain, he sent messages to Boris that he desired to live at peace with him, and would increase the territory he had received from his father. But he plotted against him how he might kill him. . . . He then commanded [emissaries] . . . to go and kill his brother Boris. . . .

These emissaries came to the Alta, and when they approached, they heard the sainted Boris singing vespers. For it was already known to him that they intended to take his life. Then he arose and began to chant, saying: "O Lord, how are they increased who came against me" (Ps. 3:1). And also, "Thy arrows have pierced me, for I am ready for wounds and my pain is before me continually" (Ps. 38:2, 17). . . . After finishing vespers, he prayed, gazing upon the eikon, the image of the Lord, with these words: "Lord Jesus Christ, who in this image hast appeared on earth for our salvation, and who, having voluntarily suffered thy hands to be nailed to the cross, didst endure thy passion for our sins, so help me now to endure my passion. For I accept it not from those who are my enemies, but from the hand of my own brother. Hold it not against him as a sin, O Lord!"

After offering this prayer, he lay down upon his couch. Then they fell upon him like wild beasts about the tent, and overcame him by piercing him with lances. . . . [They] wrapped him in a canvas, loaded him upon a wagon, and dragged him off, though he was still alive. When the impious Sviatopolk saw that he was still breathing, he sent two Varangians to finish him. When they came and saw that he was still alive, one of them drew his sword and plunged it into his heart. Thus died the blessed Boris, receiving from the hand of Christ our God the crown among the righteous. . . .

The impious Sviatopolk then reflected, "Behold, I have killed Boris, now how can I kill Gleb?" Adopting once more Cain's device, he craftily sent messages to Gleb to the effect that he should come quickly, because his father was very ill and desired his presence. Gleb quickly mounted his horse, and set out with a small company, for he was obedient to his father. When he came to the Volga, his horse stumbled in a ditch on the plain, and broke his leg. He arrived at Smolensk, and setting out thence at dawn, he embarked in a boat on the Smiadyn. At this time, Yaroslav received . . . the tidings of their father's death, and he sent word to Gleb that he should not set out, because his father was dead and his brother had been murdered by Sviatopolk. Upon receiving these tidings, Gleb burst into tears, and mourned for his father, but still more deeply for his brother. He wept and prayed with the lament, "Woe is me, O Lord! It were better for me to die with my brother than to live in this world. O my brother, had I but seen thy angelic countenance, I should have died with thee. Why am I now left alone? Where are thy words that thou didst say to me, my brother? No longer do I hear thy sweet counsel. Thou hast received affliction from God, pray for me that I may endure the same passion. For it were better for me to dwell with thee than in this deceitful world."

While he was thus praying amid his tears, there suddenly arrived those sent by Sviatopolk for Gleb's destruction. These emissaries seized Gleb's boat, and drew their weapons. The servants of Gleb were terrified, and the impious messenger, Goriaser, gave orders that they should slay Gleb with dispatch. Then Gleb's cook, Torchin by name, seized a knife, and stabbed Gleb. He was offered up as a sacrifice to God, like an innocent lamb, a glorious offering amid the perfume of incense, and he received the crown of glory. Entering the heavenly mansions, he beheld his long-desired brother, and rejoiced with him in the joy ineffable which they had attained through their brotherly love.

"How good and fair it is for brethren to live together!" (Ps. 133:1). But the impious ones returned again even as David said, "Let the sinners return to hell" (Ps. 9:17). When they returned to Sviatopolk, they reported that his command had been executed. On hearing these tidings, he was puffed up with pride, since he knew not the words of David, "Why art thou proud of thy evildoing, O mighty one? Thy tongue hath considered lawlessness all the day long" (Ps. 52:1).

After Gleb had been slain, his body was thrown upon the shore between two tree trunks, but afterward they took him and carried him away, to bury him beside his brother Boris in the Church of St. Basil. . . .

CHAPTER 6

MEDIEVAL FEUDALISM: ORGANIZED ANARCHY?

For a thousand years after the fall of the Roman Empire in the West (ca. 500 A.D.), feudalism was a way of life for the European peoples, although there was a major break in this pattern around the Millenium, with the rebirth of towns and an urban class free from feudal obligations under the direct protection of the Crown and the guilds. Even then, however, most of the people remained on the manors, subject to the feudal magnates and their incessant wars. Nevertheless, we assume that life was still better than the devastation prevailing after the Empire disintegrated and barbarian tribes overran Europe under such leaders as Attila, "the Scourge of God."

The way feudalism worked—when and if it did—was that a nobleman pledged himself to support and defend a larger magnate by becoming his vassal, in return for a piece of land (fief) and protection for himself and his "dependents"—family, knights, serfs, slaves, artisans, and anyone else on his lands. He, in turn, might receive other noblemen as vassals.

Theoretically, there was no limit to this process of infeudation and subinfeudation. Kings themselves might pledge their allegiance to other kings, emperors, or even popes. A lord might even become a vassal to two or more liege lords, in which case his contract had to specify the limits of his obligation whenever his overlords made war on each other.

The economic basis of European feudalism was the manor system. Ordinarily, each lord had one or more manors to provide himself and his dependents with food, supplies, and services. The manor also offered protection to the peasants and serfs, who were not otherwise involved in the feudal hierarchy, since only nobles could become vassals.

Vassalage was based on the word of a gentleman, backed by a religiously sanctioned oath of allegiance. If the oath were broken, therefore, the recreant was subject to the full force of God's wrath. Moreover, since the fighting was done on horseback with expensive equipment and a large staff to maintain horses and riders, and since a noble chose not to be unhorsed by any except another aristocrat, feudalism was a "privilege" of the nobility. After the Crusades, however, warfare tended to become more "democratic," employing archers, pikemen, and other foot soldiers.

Some questions: What were the Crusaders after? Did they get it? Whom were they fighting—the "infidel"? Was the Moslem less religious than the Christian?

CHARLEMAGNE

EINHARD: LIFE OF CHARLEMAGNE

Trans. A. J. Grant (London, 1907).

By his almost continuous wars, over forty years' time, and consequent demands on his vassals, Charles the Great provoked his knights into demanding more fiefs, at the same time that they sought a limit on the time (forty days) annually owed to the king's service. Charles, in turn, pressed more people into service. Einhard, a member of Charles's court, wrote this very laudatory biography of his ruler.

7. When the [Italian] war was ended, the Saxon war . . . was taken up again. Never was there a war more prolonged nor more cruel, nor one that required greater efforts on the part of the Frankish peoples. For the Saxons, like most of the races that inhabit Germany, are by nature fierce, devoted to the worship of demons, and hostile to our religion, and they think it no dishonor to confound and transgress the laws of God and man. There were other reasons too, which might cause a disturbance of the peace, for our boundaries and theirs touch almost everywhere on the open plain; . . . so that murder, robbery, and arson were frequent on both sides. . . .

War was declared [by the Franks] and fought for thirty years [772 to 804] . . . with the greatest fierceness on both sides. . . . The end might have come sooner if it had not been for the Saxons' perfidy; it is hard to say how often they admitted themselves beaten and surrendered as suppliants to King Charles; how often they promised to obey his orders, gave the required hostages, and received the ambassadors that were sent to them. . . . There was scarcely a year in which they did not both promise and fail to perform. . . .

At last, when all who had resisted had been brought under his power, [Charles] took 10,000 of the inhabitants of both banks of the Elbe, with their wives and children, and settled them in many groups in various parts of Germany and Gaul. And the war, protracted through so many years, was finished on conditions proposed by the king and accepted by them. . . .

9. While the war with the Saxons was being prosecuted, . . . [Charles] attacked Spain with the largest military expedition he could collect. He crossed the Pyrenees, received the surrender of all the towns and fortresses that he attacked, and returned

with his army safe and sound, except for a reverse which he suffered through the treason of the Gascons on his return through the passes of the Pyrenees. . . . The Gascons placed an ambuscade on top of a mountain, . . . and in the ensuing battle slew [the rear guard] to the last man. . . . In this battle Eggihard, . . . Anselm, . . . and Roland . . . were killed along with very many others. . . .*

10. [Charles] also conquered the Bretons, who . . . had been disobedient; he sent against them an expedition compelling them to give hostages and promise they would henceforth obey his orders. . . .

11. Then the Bavarian war broke out suddenly, but was swiftly ended. . . .

12. When these troubles had been settled he waged war against the Slavs, whom we are accustomed to call Wilzi [between the Elbe and the Baltic]. He so broke and subdued them . . . that they thought it no longer wise to refuse to obey his commands.

13. The greatest of all his wars, next to the Saxon, followed this, . . . the war against the Huns and Avars. He prosecuted it with more vigor than the rest and with a far greater military preparation. . . . The war was almost bloodless so far as the Franks were concerned and most fortunate in its results. . . .

14. The last war that Charles undertook was against the Northmen, called Danes, who first came as pirates, and then ravaged the coasts of Gaul and Germany with a greater naval force. Their king, Godofrid, was puffed up with the vain confidence that he would make himself master of all Germany. . . . He boasted that he would soon arrive at [Aachen, Charles's capital] with a mighty force. But he was prevented from the attempt by sudden death—killed by one of his own men—and so ended both his life and the war he began.

15. These then were the wars which the mighty King Charles waged during the course of 47 years . . . in different parts of the world with the utmost skill and success. By these wars he so nobly increased the kingdom of the Franks . . . that he almost doubled it. For . . . when he inherited it from his father Pippin [it included] only that part of Gaul bounded by the Rhine, the Loire, and the Balearic [Mediterranean] Sea; and that part of Germany inhabited by . . . the eastern Franks and bounded by Saxony, the Danube, the Rhine, and the river Saal, which separates the Thuringians and the Sorabs; and further, the Alamanni and the Bavarians. But Charles by his wars conquered and made tributary the following countries: first, Aquitania and Gascony, and the whole Pyrenean range and Spain as far as the Ebro; . . . next, all of Italy . . . as far south as Lower Calabria; . . . next, Saxony, which is a considerable portion of Germany; . . . then both provinces of Pannonia and Dacia; Histria, Liburnia, and Dalmatia, except the cities on the coast, which he left to the Greek Emperor for friendship's sake, and because of the treaty he had made with him. In fine, he vanquished and made tributary all the wild and barbarous tribes in Germany between the Rhine and the Vistula, the Ocean and the Danube, all of which speak very much the same language, but differ widely in customs and dress. . . .

*This is apparently the basis for the *Song of Roland* (p. 84, below,) with the substitution of Moslems for Gascons, although *Basques* would have been a better guess—Ed.

CHARLEMAGNE: ORGANIZATION

The following documents, in the form of royal orders, explain: first, what is expected of a vassal, in this case an ecclesiastical one: a bishop, in other words; and the second document indicates the use Charles made of some of his vassals as administrators "on mission," to control his vast empire; after all, he ruled more of Europe than any other sovereign before Napoleon.

OBLIGATIONS OF AN ECCLESIASTICAL VASSAL

From *Monumenta Germaniae Historica, Leges,* Vol. I, no. 75.

To Abbot Fulrad,
. . . Be advised that we have decided to hold our general assembly this year in eastern Saxony on the River Bode at the place called Strassfurt. We therefore enjoin you to come to this meeting place with all your men well armed and equipped on the 15th day before the festival of St. John the Baptist. Come with your men so prepared that you may be able to go thence . . . in any direction which we shall direct: that is, with arms and accoutrements and other provisions for war, such as food and clothing. Each horseman shall have a shield, lance, sword, dagger, bow and quivers with arrows; in your carts shall be implements, . . . such as axes, planes, augers, boards, spades, iron shovels, and other utensils necessary to an army. Also in the wagons should be supplies of food for three months dating from the time of the assembly, together with arms and clothing for six months. We further command that you see to it that you proceed peacefully to the aforesaid place, through whatever part of our realm you journey [i.e.,] take nothing but fodder, wood, and water. . . .

GENERAL CAPITULARY ON THE MISSI DOMENICI (802)

From Thatcher and McNeal, eds., *A Source Book for Medieval History* (New York, 1905), pp. 49–51, revised.

Concerning the representatives sent out by the Emperor:

The most serene Christian Emperor Charles has chosen certain of the ablest and wisest among his nobles, archbishops, bishops, abbots, and pious laymen to send through his realm and by these, his representatives, to give his people rules to guide them in living justly. He has ordered these men to investigate and report to him any inequity or injustice they may find in the law as now constituted, so that he might see to its correction. He has ordered that none presume to change the law by trickery or fraud or to divert the course of justice for his own ends, as many have been wont to do; or deal unjustly with the churches of God, the poor, widows and orphans, or any Christian whatsoever. . . . He has ordered his *missi,* as they desire to win the favor of Almighty God and keep the faith which they have promised, to inquire diligently into every complaint of any man's having been unfairly treated by anyone, and to render justice to all, in the fear of God. . . . Any case they cannot correct and bring to justice with the aid of the local counts, they shall make a clear report of it to the Emperor. They are not to be hindered, in doing justice, by flattery, bribery, partiality for friends, or fear of the powerful. . . .

The Emperor also directs that every man in his kingdom, lay or cleric, who has already sworn fealty to him as king shall now renew his oath to him as Emperor, and that all persons over 12 years of age who have not yet taken the oath shall do so now. The nature and extent of the promise . . . includes not only a promise of fidelity to the emperor for this life . . . but also the following: First, that each shall strive . . . to serve God according to his commandments [and] second, that no one shall ever wrongfully claim, take, or conceal anything belonging to the Emperor, such as land or slaves . . . or fugitive serfs from the royal lands.

FEUDAL RELATIONS

The following sources indicate some of the ways in which feudalism expanded and became accepted as a "normal" way of life, although its incessant warfare and violence make the word *normal* seem ironic. Apparently the only force operating to mitigate feudalism was the Church.

THE PROBLEM OF SUBINFEUDATION: JOHN OF TOUL'S OBLIGATIONS

From Cheyney, *Translations and Reprints,* 4(3):21.

I, John of Toul, make known that I am the liege man of the Lady Beatrice, countess of Troyes, and of her son, Theobald, count of Champagne, against every person, living or dead, saving my allegiance to lord Enjorand of Coucy, lord John of Arcis, and the count of Grandpré. Should it happen that the count of Grandpré make war on the countess and count of Champagne, on his own quarrel, I will aid the count of Grandpré in my own person and I will send to the count and countess of Champagne the number of knights I owe them for the fief I hold of them. But if the count of Grandpré shall make war on the countess of Champagne on his friends' behalf and not in his own quarrel, I will aid the countess and count of Champagne in my person, and send one knight to the count of Grandpré for the service I owe him for the fief I hold of him, but I will not go myself into the territory of the count of Grandpré to make war on him.

LOUIS IX: DEFINITION OF KNIGHT SERVICE

From Cheyney, *Translations and Reprints*, 4(3):30.

The barons and all vassals of the king are bound to appear before him when summoned, and to serve him at their own expense for 40 days and 40 nights, with as many knights as each one owes; he may exact these services from them when he wishes and when he needs them. And if the king wishes to keep them more than 40 days at their own expense, they are not bound to remain if they do not wish to. But if the king wishes to keep them at his expense for the defense of the realm, they are bound to remain. And if the king wishes to lead them outside the realm, they need not go unless they wish to, for they have already served their 40 days and 40 nights.

TRUCE OF GOD (1063)

Thatcher and McNeal, *Source Book*, pp. 417–418.

Drogo, Bishop of Terouanne, and count Baldwin have established this peace with the cooperation of the clergy and people of the land.

Dearest brothers in the Lord, these are the conditions you shall observe during the time of the peace called the *truce of God*, and which begins at sunset on Wednesday and lasts until sunrise on Monday.

1. During those four days and five nights, no man or woman shall assault, wound, or kill another, nor attack, seize, or destroy a castle, burg, or villa, by craft or by violence.

2. If anyone violate this peace and disobey these our commands, he shall be exiled for thirty years as a penance, but before he leaves the bishopric he shall make compensation for the damage he has done. Otherwise, he shall be excommunicated by the Lord God and denied all Christian fellowship.

3. All who associate with him in any manner, who offer advice or aid or hold converse with him, unless it be to advise him to do penance and leave the bishopric, shall be under excommunication till they make satisfaction.

4. If any violator of this peace fall sick and die before completing his penance, no Christian shall visit him or move his body . . . or receive any of his possessions.

5. Brethren, you should observe the peace in regard to lands, animals, and all things that can be possessed. If anyone take from another an animal, coin, or garment during the days of truce, he shall be excommunicated, unless he make satisfaction. If he wishes to make satisfaction for his crime, he shall first restore the thing he stole or its value in money, and do penance for seven years within the bishopric. If he dies before making satisfaction and completing his penance, his body shall not be buried nor removed from the place where it lay, unless his family shall make satisfaction for him. . . .

6. During the days of truce, no one shall make a hostile expedition on horseback,

unless summoned by the count; and all who go with the count shall take for their support only what is necessary for themselves and their horses.

7. All merchants passing through your lands . . . shall have peace from you. . . .

9. We order all priests . . . to pray for all who keep the truce and curse all violators. . . .

10. Anyone who is accused of violating the truce and denies it shall take communion and undergo the ordeal of hot iron; if found guilty, he shall do penance within the bishopric for seven years.

A LORD'S AUTHORITY OVER THE MARRIAGE OF HIS VASSALS

From Cheyney, *Translations and Reprints,* 4(3):24–25.

I, Mathilda, countess of Nevers, make known to all who see this present letter, that I have sworn upon the sacred Gospels to my dearest lord, Philip, by the grace of God, the illustrious king of France, that I will do to him good and faithful service against all living men and women, and that I will not marry without his will and grace. To keep these agreements in all faith, I have had my men pledge to the same lord king on their oath in this wise, that if I fail (which shall not happen) to keep the said agreements with the lord king, these [my vassals] are bound to come to the lord king with all their lands and fiefs, which are held from me, and take their oaths to him against me, until it shall be made good to him to his satisfaction. And whenever the lord king shall ask it, I shall obtain similar oaths to him from those of my men who were not present with me before the lord king. . . . And so that this may remain firm and lasting, I have hereby affixed my seal. Given at Melun in the year of the Lord 1221, in the month of February.

HOW THE BENEDICTINE MONKS WERE AIDED BY ST. BENEDICT

Société de l'Histoire de France, *Les miracles de Saint-Benoît,* Publications in octavo, 96 (Paris, 1858), pp. 107–109.

The following story, written around the year 1000, shows the importance of miracles in the life of the Middle Ages. It also illustrates the close relationship between the church and feudal society.

Sully Castle, three miles from our monastery at Fleury, was held by Herbert . . . the brother of the archbishop of Tours. Now, our venerable abbot . . . had given Herbert some church lands to be held as a benefice. But Herbert, not satisfied with that, had had the incredible effrontery to also take the rest of the land, which had been reserved for the benefit of our [Benedictine] order.

When the abbot and the monks all went and begged Herbert to abide by his pledge in good faith and stop occupying their land, he turned a deaf ear. So they then proceeded to lay the burden of their complaint before King Lothair and Duke Hugh [Capet], but with no better success. After another futile appeal to the perfidious Herbert to stop his oppression, . . . the monks spent the whole of Lent that year in fervent prayers to God, with solemn litanies and the beating of brass, inviting the help of all who should hear.

Continuing his wicked defiance and adding even worse deeds daily, Herbert set out one night into the Gatinais [district] with his men. Now according to the word of Truth, He that walks in darkness offends, for the light is not in him. An impious man, if he lacks the light of virtue and is surrounded by the shadows of vice, tries at least to hide himself and his deeds under the profane cloak of darkness. While he may escape the gaze of human eyes, however, he cannot escape God's; He looks down on men's ways and sees all their actions. As the blessed Job says, In the Lord are no shadows nor shades of death wherein the wicked may hide. And so it was with this impious Herbert: his light was taken from him and he himself was suddenly snatched away, an ending long overdue.

For, as he was riding his horse, along with his men, carefully choosing his way, all enveloped in the evening mist, suddenly there appeared beside him someone in monks' clothing and bearing the holy stigmata. As he himself later told his men, the figure gleamed with an ethereal light. And all at once Herbert uttered a horrible shout from being hit between the shoulders by a staff the figure seems to have had in hand. Then the vision disappeared right before his eyes. Struck by the horror of his cry, his men tried to find out what had happened.

"Saint Benedict," he exclaimed, "was beside me just now and hit me a mighty blow, which gives me great pain. You, my faithful vassals, must take me home by the way we came. Then go to the tomb of the glorious saint to beg his urgent forgiveness for me."

As instructed, they took him back to where they had started, but on the threshold of his house, in the arms of his men, he gave up the ghost. His vassals then went to the monks of St. Benedict, related what had happened, and asked the monks to receive his body for burial. Although fearing the abbot's anger, he being absent for the moment, the monks agreed to bury the body.

While they were quietly pleased at the outcome, they still felt some compassion, in all piety, for the man who had died in the first bloom of youth, for he was now deprived not only of the gifts of this life here and now, but also of the chance to atone for his wicked ways.

THE SONG OF ROLAND

Trans. I. Butler (Boston, 1904), revised.

Chansons de gestes, or songs of noble deeds, were a collective kind of art form: each singer-narrator added or revised as he went. During the High Middle Ages (1100 to 1300) troubadours traveled from castle to castle and along the pilgrim routes, relating the heroic actions of the past, always with a Christian morality and always in verse form to the accompaniment of some musical instrument.

"Roland" is based on the historical fact of Charlemagne's invasion of Spain (777 to 778) and the ambush of his rear guard under Roland's command (p. 79; above). But the Chanson reveals more about the twelfth century concept of feudalism than that of the eighth century. Oliver, who speaks first in this excerpt, is Roland's friend and lieutenant.

"I have seen the pagans," said Oliver, "Never was seen so great a multitude of living men. Those of the vanguard are upon a hundred thousand, all armed with shields and helmets, and clad in white hauberks; straight are the shafts of their lances, and bright the points thereof. Such a battle we shall have as was never before seen of man. Ye lords of France, may God give you might! And stand we firm that ye be not overcome."

"Foul fall him who flees!" then say the Franks, "for no peril of death will we fail thee."

"Great is the heathen host," saith Oliver, "and few are we. Roland, fair comrade, I pray thee sound thy horn that Charles may hear it and return with all his host."

"That were but folly," quoth Roland, "Thereby would I lose all fame in sweet France. Rather I will strike great blows with Durendal, let the blade be bloodied to the hilt."

. . . When Roland sees the battle is close upon them, he waxes fiercer than lion or leopard. . . . He saith to Oliver, "Comrade, friend, say not so. When the Emperor left us his Franks, he set apart such a 20,000 men that, certainly, is among them no coward. For his liege lord a man ought to suffer all hardship and endure great heat and cold, and give both his blood and his body. Lay on with thy lance and I will smite with Durendal, my good sword that the King gave me. If I die here, may he to whom it shall fall, say, 'This was the sword of a goodly vassal.' "

Nigh at hand is Archbishop Turpin; he now spurs his horse to the crest of a knoll and speaks to the Franks: . . . "Lords, barons, Charles put us here and it is a man's duty to die for his king. Now help ye to uphold Christianity. Certes, ye shall have a battle, for here before you are the Saracens. Confess your sins and pray for God's mercy, and that your souls may be saved I will absolve you. If ye are slain, ye will be holy martyrs and have seats in Paradise.

A king of Barbary . . . spoke to the Saracens, saying: "We shall win a fair day on these Franks for . . . such as are here shall prove themselves of small avail, nor shall one be saved alive for Charles. . . ." Archbishop Turpin hears him and to no man under Heaven has he ever borne such hate; . . . he spurs on his horse and rides upon the king with great might, cleaves his shield and hauberk, and thrusts his great lance, . . . and hurls him dead into the path.

The felon pagans . . . smite with their lances on shields and helmets. . . . Lo, how the blood and brains run down! Great is Roland's distress and grief at seeing so many knights take their end. . . . Saith he: "Sore is our battle; I will blow a blast and Charles the King will hear it."

"That would not be chivalrous!" saith Oliver, "When I did bid thee, thou disdained it. Had the king been here, we had not had these losses; but those far off are free from all reproach. . . . If I ever see my sister, I swear, thou shalt never lie in her arms."

Saith Roland: "Wherefore art thou angry?" And Oliver answereth: "Comrade, thou art thyself to blame. Wise courage is not madness. . . . Through thy folly these Franks have come to their death; nevermore shall Charles the King have service by our hands. Hadst thou taken my counsel, my liege lord had been here and this battle had been ended. . . . Henceforth Charles shall get no help of thee, but thou must die and France shall be shamed thereby. . . ."

The archbishop, hearing them dispute together, puts his pure-gold spurs to his horse and comes unto them, saying, "Sir Roland, and thou, Sir Oliver, I pray you, in God's name let be this strife. Little help shall we now have of thy horn, and yet it were better to sound it. If the king come, he will avenge us, and the pagans not go hence rejoicing.". . .

Therewith Roland sets his ivory horn to his lips, grasps it well, and blows with all the might he has. High are the hills and the sound echoes far, and for full 30 leagues they hear it resound. Charles and all his host hear it, and the king saith, "Our men are at battle."

But Count Ganelon denies it, saying, "Had any other said so, we had deemed it a great falsehood.". . .

The emperor commanded that his trumpets be sounded and now the Franks . . . spur through the passes. Each saith to the other: " If we but see Roland a living man, we will strike good blows at his side.". . .

Then the king had the [traitor] Ganelon taken and given over to the cooks of his household, saying, "Guard him well, as beseems a felon who hath betrayed my house.". . .

Now Roland feels that his sight is gone from him. With much striving he gets to his feet; the color has gone from his face. Before him lies a brown stone, and in his sorrow and wrath he smites ten blows upon it. The sword grates upon the rock, but neither breaks nor splinters, and the count saith, "Holy Mary, help me now! Ah, Durendal, alas for thy goodness! Now I am near to death, and have no more need of thee.". . .

Now he feels that death has come upon him. . . . In all haste he fares under a pine tree, and casts himself down upon his face on the green grass. Under him he has laid his sword and his horn of ivory and turned his face toward the pagan folk, for he would that Charles and his men should say that this gentle count had died a victor.

Speedily and full often did he confess his sins, and in atonement he offered his gauntlet to God. . . . His head sinks on his arm, and with clasped hands he hath gone to his end. And God sent him his cherubim and St. Michael of the Seas, and with them St. Gabriel, and they carried the soul of the count to Paradise. . . .

THE CRUSADES

URBAN II PREACHES THE FIRST CRUSADE, CLERMONT, FRANCE (1095): FULCHER OF CHARTRES'S VERSION

From F. Guizot, *Collection des mémoires relatifs à l'histoire de France* (Paris, 1825), 24:3–9 passim.

From the beginning, feudal states were expansionist, always grabbing territory and fighting with each other. But in 1095 the pope exhorted them to join forces and fight against "the infidel"—Islam, which had recently taken the Holy Land and defeated the Eastern Roman Empire in the battle of Manzikert (1071). Following are two versions of Urban's speech:

Dearest brethren, I, Urban, invested by the permission of God with the papal tiara, and spiritual ruler over the whole world, have come at this great crisis to you, servants of God, as a messenger of divine admonition. . . Since, O sons of God, you have promised the Lord to maintain peace more earnestly than heretofore and faithfully sustain the rights of Holy Church, there still remains, for you who are newly aroused by this divine correction, a very necessary work: . . . You must hasten to aid your breathren in the East, who need your help, which they have often asked. For the [Seljuk] Turks have attacked them, as some of you already know. . . .

Wherefore, I exhort you with earnest prayer . . . that, as heralds of Christ, you urge men by frequent exhortation, men of all ranks, knights and soldiers, rich and poor, to hasten to exterminate this vile race from the lands of your brethren, and to help the [Eastern Orthodox] Christians in time. . . . If those who set out thither should lose their lives on the way, by land or sea or in fighting the pagans, their sins shall be remitted. This I grant through the power vested in me by God.

Oh, what a disgrace if a race so despised, base, and demon-inspired should thus conquer a people endowed with faith in the all-powerful God and resplendent with the name of Christ! What reproaches will be charged against you by the Lord Himself if you do not help those who are counted, like yourselves, of the Christian faith! Let those who have been making private war against the faithful carry on a successful war against the infidels. Let those who have been robbers for so long now become soldiers of Christ. Let those who once fought against brothers and relatives now fight against barbarians, as they ought. Let those who have been hirelings at low wages now labor for an eternal reward. Let those who have been wearing themselves out to the detriment of body and soul now labor for a double glory. . . .

GUIBERT DE NOGENT'S VERSION

Ibid., 9:47–49.

. . . Dearest brethren, if you reverence Christ's holiness and glory, if you earnestly desire to see the shrines which are the traces of his presence on earth, then it is up to you to make the greatest efforts, with God's help, for He will lead you, fighting in your behalf, to purify the Holy City and glorious Sepulchre. . . .

If you likewise believe that the abode of the holy apostles . . . should be striven for with such efforts, why do you refuse to rescue the Cross, the Blood, and the Tomb? . . . You have been waging unjust wars, . . . you have brandished fierce weapons to destroy each other, for no reason except pride and envy. . . . We now propose to you wars with the glorious reward of martyrdom, a title of praise that will endure for ever. . . .

"Out of Zion shall go forth the law and the word of Jehovah from Jerusalem!" If Jerusalem is the source from which flows all of Christian preaching, its streams encircle the surface of the earth and the hearts of all faithful Catholics, leading them to consider wisely what they owe to such a bountiful source. . . .

ISLAM: SUBMISSION TO ALLAH

If you thought that Urban's crusade against "the infidel" was some sort of phony diversion, the following excerpts from the Koran may convince you that the soldiers of the Prophet were at least as dedicated as the Christians when it came to spreading the faith. After they had defeated the Byzantine Empire at Manzikert (1071), they went on to take Constantinople in 1453 (what's 382 years in the Moslem calendar?) and they were besieging Vienna during the Reformation of the sixteenth century.

According to tradition, the Koran was revealed by God to His Prophet Mohammed, after whose death (632 A.D.), 114 suras or chapters were collected from various sources to make up the Sacred Book, the bible of some 600 million Moslems today.

THE KORAN

Le Koran, trans. M. Kasimirski (Paris, 1859), pp. 415–418.

Sura 47, Titled Mohammed, Revealed at Medina

In the Name of Allah, the Compassionate, the Merciful.

Allah will nullify the works of those who disbelieve and who turn others away from his path. As for those who have faith, do good, and believe in that which was revealed to Mohammed—for it is the Lord's truth—Allah will expiate their sins and ennoble their hearts. This is because the unbelievers follow falsehood, while the faithful follow the truth from their Lord. Thus Allah propoundeth their examples unto mankind.

When you meet the unbelievers, strike off their heads until you have made a great slaughter, and bind securely those you take captive. Then either set them free or take their ransom after the war has ended. This you shall do. If Allah had wished he could have destroyed them himself, but he ordained it thus in order to test you, one by the other. For them who die in Allah's cause, he will not let their deeds be in vain. He will guide them and ennoble their hearts. He will lead them into the paradise he has already told you about.

O believers, if you will help Allah in his war against the wicked, he will help you too and make you steadfast. As for the unbelievers, may they perish and their works as well. It will be their retribution for having rejected his revelation. Have they not traveled through the earth and seen what was the end of those who were before them? Allah destroyed them utterly; a like fate awaits the unbelievers of our day. For Allah is the patron of the true believers, but the unbelievers have no patron.

Allah will admit those who believe and do good works to gardens watered by flowing rivers; as for the unbelievers, let them indulge themselves and eat as animals eat: Hell shall be their abode.

How many cities, [O Mohammed,] cities mightier than your own city which expelled you: how many cities have we destroyed, and there was none to help them!

Shall he who follows the guidance of his Lord be compared to him who pursues his appetites and does foul deeds?

This is the garden which the righteous have been promised: Rivers of the purest water flow there, rivers of milk that is forever fresh, rivers of the most delectable wine, and rivers of the clearest honey. They shall eat of every fruit and receive pardon for their sins. Is this comparable to the lot of those who shall abide in Hell forever and drink scalding water which will tear their bowels?

What are the unbelievers waiting for? Are they waiting for the Hour of Doom to overtake them unawares? Portents of that day have already appeared; but what is the use of warnings to them?

Know that there is no god but Allah; implore him to forgive your sins and the sins of the men and women who are the true believers. Allah knows your every movement and all your resting places. . . .

As for the apostates, who return to unbelief after the true way has been revealed to them, they are seduced by Satan. That is because they say to those who abhor the word of Allah: We shall obey you in certain things [only]. Allah knows their secret thoughts. What will they do when the angels, taking their lives from them, strike them on their heads and backs?

Allah will not forgive the unbelievers who have sought to turn others away from his path and who die unbelievers. Never be cowardly and never sue for peace when you have the upper hand and Allah is on your side. He will not grudge you the reward of your labor. . . .

You are called upon to spend your wealth for the cause of Allah, and there are among you some who are miserly; but those who are ungenerous to this cause are ungenerous to themselves, for Allah is rich and you are poor. If you equivocate, he will raise up another people to replace you, a people that will be entirely different from you.

FULCHER OF CHARTRES: THE CAPTURE OF JERUSALEM (1099)

Foulcher de Chartres, *Histoire des Croisades,* in F. Guizot, *Collections des mémoires relatifs à l'histoire de France* (Paris, 1825), 24:70–74.

Bishop Fulcher accompanied the First Crusade and described its successful conclusion in the capture of Jerusalem. He was later made chaplain to Baldwin, the new king of Jerusalem (1100).

When the Franks saw the city and that it would be difficult to take, our princes ordered wooden ladders made. By putting these against the walls, they hoped to scale them and enter the city, with God's help. After they had made them, at a signal from the leaders,

. . . they rushed the city from all sides. . . . But though they attacked until the sixth hour of the day, they were unable to enter . . . and sadly abandoned the assault. . . .

Then craftsmen were ordered to make machines, such that by moving them close to the walls, they might with God's help obtain the desired end. . . . When the machines—battering rams, movable sheds, and the like—were ready, they again prepared to attack the city. Besides other siege craft, they built a tower from small pieces of wood, because large pieces were not available, . . . and carried it piecemeal to a corner of the city. Early in the morning, . . . they quickly erected the tower not far from the wall. . . . Then a few brave soldiers climbed to the top of it. But the Saracens defended themselves from them and used slings to hurl firebrands dipped in grease and oil at the tower. After that, death was present and sudden for many on both sides. . . .

On the next day, at the blast of the trumpets, they took up the same work more vigorously, so that by hammering in one place with the battering rams, they breached the wall. One stone tower on the wall was already afire from our machines hurling firebrands. . . .

Then on Friday noon the Franks entered the city magnificently . . . with trumpets sounding and everything in an uproar; straightway they raised the banner on top of the wall. All the heathen, utterly terrified, changed their bravado to swift flight through the narrow streets. . . . Count Raymond and his men, assailing the city in another sector, . . . saw the Saracens jumping from the walls. Thereupon he and his men ran joyfully into the city to help pursue and kill the wicked enemy. . . . In Solomon's Temple [alone] about 10,000 were beheaded. . . . They did not spare the women and children.

CHAPTER 7

THE MEDIEVAL CHURCH: HOW GREAT A FORCE?

In the Middle Ages the church was the chief humanizing agency. There was almost nothing in which it was not involved, from art to agriculture, from holding fiefs to owning serfs, from running governments to fighting wars—things that would hardly seem to be clerical functions today.

In the Middle Ages as now, there were two divisions of the clergy: secular and regular. The secular clergy were those who were out in the world doing the business of curing souls: priests, deacons, bishops, even the pope. The regular clergy were the monks and nuns, living in cloisters and therefore insulated from the contaminating influences of the world. In those self-sufficient communities they cultivated no souls but their own. They followed a rule *(regula)* laid down by St. Benedict (c. 530 A.D.) which, rigorously obeyed, almost guaranteed entrance into heaven. Being so near to sainthood, therefore, they might be excused for looking down on their brothers in the secular clergy.

But the price of sainthood is eternal vigilance, and by the tenth century monasticism was badly in need of reform. Fortunately, a layman, Duke William of Aquitaine, was prepared to sponsor a new monastery dedicated to the revitalization of the whole church: by enforcing clerical celibacy, prohibiting the buying and selling of church offices, and making the pope in Rome the sovereign ruler of the entire organization.

To generate this movement, William gave one of his fiefs at Cluny, in southeastern France, to the formation of a new monastery under a reforming abbot. Before many decades the Cluniac idea had spread throughout France and other countries, and a former Cluniac monk became the head of Christendom. He soon put the reform into high gear by excommunicating all bishops who did not fit the Cluniac ideal. When their suzerain, the Holy Roman Emperor, came to their defense, Pope Gregory excommunicated him too!

In reading these documents, you should remember that the Middle Ages is like a foreign country to us, with its unique pattern of customs, goals, values, and even technology all very different from ours and—who knows?—maybe better. Henry Adams, descended from Presidents John and John Quincy, concluded that he would rather have lived in the twelfth century than in the twentieth.

LEO I: THE PRIMACY OF THE ROMAN SEE (ca. 450)

Sermons of Leo the Great, trans. C.L. Feltoe, in *Library of Nicene and Post-Nicene Fathers* (New York, 1895), 12:117.

Four cities claimed primacy in the Christian religion: Rome, Jerusalem, Antioch, and Byzantium (Constantinople). In the end the honor was split between the Roman and Greek (Byzantine) churches. Rome's claim was based on the fact that it had been the capital of Roman culture for a thousand years; that Peter, chief of the apostles, was also the first bishop of Rome, and that that city had been the site of both Peter's and Paul's martyrdom. In the fifth century Pope Leo I delivered a sermon in which he gave classic expression to the Petrine doctrine.

. . . When the Lord asked the disciples whom they believed him to be amid the various opinions that were held, the blessed Peter replied, Thou art the Christ, Son of the living God. And the Lord said, Blessed art thou, Simon Bar-Jona, because not flesh and blood but My Father, which is in heaven, hath revealed it to thee. And I say to thee that thou art Peter, and upon this rock will I build My church, and the gates of Hades shall not prevail against it. And I will give unto thee the keys of the kingdom of heaven. And whatsoever thou shalt bind on earth shall be bound in heaven; and whatsoever thou shalt loose on earth shall be loosed also in heaven.

MONASTICISM

THE RULE OF ST. BENEDICT (ca. 530)

From E. F. Henderson, ed., *Select Historical Documents of the Middle Ages* (London, 1905), pp. 274–96, passim.

Disgusted with the degenerate life of sixth-century Rome, Benedict withdrew to become a hermit. But he was followed by so many admirers that he set up the first monastery in the West (at Monte Casino, Italy) and drew up the Rule that was to become a model for later orders. Because of its length (forty pages), section titles, if clear, are sometimes used below, with explanatory text omitted.

Prologue. . . . We are about to found a school for the Lord's service, in the organization of which we trust that we shall ordain nothing severe or burdensome. . . . As one's way of life and one's faith progress, the heart becomes broadened and, with the ineffable sweetness of love, the way of the Lord's mandates is traversed. Thus, . . . continuing in the monastery in His teaching until death, through patience we are made sharers in Christ's passion, in order that we may merit to be companions in His kingdom.

1. *Concerning the kinds of monks and their manner of life.*

2. *What the abbot should be like.* An abbot should always remember what he is called [Father]. . . . His teaching should be sprinkled with the ferment of divine justice. . . .

5. *Concerning obedience.* The first grade of humility is obedience without delay . . . so that as soon as anything is commanded by their superior, they [cannot] suffer delay in doing it, even as if it were a divine command. . . .

7. *Concerning humility.* . . . A monk should be contented with all lowliness or extremity, and consider himself, with regard to everything which is enjoined on him, as a poor and unworthy workman. . . . And everywhere, sitting or walking or standing, let him always be with head inclined, his eyes fixed upon the ground; remembering every hour that he is guilty of his sins. . . .

16. *How divine service shall be held through the day.*

19. *Concerning the art of singing.*

22. *How the monks shall sleep.*

23. *Concerning excommunication for faults.*

25. *Concerning those who . . . associate with excommunicants.*

31. *Concerning the cellarer of the monastery.* . . . Elected from the congregation, one who is wise, mature, sober, not given to much eating, not proud, not turbulent, . . . but fearing God: a father, as it were, to the whole congregation. . . . He shall have charge of what things are ordered: he shall not rebuff the brethren. If a brother by chance demand anything unreasonable, he shall humbly deny him who wrongly seeks. . . .

33. *Whether a monk should have anything of his own.* . . . He should have absolutely nothing: neither books nor tablets nor pen. Nothing at all. For indeed monks are not allowed to have their own bodies or wills. . . .

36. *Concerning infirm brothers.* Before all and above all, attention shall be paid to the care of the sick; so that they shall be served as if it were actually Christ. For He Himself said: "I was sick and ye visited me." . . .

38. *Concerning the weekly reader.* When the friars are eating at the tables, there should always be reading. . . . He who is about to read for the whole week . . . shall ask everybody to pray for him. . . . And there shall be complete silence at the tables . . . so that no voice will be heard but that of the reader. . . . Nor shall anyone presume to ask questions concerning the reading or anything else. . . .

40. *Concerning the amount of drink.* . . . In view of the weakness of the infirm we believe that one hemina [½ liter] of wine per day is enough for each one.

44. *How those who are excommunicated shall render satisfaction.* He who is excommunicated from the oratory and from table shall, when the divine service is being celebrated in the oratory, lie prostrate before the oratory doors, saying nothing, his head on the ground and his body before the feet of all those going out from the oratory. He shall continue this until the abbot judge him to have rendered satisfaction. . . .

45. *Concerning those who make mistakes in the oratory.* If anyone, in saying a psalm, response, antiphone, or lesson, make a mistake: unless he humble himself before all, giving satisfaction, he shall be subjected to greater punishment, as one who was unwilling to correct by humility that in which he had erred by neglect. Children, for such a fault, are whipped.

46. *Concerning those who err in other matters.* If anyone commit any fault while at labor in the kitchen, the cellar, the offices, the bakery, or any [other] place; or break or lose anything, or commit any excess whatever, and do not himself, coming before the abbot or the congregation, of his own accord give satisfaction and declare his error: if it become known through another, he shall be subjected to greater amends. But if the cause of his sin lie hidden in his soul, he may declare it to the abbot or to his spiritual elders, who may know how to cure his wounds, without making them public. . . .

47. *Concerning the daily manual labor.* Idleness is the enemy of the soul. Therefore at fixed times the brothers ought to be occupied in manual labor, and again at fixed times in sacred reading.

53. *Concerning the reception of guests.* All guests shall be received as though they were Christ. . . . "I was a stranger and ye took me in.". . . Run to meet them with all . . . love.

54. *Whether a monk should be allowed to receive letters or anything.* By no means shall a monk be allowed to receive—either from relatives or from any man or from one of his fellows—letters, presents, or any gift, without order of the abbot. . . .

55. *Concerning priests who may chance to dwell in the monastery.*

69. *That in the monastery one shall not presume to defend another.*

70. *That no one shall presume to strike promiscuously.* . . . No one shall be allowed to excommunicate or strike any of his brothers. . . .

72. *Concerning the good zeal which the monks ought to have.* As there is an evil zeal of bitterness, which separates from God and leads to Hell, so there is a good zeal, which separates from vice and leads to God and eternal life. Let the monks therefore exercise this zeal with the most fervent love: that is, let them mutually surpass each other in honor. . . .

73. *Concerning the fact that not every just observance is decreed in this Rule.* . . . For the perfection of living, there are the teachings of the holy fathers, the observance of which leads to the heights of perfection. And what page of . . . the Old or New Testament is not a perfect rule for human life?

DUKE WILLIAM OF AQUITAINE FOUNDS CLUNY (910)

From A. Bernard, *Recueil des chartes de l'Abbaye de Cluny*, 6 vol. (Paris, 1876–1903), 1:124–128.

By the end of the ninth century the Church had fallen into the same decay that beset the Carolingian Empire after the death of Charlemagne. Priests and bishops were living with their wives or, worse still, with concubines; monks were flaunting their vows; and the people generally were attacked by waves of Norsemen, wolves, or brigands. It was at this low point in Western civilization that things began to change. One factor in the new spirit was Duke William the Pious of Aquitaine, who donated a portion of his holdings in Burgundy to the founding of a new order, destined to reform the clergy and, eventually, the state. We are fortunate to have William's original charter, from which the following excerpts:

. . . To all who live in the unity of the faith and implore the mercy of Christ, . . . I make known that for the love of God and our Saviour Christ Jesus I give and deliver to the Apostles Peter and Paul the village of Cluny on the river Grosne, with its curtilage and house, with the chapel that is dedicated to St. Mary Mother of God and St. Peter, Prince of the Apostles, with everything pertaining thereunto: cottages, chapels, serfs of both sexes, vines, fields, meadows, land tilled and untilled, with no reservations. I and my wife Ingelberga . . . give so that a regular monastery may be instituted at Cluny in honor of the Apostles Peter and Paul; that monks shall form a congregation there under the rule of St. Benedict; that they shall forever possess, hold, and order the property given in such wise that this honorable house shall be unceasingly full of vows and prayers.

. . . May the monks and all the aforesaid possessions be under the power and dominion of Abbot Berno, who shall rule according to his knowledge and power so long as he shall live. After his death may the monks have the power and freedom to elect as abbot and ruler the monk of their order whom they shall prefer, according to the good pleasure of God and the rule laid down by St. Benedict, with no contradiction or impediment of this election by our power or any other. Nevertheless, every five years they shall pay to Rome ten goldpieces for the maintenance of the candles of the Church of the Apostles. May the Apostles and the Roman Pontiff afford them protection. . . . The congregation of Cluny shall be wholly free of our power, our kindred's power, or that of royal jurisdiction, and never shall submit to the yoke of any earthy force. I beg and pray that no secular prince, count, bishop, or any . . . pontiff . . . may ever invade the possessions of these servants of God. . . . That this prohibition may bind the bold and evil with straiter bonds, . . . I conjure you, ye Holy Apostles . . . and thou Pontiff of the Apostlic See, do ye cut off from the communion of the . . . Church and life eternal all who steal [or] invade or sell things from these monks.

EMPIRE AND PAPACY

PAPAL ELECTION OF 1046

From C. Mirbt, *Quellen zur Geschichte des Papstums* (Freiburg, 1895), p. 107.

The following contemporary account describes Henry III's visit to Italy in 1046; he went there as King of Germany and returned as Holy Roman Emperor.

The first great synod was held in Pavia before the lord Henry, then king. At the second synod at Sutri, also in the king's presence, . . . two popes were deposed. At the third synod in Rome, . . . just before the Nativity of our Lord, Pope Benedict was canonically and synodically deposed, and by the unanimous election of the clergy and the people, Suidger . . . was substituted for him. On the next day Suidger was consecrated pope with the name of Clement [II]. Then, by the will and obvious approval of the Roman people, he crowned the lord Henry emperor.

DECREE ON PAPAL ELECTIONS (1059)

Henderson, *Select Documents,* pp. 361–62 passim.

To avoid this kind of lay interference with the choice of a pope, Nicholas promulgated a new set of rules at the Lateran Council of 1059. This is the basic procedure by which popes are elected today.

. . . We [Pope Nicholas II] decide and establish that on the death of the pontiff, . . . first the cardinal bishops shall discuss . . . and then shall summon the cardinal clergy to join them; afterwards the rest of the clergy and the people shall give their assent to the new election. . . .

Since the apostolic see is raised above all churches in the world, the cardinal bishops . . . perform the function of a metropolitan when they raise the pontiff elect to the apostolic eminence. They shall elect someone from amongst this [Roman] church, if a suitable candidate be found; if not, from another church. Saving the honor and reverence due our beloved son Henry, who is presently acknowledged king and, it is hoped, will be emperor, God willing, as we grant [such] right in person from the apostolic see.

If, however, the perversity of evil men shall make it impossible to hold a pure, sincere, and uncorrupt election in this city, the cardinal bishops with the godly chosen clergy and catholic laymen . . . shall have the power to elect the pontiff . . . in any place they consider more convenient. . . .

GREGORY VII: DECREES AGAINST SIMONY, CLERICAL MARRIAGE, AND LAY INVESTITURE

From Thatcher and McNeal, *Source Book,* pp. 134–35; Robinson, *Readings,* 1:276.

In 1073 a Cluniac monk, Hildebrand succeeded to the papacy as Gregory VII. Ironically, however, he was not chosen by the cardinals, as proposed by the decree of 1059, but by acclamation of the Roman people—something that would return to haunt him later on. Nevertheless, he proceeded with his reform program, just as if he had been regularly elected under the new procedure.

Below are three of his reforming decrees, which hit the German bishops especially hard because many had been recently appointed by a king who was also bent on reform, but in a different direction. Henry IV, just turned eighteen, wanted to centralize authority in the royal government, the way the French and English kings were doing, in a

Gregory VII *receiving an abbot under his protection. From a line drawing of the twelfth century.*

process we now call modernization. But since bishops and other church magnates usually ruled large feudal estates, Henry's need to control them came into conflict with Gregory's clerical reform effort.

Decree against simony (1074). Those who have been advanced to any grade of holy orders, or to any office, through simony, that is, by the payment of money, shall hereafter have no right to officiate in the holy church. . . .

Against marriage of the clergy (1074). If there be any priests, deacons, or subdeacons who are married, we, by the power of omnipotent God and the authority of Saint Peter, forbid them to enter a church until they repent and mend their ways. But if any remain with their wives, no one shall dare hear them, because their benediction is turned into a curse and their prayer into sin. For the Lord says through the prophet, I will curse your blessings [Mal. 2:2]. Whoever shall refuse to obey this most salutary command shall be guilty of the sin of idolatry. For Samuel says, . . . Rebellion is as the sin of witchcraft, and stubbornness is as iniquity and idolatry [1 Sam. 15:23].

Against lay investiture (1078). . . . If anyone shall henceforth receive a bishopric or abbey from the hands of any lay person, he shall by no means be reckoned among the bishops and abbots; . . . Moreover, we further deny him the favor of Saint Peter and entrance to the church, until, coming to his senses, he shall surrender the position he has appropriated through criminal ambition and disobedience—which is the sin of idolatry. Likewise, if any emperor, king, duke, margrave, count, or any secular . . . person shall presume to bestow the investiture with bishoprics or with ecclesiastical office, let him know that he is bound by the same condemnation.

DICTATUS PAPAE (DICTATES OF THE POPE), 1075

From E. Casper, *Das Register Gregors VII* (2 vols., Berlin, 1920–23), 1:202–207 passim.

The following excerpts from the Register of Pope Gregory VII indicate that the papacy was interested in something more than just moral reform.

1. That the Roman church was founded by God alone.
2. That the Roman bishop alone is properly called universal.
3. That he alone may depose bishops and reinstate them.
8. That he alone may use the insignia of the Empire.
9. That the pope is the only person whose feet are kissed by princes.
11. That his title is unique in the world.
12. That he may depose emperors.
16. That no council may be called "general" without his consent.
17. That no book or chapter may be regarded as canonical without his authority.
18. That his decrees may be annulled by no one, and he is the only one who may retract them.
20. That no one shall dare to condemn anyone who appeals to the papal see.
22. That the Roman church has never erred, nor ever, as witness Scripture, shall err.
26. That no one may be regarded as catholic if he is not in agreement with the Roman church.
27. That the pope may absolve subjects from their fealty to wicked men.

CHURCH VERSUS STATE: GREGORY VII AND HENRY IV

The German bishops defied the pope's reforming decrees, and continued in their support of King Henry. When the pope excommunicated them, Henry "excommunicated" the pope!

HENRY IV: DEPOSITION OF GREGORY VII (JANUARY 24, 1076)

Thatcher and McNeal, *Source Book,* pp. 151–152.

Henry, king not by usurpation but by the holy ordination of God, to Hildebrand, not pope but false monk.

This is the salutation you deserve, for you have never held any office in the church without making it a source of confusion and a curse to Christian men instead of an honor and a blessing. To mention only the most obvious case out of many, you have not only dared to touch the Lord's anointed, the archbishops, bishops, and priests; but you have scorned them and abused them as if they were ignorant servants unfit to know what their master was doing. . . . You have declared that the bishops know nothing and that you know everything. . . .

All this we have endured because of our respect for the papal office, but you have mistaken our humility for fear and have dared to make an attack upon the royal and imperial authority which we received from God. . . .

You have incited subjects to rebel against their prelates by teaching them to despise the bishops, their rightful rulers. . . . You have attacked me who, unworthy as I am, have yet been anointed to rule among the anointed of God, and who, according to the teaching of the fathers, can be judged by no one save God alone. . . .

Come down, then, from that apostolic seat which you have obtained by violence; for you have been declared accursed by St. Paul for your false doctrines and have been condemned by us and our bishops for your evil rule. Let another ascend the throne of St. Peter, one who will not use religion as a cloak for violence but will teach the life-giving doctrine of that prince of the apostles. I, Henry, king by the grace of God, with all my bishops say unto you: Come down, come down, and be accursed through all the ages.

GREGORY'S FIRST DEPOSITION AND EXCOMMUNICATION OF HENRY IV (1076)

Ibid., pp. 155–156.

St. Peter, prince of the apostles, incline thine ear unto me, I beseech thee, and hear me, thy servant, whom thou hast nourished from mine infancy and hast delivered from mine enemies that hate me for my fidelity to thee. Thou art my witness, as are also my mistress, the mother of God, and St. Paul thy brother, and all the other saints, that thy holy Roman church called me to its government against my own will, and that I did not gain thy throne by violence; that I would rather have ended my days in exile than have obtained thy place by fraud or for worldly ambition. . . .

Confident of my authority and integrity, I now declare in the name of omnipotent God, the Father, Son, and Holy Spirit, that Henry, son of the emperor Henry, is deprived of his kingdom of Germany and Italy. I do this by thy authority and in defense of the honor of thy church, because he has rebelled against it. . . . He has refused to obey as a Christian should, he has not returned to God from whom he had wandered, he has had dealings with excommunicated persons, he has done many iniquities, he has despised the warnings which, as thou art witness, I sent him for his salvation, he has cut himself off from the church and has attempted to rend it asunder; therefore, by thy authority, I place him under the curse. It is in thy name that I curse him, that all people may know that thou art Peter, and upon thy rock the Son of the living God has built his church, and the gates of hell shall not prevail against it [Matthew 16:18].

GREGORY VII TO THE GERMAN PRINCES CONCERNING THE PENANCE OF HENRY IV AT CANOSSA (JANUARY 1077)

Ibid., pp. 157–159.

Henry's excommunication freed his vassals from their allegiance to him, with the result that he faced the immediate loss of his kingdom to his rivals. In the attempt to forestall the pope's coming to Germany to hold a public trial, Henry crossed the Alps in the dead of winter and met the pontiff at Canossa in northern Italy, where he pleaded as a penitent sinner for release from excommunication. Pope Gregory tells how it went from there:

Gregory, bishop, servant of the servants of God, to all the archbishops, bishops, dukes, counts, and other princes of the German kingdom, defenders of the Christian faith, greeting and apostolic benediction. . . .

According to the agreement made with your representatives, we had come to Lombardy and were there waiting those whom you were to send to escort us into your land. . . . [when] we learned that the king was approaching. Now before he entered Italy he had sent to us and had offered to make complete satisfaction for his fault, promising to reform and henceforth to obey us in all things, provided we would give him our absolution and blessing. We hesitated for some time, taking occasion to reprove him sharply for his former sins. Finally he came in person to Canossa, where we were staying, bringing with him only a small retinue and manifesting no hostile intentions. Once arrived, he presented himself at the gate of the castle, barefoot and clad only in wretched woollen garments, beseeching us with tears to grant him absolution and forgiveness. This he continued to do for three days, until all those about us were moved to compassion at his plight and interceded for him with tears and prayers. Indeed, they marvelled at our hardness of heart, some even complaining that our action savored rather of heartless tyranny than of chastening severity. At length his persistent declarations of repentance and the supplications of all who were there with us overcame our reluctance, and we removed the excommunication from him and received him again into the bosom of the holy mother church. But first he took the oath, which we have subjoined to this letter, confirmed by the abbot of Cluny, the countess Matilda, the countess Adelaide, and many other ecclesiastic and secular princes.

KING HENRY'S OATH

I, Henry, king, promise to satisfy the grievances which my archbishops, bishops, dukes, counts, and other princes of Germany or their followers may have against me, within the time set by pope Gregory and in accordance with his conditions. . . . I will never enter into any plan for hindering him or molesting him, but will aid him in good faith and to the best of my ability if anyone else opposes him.

CONCORDAT OF WORMS (1122)

Ibid., p. 165.

The issue of lay investiture was not to be settled in the lifetimes of Gregory VII and Henry IV, but in 1122 a compromise was reached between the Emperor Henry V and Pope Calixtus II. In the so-called "Concordat of Worms" the two sides tried to distinguish the material aspects of the church from its spiritual aspects.

The Emperor's Privilege

In the name of the holy and indivisible Trinity.

For the love of God and his holy church and of Pope Calixtus, and for the salvation of my soul, I Henry, by the grace of God Emperor of the Romans, Augustus, hereby surrender to God and his apostles, Sts. Peter and Paul, and to the holy Catholic church, all investiture by ring and staff. I agree that elections and consecrations shall be free from all interference. I surrender also the possessions and regalia of St. Peter which have been seized by me during this quarrel, or by my father in his lifetime, and which are now in my possession, and I promise to aid the church to recover such as are held by any other persons. . . .

Finally, I make true and lasting peace with Pope Calixtus and with the holy Roman church and with all who are or have ever been of his party. I will aid the Roman church whenever my help is asked, and will do justice in all matters in regard to which the church may have occasion to make complaint.

All these things have been done with the consent and advice of the princes whose names are written below: Adelbert, archbishop of Mainz: Frederick, archbishop of Cologne, etc.

The Pope's Privilege

Calixtus, bishop, servant of the servants of God, to his beloved son, Henry, by the grace of God emperor of the Romans, Augustus.

We hereby grant that in Germany the elections of the bishops and abbots who hold directly from the crown shall be held in your presence, such elections to be conducted canonically and without simony or other illegality. In the case of disputed elections you shall have the right to decide between the parties, after consulting with the archbishop of the province and his fellow-bishops. You shall confer the regalia of the office upon the bishop or abbot elect by giving him the sceptre, and this shall be done freely without exacting any payment from him; the bishop or abbot elect on his part shall perform all the duties that go with the holding of the regalia. . . .

INNOCENT III: ON PAPAL AUTHORITY (1198)

Ibid., p. 208.

Perhaps the ultimate statement of papal supremacy came a century after Gregory in the following words of that most powerful of medieval popes, Innocent III.

Innocent III to Acerbius, prior, and to the other clergy in Tuscany.

As God, the creator of the universe, set two great lights in the firmament of heaven, the greater light to rule the day, and the lesser light to rule the night [Genesis 1:15–16], so He set two great dignities in the firmament of the universal church, . . . the greater to rule the day, that is, souls, and the lesser to rule the night, that is, bodies. These dignities are the papal authority and the royal power. And just as the moon gets her light from the sun, and is inferior to the sun in quality, quantity, position, and effect, so the royal power gets the splendor of its dignity from the papal authority. . . .

FRANKFORT DIET: ON IMPERIAL AUTHORITY, 1338

Henderson, *Select Documents,* pp. 437–438.

But the controversy continued; the imperial position is well stated in this action by the Imperial Diet.

Although both civil and canon law manifestly declare that the imperial dignity and power proceeded from of old directly through the Son of God, and that God openly gave laws to the human race through the emperor and the kings of the world; and since the emperor is made true emperor by the election alone of those to whom it pertains, and needs not the confirmation or approbation of anyone else, since on earth he has no superior as to temporal things, but to him peoples and nations are subject, and our Lord Jesus Christ Himself ordered to be rendered unto God the things that are God's, and unto Caesar the things that are Caesar's; because, nevertheless, some, led by the blindness of avarice and ambition, and having no understanding of Scripture, but turning away from the path of right feeling into certain iniquitous and wicked deceptions . . . do wage war against the imperial power and authority and against the prerogatives of the emperors, electors, and other princes and of the faithful subjects of the empire, falsely asserting that the imperial dignity and power come from the pope and that he who is elected emperor is not true emperor or king unless he be first confirmed and crowned through the pope or the apostolic see; and since, through such wicked assertions and pestiferous dogmas the ancient enemy moves discord, excites quarrels, prepares dissensions and brings about sedition;—therefore, for the purpose of averting such evil, by the counsel and consent of the electors and of the other princes of the empire we declare that the imperial dignity and power comes directly from God alone; and that, by the old and approved right and custom of the empire, after anyone is chosen as emperor or king by the electors of the empire concordantly, or by the greater part of them, he is, in consequence of that election alone, to be considered and called true king and emperor of the Romans, and he ought to be obeyed by all the subjects of the empire. And he shall have full power of administering the laws of the empire and of doing the other things that pertain to a true emperor; nor does he need the approbation, confirmation, authority or consent of the apostolic see or of anyone else.

THE FRIARS

THE RULE OF ST. FRANCIS (1223)

Henderson, *Select Documents*, pp. 344–349.

The monk of the early Middle Ages deserted the world and entered a monastery to save his own soul. By the twelfth century, however, new orders—Cistercians, Dominicans, Franciscans—came along with a fresh vision of reform. Of these the most original was the Poor Friars of St. Francis. Instead of shutting themselves away from the world, they went out into it, barefoot and in rags, preaching the gospel of love directly to the people. Following is the rule of Francis, as confirmed by Pope Honorius III.

1. This is the rule and life of the Minor Brothers, namely, to observe the holy gospel of our Lord Jesus Christ by living in obedience, in poverty, and in chastity. . . .

2. . . . Any wishing to adopt this life . . . shall be sent to the provincial ministers, who alone have the right to receive others into the order. The provincial ministers shall carefully examine them in the catholic faith and the sacraments of the church. And . . . if they have no wives, or if they have wives and the wives have . . . already entered a monastery and taken the vow of chastity, . . . let the provincial minister repeat to them the word of the holy gospel, to go and sell all their goods and give to the poor [Matt. 19:21]. . . . Then the ministers shall give them the dress of a novice. . . . After the year of probation is ended they shall be received into obedience, by promising to observe this rule and life forever and . . . they shall never be permitted to leave the order and give up this life and form of religion. . . .

3. The clerical brothers shall perform the divine service according to the order of the holy Roman Church. . . . When they go into the world, they shall not quarrel, nor contend with words, nor judge others. But they shall be gentle, peaceable and modest, merciful and humble, honestly speaking with all, as is becoming. . . .

4. I firmly command all the brothers by no means to receive coin or money, of themselves or through an intervening person. . . .

5. Those brothers to whom God has given the ability to labor, shall labor faithfully and devoutly, in such a way that idleness, the enemy of the soul, being excluded, they may not extinguish the spirit of holy prayer and devotion, to which other temporal things should be subservient. . . .

6. The brothers shall appropriate nothing to themselves, neither a house nor a place nor anything, but as pilgrims and strangers in this world, in poverty and humility

serving God, they shall confidently go seeking for alms. Nor need they be ashamed, for the Lord made Himself poor for us in this world. This is that height of most lofty poverty, which has constituted you my most beloved brothers heirs and kings of the kingdom of Heaven, has made you poor in possessions, has exalted you in virtues. . . .

7. But if any of the brothers at the instigation of the enemy shall mortally sin: for those sins concerning which it has been ordained among the brothers that recourse must be had to the provincial ministers, the aforesaid brothers shall be bound to have recourse to them, as quickly as they can, without delay. . . .

8. All the brothers shall be bound always to have one of the brothers of that order as general minister and servant of the whole fraternity, and shall be firmly bound to obey him. . . . And if at any time, it shall be apparent to the whole body of the provincial ministers and guardians that the aforesaid minister does not suffice for the service and common utility of the brothers, the aforesaid brothers to whom the right of election has been given shall be bound, in the name of God, to elect another as their guardian. . . .

9. The brothers may not preach in the bishopric of any bishop if they have been forbidden to by him. And no brother shall dare to preach at all to the people unless he have been examined and approved by the general minister of this fraternity. . . .

10. The brothers who are the ministers and servants of the other brothers shall visit and admonish their brothers and humbly and lovingly correct them. . . . I warn and exhort, in Christ Jesus the Lord, that the brothers be on their guard against all pride, vainglory, envy, avarice, solicitude for this world, detraction, and murmuring; . . . that they always pray to God with a pure heart; that they have humility and patience in persecution; and that they love those who persecute, revile, and attack us. . . .

11. I firmly forbid all brothers to have any association or conversation with women that may cause suspicion. . . . Neither let them become intimate friends with men or women, lest from this cause a scandal may arise among the brothers or about the brothers.

12. Whoever of the brothers may be divinely inspired to go among the Saracens and other infidels shall seek permission to do so from their provincial ministers. . . . In addition, I command the ministers to ask the pope to assign them a cardinal of the holy Roman Church to be their guide, corrector, and protector of the brotherhood, so that . . . they may observe poverty, humility, and the holy gospel of our Lord Jesus Christ, as we have firmly promised.

ST. FRANCIS: CANTICLE OF BROTHER SUN

Francis, *Speculum perfectionis* (Paris, 1898), p. 18.

The following hymn to nature by St. Francis not only reveals another side of his character but also illustrates the new spirit of the High Middle Ages.

Most high, omnipotent, good Lord, Thine is the praise, the glory, the honor, and every benediction;

To Thee alone, Most High, these do belong, and no man is worthy to name Thee.

Praised be Thou, my Lord, with all Thy creatures, especially my lord Brother Sun that dawns and lightens us;

And he, beautiful and radiant with great splendor, signifies Thee, Most High.

Be praised, my Lord, for Sister Moon, and the stars that Thou hast made bright and precious and beautiful.

Be praised, my Lord, for Brother Wind, and for the air and cloud and the clear sky and for all weathers through which Thou givest sustenance to Thy creatures.

Be praised, my Lord, for Sister Water, that is very useful and humble and precious and chaste.

Be praised, my Lord, for Brother Fire, through whom Thou dost illumine the night, and comely is he and glad and bold and strong.

Be praised, my Lord, for Sister, Our Mother Earth, that doth cherish and keep us, and produces various fruits with colored flowers and the grass.

Be praised, my Lord, for those who forgive for love of Thee, and endure sickness and tribulation; blessed are they who endure in peace; for by Thee, Most High, shall they be crowned.

Be praised my Lord, for our bodily death, from which no living man can escape; woe unto those who die in mortal sin.

Blessed are they that have found Thy holy will, for the second death shall do them no hurt.

Praise and bless my Lord and render thanks and serve Him with great humility.

CHAPTER 8

THE MEDIEVAL UNIVERSITY: SCHOLASTIC PHILOSOPHY

Today's university had its birth in the twelfth century. We cannot give its birth date precisely, because it seems to have gestated slowly in response to a felt need, one beginning with the Cathedral schools of Charlemagne. But the fully developed concept of the free and independent university as a marketplace of ideas occurred between the teaching of Peter Abelard (1110–1140) and Philip II's charter of 1200.

Neither can we give an exact birth place, the honor being shared between Paris, France, and Bologna, Italy. Unless we are loyal to France or Italy, then, we shall honor both, *summa cum laude*. Because we happen to have more data on Paris, however, our documents apply to that school. It was also there that the greatest scholastic philosopher of all time studied and taught—and he was Italian: Tomaso d'Aquino, or St. Thomas Aquinas. We give him major attention not only because he was the greatest, but also because he combined, in himself, both the French and the Italian strains—a "medieval synthesis" of the two schools.

We should apologize for that remark, though: it is a bad medieval pun. The scholastic philosophy as perfected by Thomas Aquinas was a synthesis of Classical Greek learning and the Christian thinking of the Church Fathers. The philosophy was called *scholastic* both because it was developed in the new colleges and universities and because it was based on methods of reasoning perfected in the schools of Athens in the days of Aristotle and Plato. To see this you have only to read the words of Thomas himself, several of whose writings are included here. Incidentally, scholastic philosophy is not limited to the Middle Ages. Many secular and all Catholic universities today teach it in one form or another, frequently under titles such as Neo-Thomism or Neo-Scholasticism.

The ferment of ideas in Paris did not begin with Aquinas, however. A century before him, Peter Abelard had come to Paris to debate with the leading scholars of the day—and to beat them in the science of dialectics so severely that he was driven "into the wilderness," as he put it, where the students followed him and made him famous throughout Europe. He was also one of the world's most tragic lovers, along with his beloved Heloise. But he tells the story much better himself. (By the way, the tomb of Abelard and Heloise in the Père Lachaise cemetery, Paris, is a mecca for lovers around the world.)

Questions for thought: What are some of the differences between the Medieval and the modern university? Can you explain the significance of the Scholastic Philosophy?

PETER ABELARD: AUTOBIOGRAPHY

Historia suarum Calamitatum, in *Patrologiae,* ed. J.P. Migne (Paris, 1855), 178:115–136 passim.

I came to Paris, where above all at that time the art of dialectics was flourishing, and there I met William of Champeaux, my teacher, a man who was distinguished in his science both by his merit and his renown. I remained with him for some time, at first well liked by him, but later when I undertook to refute some of his opinions, I caused him much unhappiness. I frequently attacked him in disputation and from time to time was judged the victor. Now, to my fellow students who ranked the highest, this seemed quite intolerable, both because of my youth and because of the short time I had been studying.

From this came the beginning of my misfortunes, which have followed me even to the present day. The more widely my fame was spread abroad the greater the envy kindled against me. It was rumored that I, presuming on my gifts far beyond my tender years, was aspiring to the leadership of a school; and, indeed, that I was already preparing the very place where I would undertake this task, the place being the castle of Melun, at that time a royal seat. My teacher himself, gaining advanced knowledge of my plan, tried to have my school removed as far as possible from his own. By working in secret, he tried in every way before I left his following to bring to naught the school I had planned and the place I had chosen for it. Since he had many rivals in that place, however, and some of them men with influence among the powers that be, I saw my wish filfilled with their help. His unconcealed envy brought me the support of many others. From this small beginning of my school, my fame in the art of dialectics spread, so that little by little the renown of those who had been my fellow students, as well as that of our teacher himself, grew dim and was like to fade away completely. Thus, becoming still more confident of myself, I moved my school as soon as feasible to the castle of Corbeil, which is nearer the city of Paris, for there I knew I would have more frequent opportunities for my assaults in our battle of disputation. . . .

I returned to him . . . because I was eager to learn more of rhetoric from his lips, and in the course of our many arguments on various subjects, I compelled him by the force of my reasoning to change his former opinion in the matter of Universals, and finally to abandon it altogether. Now, the basis of this old concept of his regarding the reality of universal ideas was that the same quality formed the essence alike of the abstract whole and of the individuals that were its parts; in other words, that there could be no essential differences among those individuals, all being alike save for such variety as might stem from the many accidents of existence. Subsequently, however, he corrected this opinion, no longer maintaining that the same quality was the essence of all things, but that, rather, it manifested itself in them. This problem of Universals is always a most vexed one among logicians, to such a degree, indeed, that even Porphyry [a Neoplatonist, d. 304] did not attempt a final pronouncement, . . . saying rather: This is the deepest problem of its kind. Whence it followed that when William at first revised and then abandoned altogether his views on this subject, his lecturing sank into such a state of careless reasoning that it could hardly be called lecturing on the science of dialectics at all. It was as if his whole knowledge had been bound up in this one question of the nature of Universals.

Thus it came to pass that my teaching won such fame and authority that even those who had previously clung most tenaciously to my former master, attacking my doctrines in the bitterest terms, now came flocking to my school. . . .

In the midst of these things, I had to return to my old home on account of my dear mother Lucia; after my father's conversion to the monastic life, she was arranging to do likewise. When these matters had been settled, I returned to Paris to study theology. . . .

Now in this same city of Paris there dwelt a maiden named Heloise, the niece of Canon Fulbert. His love for her was such that he wanted to give her the best education possible. Besides her beauty, she was remarkable for her intellect and her knowledge of letters. This virtue being rare among women, it doubled her grace and made her the most worthy of renown in the whole kingdom. I determined to unite this girl with myself in the bonds of love, something that seemed to me very easy to do. My name was so distinguished and I had such advantages of youth and comeliness that I never feared rejection from any woman I might favor. . . .

Consumed with passion for this girl, I sought some means of daily intercourse with her, the more easily to win her consent. Therefore I persuaded her uncle, with help from some of his friends, to take me into his household in return for a small payment. My excuse for this was that caring for a household myself was a handicap to my studies. Since he was avaricious and also desirous that his niece's study of letters should proceed as rapidly as possible, I easily won his consent, he being fairly agape at my money, at the same time believing that his niece would greatly profit from my teaching. Moreover, he fell in with my desires beyond my fondest hopes, begging me to give her instruction whenever I might be free, . . . day or night, and to punish her sternly if I found her negligent of her tasks. In all, the man's naiveté was nothing less than astounding; I should not have been more thunderstruck if he had entrusted the care of a tender lamb to a ravenous wolf. . . .

[Heloise became pregnant, a child was born; Abelard proposed marriage, but Heloise refused for fear of ruining Abelard's clerical career. Finally married in secret, Abelard sent her to a convent to protect her from her uncle's fury and the gossip of the Parisians.]

When her uncle and his kinsmen discovered this, they were convinced that I had tricked them and that I had rid myself of Heloise by forcing her to become a nun. Infuriated, they hatched a plot against me. One night, as I lay all unsuspecting in my secret room in my lodgings, they broke in with the help of one of my servants, whom they bribed. There they had vengeance on me with a most shameful and cruel punishment, such as astounded the whole world; for they cut off those parts of my body with which I had done that which caused their sorrow. Then they fled, but two of them were caught and suffered the loss of their eyes and genitals. One was the aforesaid servant. . . .

When morning came, the whole city was assembled before my dwelling. It is difficult—nay, impossible—for words to describe their amazement, their lamentations, and the uproar with which they harassed me, or the grief with which they increased my own suffering. Mainly the clerics, and above all my students, tortured me with their intolerable lamentations, so that I suffered more from their compassion than from the pain of my wounds. In truth, I felt the disgrace more than the hurt to my body. . . . I saw how justly God had punished me in that very part of my body whereby I had sinned. . . .

I must confess that in my misery it was the overwhelming sense of disgrace rather than any ardor for conversion to the religious life that drove me to seek the seclusion of the cloister. Heloise had already taken the veil and entered a convent, at my bidding. Thus it was that we both put on the sacred garb, I in the abbey of St. Denis, she in the convent of Argenteuil. . . .

PETER ABELARD: YEA AND NAY

Robinson, *Readings*, 1:450–452.

Abelard's most significant work was the *Sic et Non* (Yea and Nay), a collection of contradictory writings from the church fathers. Showing the influence of Plato and Aristotle, the work also exhibits the quality of Abelard's philosophic spirit. From the excerpt below, try to define that spirit and explain why Abelard might represent a turning point in the thought of the Middle Ages.

There are many seeming contradictions and even obscurities in the innumerable writings of the church fathers. Our respect for their authority should not stand in the way of an effort on our part to come at the truth. The obscurity and contradictions in ancient writings may be explained upon many grounds and may be discussed without impugning the good faith and insight of the fathers. A writer may use different terms to mean the same thing, in order to avoid a monotonous repetition of the same word. Common, vague words may be employed in order that the common people may understand, and sometimes a writer sacrifices perfect accuracy in the interest of a clear general statement. Poetical, figurative language is often obscure and vague.

Not infrequently, apochryphal works are attributed to the saints. Then, even the best authors often introduce the erroneous views of others and leave the reader to distinguish between the true and the false. Sometimes, as Augustine confesses in his own case, the fathers ventured to rely on the opinions of others.

No doubt the fathers might err; even Peter, the prince of the apostles, fell into error;

what wonder that the saints do not always show themselves inspired? The fathers did not themselves believe that they or their companions were always right. Augustine found himself mistaken in some cases and did not hesitate to retract his errors. He warns his admirers not to look upon his letters as they would upon the Scriptures, but to accept only those things which, upon examination, they find to be true.

All writings in this class are to be read with full freedom to criticize and with no obligation to accept without question; otherwise, the way would be blocked to all discussion and posterity be deprived of the excellent mental exercise of debating difficult questions of language and presentation. But an explicit exception must be made in the case of the Old and New Testaments. In the Scriptures, when anything strikes us as absurd, we may not say that the writer erred, but that the scribe made a mistake in copying the manuscript, or that there is an error in interpretation, or that the passage is not understood. The fathers made a very careful distinction between the Scriptures and later works. They advocate a discriminating, not to say suspicious, use of the writings of their own contemporaries.

In view of these considerations, I have ventured to bring together various sayings of the holy fathers as they came to mind, and to formulate certain questions which were suggested by the seeming contradictions in the statements. These questions ought to excite young readers to a zealous inquiry into truth and sharpen their wits. The master key of knowledge is, indeed, a persistent and frequent questioning. Aristotle, the most clearsighted of all philosophers, was desirous above all to arouse this questioning spirit, for in his *Categories* he exhorts the student as follows: "It may well be difficult to reach a positive conclusion in these matters unless they be frequently discussed. It is by no means fruitless to be doubtful on particular points." By doubting we come to examine; by examining we reach the truth.

[Following are some questions Abelard raised in *Sic et Non*.]

Should human faith be based on reason, or no?

Is God one, or no?

Is God a substance, or no?

Does the first Psalm refer to Christ, or no?

Is sin a pleasure to God, or no?

Is God the author of evil, or no?

Is God all-powerful, or no?

Can God be resisted, or no?

Has God free will, or no?

Was the first man persuaded to sin by the devil, or no?

Was Adam saved, or no?

Did all the apostles have wives except John, or no?

Are the flesh and blood of Christ in very truth and essence present in the sacrament of the altar, or no?

Do we sin willingly, or no?

Does God punish the same sin both here and in the future, or no?

Is it worse to sin openly than secretly?

THE UNIVERSITY OF PARIS

Abelard may have given the impetus to the University of Paris, but its official recognition did not come until 1200, when King Philip II (Augustus) issued the following charter in the wake of a tavern brawl: five German students were killed by the townspeople, and the city provost, or police chief, sided with the citizens.

That the dead students were German is significant only in showing that the university was a center for scholars from all over Europe: Thomas from Aquino, Italy; John of Salisbury, England; and the bishop-elect of Liège, in the Holy Roman Empire, who was among the five dead. Half the population of Paris at that time were probably students, perhaps as many as twenty thousand. When they went on strike for two years in 1229, Paris suffered, and many of its scholars went to other universities, such as Cambridge, England, in the interim.

PHILIP II (AUGUSTUS): CHARTER TO THE UNIVERSITY OF PARIS (1200)

Munro, *Translations and Reprints,* 2(3):4–6.

In the name of the sacred and indivisible Trinity, amen.

Philip, by the grace of God, King of the French, Let all men know, now and in the future, that for the terrible crime owing to which five of the clergy and laity of Paris were killed by certain malefactors, we shall do justice as follows: that Thomas, then provost, . . . we shall consign to perpetual imprisonment. . . .

Concerning the safety of the students at Paris in the future, . . . we have ordained as follows: we will cause all the citizens of Paris to swear that if anyone see an injury done to any student by a layman, he will testify truthfully to this. . . . And if it shall happen that anyone strike a student, except in self-defense, especially . . . with a weapon, club, or stone, all laymen who see it shall in good faith seize the malefactor or malefactors and deliver them to our judge. . . .

Also, neither our provost nor our judges shall lay hands on a student for any offense whatever; nor shall they place him in our prison, unless such a crime has been committed by the student that he ought to be arrested. And, in that case, our judge shall arrest him on the spot, without striking him at all unless he resists, and shall hand him over to the ecclesiastical judge, who ought to guard him in order to satisfy us and the one suffering the injury. . . .

We have decided that our provost and the people of Paris shall affirm by an oath, in the presence of the scholars, that they will carry out in good faith all the above-mentioned. And always in the future, whosoever receives from us the office of the Provost of Paris, among his other initiatory acts . . . in one of the churches of Paris . . . shall affirm by an oath, publicly, in the presence of the scholars, that he will keep in good faith all the above-mentioned. And that these decrees may be valid forever, we have ordered this document to be confirmed by the authority of our seal and by the characters of the royal name, signed below. . . .

THOMAS AQUINAS

After having studied at Paris under Albertus Magnus, who introduced him to the greatness of Aristotle, Aquinas himself became professor of philosophy there in 1252, where he soon gained a reputation as a brilliant lecturer and clear thinker. Aquinas's synthesis of faith and reason, Christian thought with Classical, especially Aristotelian, is evident in all his works; his *Summa theologica* and *Summa contra Gentiles* constitute a medieval encyclopedia of all then-existing knowledge. He is the founder of scholasticism, which Leo XII called the official Catholic philosophy. Following are examples from both of the above works; in the beginning you may be confused by Thomas's dialectical method, but he indicates his own thinking by the personal pronoun *I*.

WHETHER MATRIMONY IS OF NATURAL LAW?

From *Summa theologica*, in *Opera omnia*, 16 vols. (Rome, 1882–1906), 16 (supp.): 78–79.

We analyze this question as follows:

Objection 1. It would seem that matrimony is not natural, because natural law is what nature has taught all animals. But in other animals the sexes are joined without matrimony. Therefore matrimony is not of natural law. . . .

I answer that, A thing is said to be natural in two ways: First, as a necessary result of the principles of nature: thus, for example, upward movement is natural to fire. In this sense matrimony is not natural, nor is anything else that comes about as a result of the intervention of the free will.

Secondly, that to which nature inclines is said to be natural, even though it may come about through the intervention of the free will; thus, acts of virtue are called natural; and in this way matrimony is natural, because natural reason leads to it: first, in relation to the chief end of marriage, which is the good of the offspring. Nature intends not only the begetting of offspring, but also their education and upbringing until they reach the perfect state of the human being, which is the state of virtue. Now, according to the Philosopher (Aristotle, *Ethics,* 8:12), we receive three things from our parents: existence, nourishment, and education. But a child cannot be brought up unless it have certain definite parents, which would not be the case unless there were a bond between the man and one particular woman, which marriage provides.

Second, in relation to the other function of matrimony, which is the mutual services the married people render each other in household affairs: Inasmuch as natural reason dictates that human beings should live together, since no one is self-sufficient in all things in life—for which reason man is said to have a *political nature*—so too, among those things that are necessary for human life, some are appropriate for men, others for women. Wherefore nature inculcates the association of man and woman which is marriage. And these two reasons are set forth by the Philosopher in the *Ethics* (ch. 8).

Reply to Objection 1. Man's nature inclines to a thing in two ways: In one way, because the thing is appropriate to his generic nature and this is common to all animals; and in another way, because it is appropriate to the *difference* in the nature of the human species, which, being rational, goes beyond its genus as, for example, in acts of prudence or forebearance. Just as the generic nature, though one and the same in all animals, yet is not in all in the same way, so neither does it incline in the same way, but in a way that is befitting to each one.

Accordingly, man's nature inclines to marriage because of the difference, as regards the second reason given above. Wherefore the Philosopher (ibid., and *Politics,* 1) gives this reason in man, above the other animals. But as regards the first reason, it inclines on the part of the genus, wherefore he states that the begetting of children is common to animals. Yet nature does not incline thereto in the same way in all animals, since some have offspring that are able to seek food immediately after birth, or are adequately fed by the mothers alone; and in these there is no tie between male and female. But in those whose young need the support of both parents, although only for a short time, there is a certain tie, as may be seen in certain kinds of birds. Since the human offspring, however, needs the parents' care for a very long time, there is a strong tie between male and female, to which even man's generic nature inclines him.

WHETHER, BESIDES PHILOSOPHY, ANY FURTHER DOCTRINE IS NEEDED?

Summa theologica, Question 1, in ibid., 4:6–8.

We analyze this question as follows:

Objection 1. It would seem that, besides philosophy, we have no need of any further knowledge. Man should not strive to know what is above reason: "Seek not for things that are too high" (Eccl. 3:22). And everything that is not above reason is fully dealt with in philosophical science. Therefore any other knowledge is superfluous.

Obj. 2. Moreover, knowledge can be concerned only with being, since nothing can be known except what is true and all that is, is true. Now, everything that is, is included in philosophical science, even God Himself—theology, or the divine science, as Aristotle has shown (Metaph. 6), is a branch of philosophy. Hence, there is no need of any further knowledge beyond that science.

On the contrary, it is said, "All Scripture is given by inspiration of God and is profitable for doctrine, for reproof, for correction, for instruction in righteousness" (2 Tim. 3:16). Scripture, being inspired of God is not part of philosophical science, which is constructed out of human reason. Therefore, besides philosophy, there has to be other knowledge inspired of God.

I answer that, for man's salvation, there has to be a knowledge revealed by God besides philosophical science built on human reason. Firstly, because man is ordained to God, as to an end that surpasses his understanding: "The eye hath not seen, besides Thee, O God, what things Thou has prepared for them that wait for Thee" (Isa. 64:4). For men who are to direct their thoughts and actions to an end, the end must first be known. Hence, for man's salvation, certain truths that exceed human reason had to be communicated to him by divine Revelation. Even for those truths which human reason could have discovered about God, divine Revelation was necessary: for the truths that human reason could have discovered would be known to only a few people, after a long time, and with an admixture of many errors, while man's whole salvation, which is in God, depends upon the knowledge of *that* Truth. In order, therefore, that man's salvation be achieved more properly and more surely, it was necessary that he be taught divine Truths by divine Revelation. Besides philosophical science built up by reason, therefore, there had to be a sacred science learned by Revelation.

THAT MAN'S ULTIMATE HAPPINESS LIES NOT IN THIS LIFE

From *Summa contra Gentiles,* Bk. 3, Ch. 48, in ibid., 14:130–132.

Since man's ultimate happiness does not consist in that knowledge of God whereby He is known to all or to many in some vague kind of way; nor in that knowledge of God whereby He is known through demonstration in the speculative sciences; nor in that knowledge whereby He is known through faith, as we have proved above; and since it is not possible in this life to reach a higher understanding of God in His essence, or at least so that we understand other separate substances, thus knowing God through that which is nearest to Him, in a manner of speaking, as we have also proved; and since we must found our ultimate happiness upon some kind of knowledge of God, as we have shown:—it is not possible for man's happiness to be in this life.

Again: Man's ultimate end is the termination of his natural appetite, so that when he has obtained it, he desires nothing more, because if he still had a movement toward something, he would not yet have reached the end and be at rest. Now, this cannot happen in this life, since the more man understands the more his desire to understand increases—for this is natural in man—unless there were someone who understood all things. But in this life this can never happen to anyone who is a mere man, since in this life we are incapable of knowing separate substances, which in themselves are most intelligible, as we have proved. Therefore man's ultimate happiness cannot be in this life.

Furthermore, whatever is in motion towards some end has a natural desire to be stabilized and at rest in that end. Hence, a body does not draw away from the place towards which it is naturally moving except because of some powerful force which is contrary to its desire. Since happiness is the final goal which man naturally desires, it is his natural wish to see his happiness stabilized. Consequently unless he acquires a state of immobility with his happiness, he is not yet happy, since his natural desire is not yet at rest. Hence, when one acquires happiness, he also acquires stability and rest; so that all agree in conceiving stability as a necessary condition of happiness. As the

Philosopher says, "We do not look upon the happy man as some sort of chameleon." Now, in this life there is no sure stability, since, however happy a man may be, sickness and misfortune may befall him, so that he is hindered in the operation of whatever his happiness consisted. Therefore man's ultimate happiness cannot be in this life.

Moreover, it would seem inappropriate and unreasonable for something to take a long time in becoming, only to have but a short time in being; for it would follow that for a longer period of time nature would be deprived of its end. Hence we see that animals which live only a short while reach their perfection in a short time. But if happiness consists in a perfect operation according to perfect virtue [as Aristotle says], whether intellectual or moral, man cannot reach it except after a long time. This is evident in speculative matters, wherein man's ultimate happiness consists, as we have proved; for hardly is man able to attain perfection in the speculations of science even by the time he reaches the last stages of his life, and then, in most cases, he has but a short space of time remaining to him. Therefore man's ultimate happiness cannot be in this life.

In addition, everyone will admit that happiness is a perfect good or else it would not set the appetite to rest. Now perfect good is that which is wholly free of evil admixtures, just as that which is perfectly white is totally free of any admixture of black. But man cannot be wholly free from evils in this state of life, not only from evils of the body, like hunger, thirst, and cold, but also from evils of the soul. For there is no one who is not disturbed at some time by inordinate passions; no one who does not sometimes go beyond the golden mean of virtuous behavior, either in the direction of excess or of deficiency; no one who is not deceived in one way or another, or who is ignorant of things he would like to know, or does not have doubts about an opinion he would like to be confident of. Therefore no man is happy in this life.

Again, man naturally shuns death and is saddened by it. He not only shuns it when he feels its presence, but also whenever he thinks about it. But in this life man cannot avoid death. Therefore it is not possible for man to be happy in this life.

Besides, ultimate happiness consists not in a habit but an operation, since habits are for the purpose of action. But in this life one cannot perform any action continuously. Therefore man cannot be entirely happy in this life. . . .

Now, someone might say that, since happiness is a good of an intellectual nature, perfect and true happiness is for those in whom the intellectual nature is perfect, namely, in separate substances, and that in man it is perfect by a kind of participation. For man can arrive at a full understanding of the truth only by a sort of movement of inquiry, and he fails entirely to understand things that are by nature most intelligible, as we have proved. Therefore, neither is happiness, in its perfect form, possible to man, but he has a certain participation in it even in this life. This seems to have been Aristotle's opinion about happiness: inquiring whether misfortunes destroy happiness, he shows that happiness appears to consist primarily in deeds of virtue, which seem to be most stable in this life, and concludes that those who attain to that perfection in this life are happy *as men,* as though not attaining to happiness absolutely but only in a *human* way.

We must now show that his explanation does not refute the foregoing arguments.

Although man is below the separate substances according to the order of nature, he is above the irrational creatures. Hence, he attains his ultimate end in a more perfect way than they. But these attain their last end so perfectly that they seek nothing further. Thus a heavy body rests when it is in its proper place, and when an animal enjoys sensual pleasure, its natural desire is at rest. Much more, therefore, when man has obtained his last end, must his natural desire be at rest. But this cannot happen in this life. Therefore man in this life does not obtain happiness considered as his proper end, as we have proved. Hence, he must obtain it after this life.

Again: Natural desire cannot be empty, since "nature does nothing in vain," [as Aristotle says]. But nature's desire would be empty if it could never be fulfilled. Therefore man's natural desire can be fulfilled. But not in this life, as we have shown, so it must be fulfilled after this life. Therefore man's ultimate happiness is after this life.

Furthermore, as long as a thing is in motion towards perfection, it has not reached its last end. Now, in the knowledge of truth all men are always in motion and tending towards perfection, because those who follow make discoveries in addition to those made by their predecessors, as is also stated in [Aristotle's] *Metaphysics,* 2. In the knowledge of truth, therefore, man is not situated as though he had reached his final end. Since, then, as Aristotle himself shows, man's ultimate happiness in this life consists apparently in speculation, whereby he seeks knowledge of the truth, we cannot possibly agree that man obtains his last end in this life.

Moreover, whatever exists in potential tends to become actual, and so long as it is not wholly actual, it has not reached its last end. Now, our intellect, in its potential, seeks to know all the forms of things, and it becomes actual when it knows any *one* of them. Consequently it will not be wholly actual, not in possession of its last end until it knows all things, at least all material things. But man cannot obtain this through the speculative sciences, by which we know the truth in this life. Therefore man's ultimate happiness cannot be in this life. . . .

Therefore man's ultimate happiness will consist in that knowledge of God which the human mind possesses *after* this life, a knowledge similar to that by which separate substances know Him. Hence our Lord promises us a "reward . . . in heaven" (Matt. 5:12) and states (22:30) that the saints "shall be as the angels," who always see God in heaven (18:10).

STUDENTS

JACQUES DE VITRY: STUDENT LIFE AT PARIS (THIRTEENTH CENTURY)

From Munro, *Translations and Reprints,* 2(3):19–21.

After he became a bishop, Jacques de Vitry recalled his student days, without the usual nostalgia of an alumnus.

Student life in the medieval university, *illlustrations from a fifteenth century manuscript showing scenes of gambling, debating, and dormitory life*—Plus ça change . . . *(University Library of Freiburg-im-Bresgau.)*

Almost all the students at Paris, foreigners and natives, did absolutely nothing except learn or hear something new. Some studied merely to acquire knowledge, which is curiosity; others to acquire fame, which is vanity; others still for the sake of gain, which is cupidity and the vice of simony. Very few studied for their own edification or that of others. They wrangled and disputed not only about various sects or discussions, but the differences between countries, [which] caused dissensions, hatreds, and virulent animosities among them. . . .

They affirmed that the English were drunkards and had tails; the sons of France proud, effeminate, and carefully adorned like women. They said the Germans were violent and obscene at their feasts; the Normans vain and boastful; the Poitevins, traitors and adventurers. The Burgundians they considered vulgar and stupid. The Bretons, reputed to be fickle, were often reproached for the death of Arthur. The Lombards were called avaricious, vicious, and cowardly; the Romans seditious, turbulent, and slanderous; the Sicilians, tyrannical and cruel; the inhabitants of Brabant, men of blood, incendiaries, brigands, and ravishers; the Flemish, fickle, prodigal, gluttonous—from insults they came to blows.

I will not speak of those logicians before whose eyes flitted constantly "the lice of Egypt," that is, all the sophistical subtleties, so that no one could comprehend their eloquent discourses in which "there is no wisdom," as Isaiah says. As for the doctors of theology, "seated in Moses's seat," they were swollen with learning, though lacking in charity. Teaching and not practicing, they have "become as sounding brass or a tinkling cymbal," or like a stone canal, always dry, which ought to carry water to "the bed of spices." They not only hated one another but used flattery to entice away the students of others; each one seeking his own glory, and caring not a whit about the welfare of souls.

Having listened intently to the words of the Apostle, "If a man desire the office of a bishop, he desireth a good work," they kept multiplying the prebends and seeking after the offices; and yet they sought the work decidedly less than the preeminence, desiring above all "the uppermost rooms at feasts and the chief seats in the synagogue. . . ." Although the Apostle James said, "My brethren, be not many masters," they, on the contrary, were in such haste to become masters, that most of them were not able to have any students except by entreaties and payments. Now, it is safer to listen than to teach and a humble listener is better than an ignorant and presumptuous doctor.

THE WANDERING SCHOLARS

From J.A. Symonds, *Wine, Women, and Song* (London, 1884).

Many students, tired of attending classes, wandered about the country enjoying their status as scholar-clerics, drinking, wenching, and singing songs in Latin that they composed themselves, frequently shocking that "age of faith."

Let us live then, and be glad
While young life's before us!
After youthful pastime had,
After old age hard and sad,
Earth will slumber o'er us.

Where are they who in this world,
Ere we kept, were keeping.
Go ye to the gods above;
Go to hell; inquire thereof:
They are not; they're sleeping.

* * * *

Live this university,
Men that learning nourish;
Live each member of the same,
Long live all that bear its name;
Let them ever flourish!

Live all girls! A health to you,
Melting maids and beauteous!
Live the wives and women too,
Gentle, loving, tender, true,
Good, industrious, duteous!

We in our wandering,
Blithesome and squandering,
Tara, tantara, teino!
Eat to satiety,
Drink to propriety,
Tara, tantara, teino!
Rags on our hides we fit,
Laugh till our sides we split;
Tara, tantara, teino!

* * * *

Jesting eternally,
Quaffing infernally,
Tara, tantara, teino!
Brother catholical,
Man apostolical,
Tara, tantara, teino!
Clasped on each other's breast,
Brother to brother pressed,
Tara, tantara, teino!

CHAPTER 9

OF TOWNS AND BURGESSES

During the barbarian invasions (ca. 400–1000), towns and the urban way of life practically disappeared from Western Europe. Feudalism, by contrast, was a rural culture, merely providing islands of order in a sea of chaos. But some time around the first millenium, for reasons that we can only speculate, town life revived, along with other manifestations of increasing energy in the West: reform movements such as Cluny, the Norman Conquest of England, the rise of mass movements like pilgrimages and Crusades, increased agricultural output and population growth, and the revival of trade over great distances.

The new towns produced a new man. Neither noble nor serf, he was called variously *burgher, bourgeois,* or *burgess,* depending on the language and the country. To paraphrase an American president, The business of an urban society is business. The towns were organized by and for commercial interests and they soon obtained royal charters granting them immunity—immunity, that is, from feudal barons who wanted to take them over and use this new wealth for selfish purposes. To this end, they put chains across rivers and harbors, hijacked their boats and caravans, and hired lawyers to claim title to the towns as part of their feudal estates (fiefs.).

For a sizable fee, the king would put the towns under his protection and grant them, for additional fees, whatever concessions the merchants wanted, as illustrated by King John's charter to the Borough of Gloucester, below. When the Model Parliament was called in 1295 the towns were allowed to send two representatives each, along with the shires, the nobility, and the clergy.

The major political and economic force in the new towns was usually the guilds,* both merchant and craft. The following documents provide examples of both types, although when it comes to guilds, as with every other medieval institution, nothing is ever typical. But the sources indicate solid evidence of both craft and merchant guilds, for whatever they may be worth, in every town and country.

It will also be evident that the towns were a breeding ground for freedom, not only because they escaped from the tyranny and irresponsibility of the feudal

*Exceptions were capital cities, such as Paris and London, where the royal government predominated.

nobility, but also because any serf who lived in a town for a year and a day was declared a bourgeois, meaning a free man.

Questions to ponder as you read these sources of today's urban culture: How different are our problems from theirs? Do we have St. Godrics today who make a fortune in business and then find it meaningless? How close to home is St. Thomas on the issue of (high) interest-taking? profit-taking?

KING JOHN: CHARTER TO THE BURGESSES OF GLOUCESTER (1200)

From A. Ballard, ed., *British Borough Chapters* (2 vols., Cambridge University Press, 1913–1923).

John, by the Grace of God King etc.

Know ye that we have granted and by this charter confirmed to our burgesses of Gloucester the whole borough of Gloucester with its appurtenances to be held of us and our heirs for ever at farm, rendering every year 55 pounds sterling as they were wont to render and 10 pounds by tale as increments of the farm at our Exchequer in the Easter term and in the Michaelmas term.

We also grant to our burgesses of Gloucester of the Merchant Guild that none of them shall plead outside the walls of the borough of Gloucester on any plea, except pleas of foreign tenure and except the minters and our ministers. . . .

We also grant to them that all the burgesses of the Merchant Guild shall be quit of toll, lastage, pontage, and stallage in and out of fairs and throughout the seaports, . . . saving in all things the liberties of the city of London. . . .

And that they shall justly have their lands and tenures and mortgages and all debts, whosoever owes them to them. . . .

And if any in all our land take toll or custom from the men of Gloucester of the Merchant Guild, after he has failed to redress, the sheriff of Gloucester . . . shall take distress therefor at Gloucester. . . .

And whoever shall seek the borough of Gloucester with his merchandise, . . . they may come, sojourn, and depart in our safe peace on paying the due customs, and no one shall unjustly disturb them. . . . And we forbid anyone to commit wrong or damage or molestation against them on pain of forfeiture of 10 pounds to us. . . .

We also will and grant that our same burgesses of Gloucester . . . shall elect two of the more legal and discreet burgesses of the borough . . . and present them to our chief justice at Westminster, and these men . . . shall well and faithfully keep the provostship of the borough and shall not be removed so long as they administer things well in their bailiwick, except by the common counsel of the borough.

We will also that . . . there shall be elected by the common counsel of the burgesses four of the more legal and discreet men of the borough to keep the pleas of the crown and the other matters which pertain to us and our crown. . . . And to see that the reeves or reeve of that borough justly and lawfully treat both poor and rich.

Witness: . . . etc.

GUILDS

ORDINANCES OF THE GUILD MERCHANT OF SOUTHAMPTON (ca. 1300)

From the University of Pennsylvania, *Translations and Reprints* (1895), 2(1):12–17 passim.

1. In the first place, there shall be elected from the Gild Merchant, and established, an alderman, a steward, a chaplain, four skevins [bailiffs], and an usher. . . . The alderman shall receive from each one entering the Gild fourpence, the steward twopence; the chaplain, twopence; and the usher, one penny. And the Gild shall meet twice a year: that is to say, on Sunday . . . after St. John the Baptist's day, and on Sunday after St. Mary's day.

3. And when the Gild shall sit, the alderman is to have each night . . . two gallons of wine and two candles, and the steward the same; and the four skevins and the chaplain, each of them one gallon of wine and one candle. . . .

4. And when the Gild shall sit, the lepers of La Madeleine shall have of the alms of the Gild, two sesters of ale, and the sick of God's House and of St. Julian shall have two sesters of ale. And the Friar's Minor . . two of ale and one of wine. . . .

6. If a gildsman is ill, . . . wine shall be sent to him, two loaves of bread and a gallon of wine and a dish from the kitchen; and two men of the Gild shall go to visit him. . . .

7. And when a gildsman dies, all those who are of the Gild . . . shall attend the service for the dead, and gildsmen shall bear the body . . . to the place of burial. . . . So long as the service of the dead shall last, . . . there ought to burn four candles of the Gild, each candle of two pounds or more, until the body is buried. . . .

9. When a gildsman dies, his eldest son or his next heir shall have the seat of his father. . . . No husband can have a seat in the Gild by right of his wife, nor demand a seat by right of his wife's ancestors.

12. And if any gildsman strikes another with his fist and is convicted thereof, he shall lose the Gild until he shall have bought it back for ten shillings, and taken the oath like a new member. . . .

19. And no one in the city of Southampton shall buy anything to sell again in the same city, unless he is of the Gild Merchant or of the franchise. . . .

20. And no one shall buy honey, fat, salt herrings, or any kind of oil, millstones, or fresh hides, or any kind of fresh skins, unless he is a gildsman; nor keep a tavern for wine, nor sell cloth at retail, except in market or fair days; nor keep grain in his granary beyond five quarters, to sell at retail, if he is not a gildsman. . . .

22. If any gildsman falls into poverty and . . . is not able to work to provide for himself, he shall have one mark from the Gild to relieve his condition when the Gild sits. . . .

ARTICLES OF THE GUILD OF LONDON HATTERS

From H.T. Riley, *Memorials of London and London Life, 1276–1419* (London, 1868), pp. 239–240.

In the first place, that six men of the most lawful and most befitting of the said trade shall be assigned and sworn to rule and watch the trade, in such manner as other trades of the said city are ruled and watched by their Wardens.

Also, that no one shall make or sell any manner of hats within the franchise of the aforesaid city if he be not free of the same city; on pain of forfeiting to the Chamber the hats which he shall have made. . . .

That no one shall be made apprentice in the said trade for a less term than seven years, and that, without fraud or collusion. And he who shall receive any apprentice in any other manner, shall lose his freedom, until he shall have bought it back again. . . .

That the aforesaid Wardens shall have power to take all manner of hats that they shall find defective and not befitting, and to bring them before the Mayor and Alderman of London, so that the defaults which shall be found may be punished by their award.

Also, whereas some workmen in the said trade have made hats that are not befitting, in deceit of the common people, from which great scandal, shame and loss have often arisen to the good folks of the said trade, they pray that no workman in the said trade shall do any work by night touching the same but only in the clear daylight; that so, the aforesaid Wardens may openly inspect their work. And he who shall do otherwise, and shall be convicted thereof before the Mayor and Aldermen, shall pay to the Chamber of the Guildhall, the first time 40 pence, the second time half a mark, and the third time he shall lose his freedom.

Also, that no one of the said trade shall be admitted . . . to work in the said trade . . . or to sell any manner of hats . . . if he be not attested by the aforesaid Wardens as being a good and lawful person, and as a proper workman.

Also, that no one of the said trade shall receive the apprentice . . . until he has fully completed his term. . . .

Also, that no one of the said trade shall receive the serving-man of another to work, so long as he is in debt to his master. . . .

Also, whereas foreign folk of divers countries do bring to the said city divers manners of hats to sell, and carry them about in the streets, as well before the houses of freemen of the said trade, as elsewhere; and thereby bar them of their dealings and of their sale, so that the freemen of the said trade in the City are greatly impoverished thereby; it is agreed that no strange person bringing hats to the said city for sale, shall sell them by retail, but only in gross, and that, to the freemen of the City; on pain of losing same.

THOMAS AQUINAS

WHETHER IT IS LAWFUL TO SELL A THING FOR MORE THAN IT IS WORTH

Summa theologica, Part 2, Questions 77 and 78.

The Church's official position, as expounded by Aquinas, was in direct opposition to the new economic forces of the towns and the burgesses.

We analyze this question as follows:

Objection 1. It appears that it is lawful to sell a thing for more than it is worth. For in the exchanges of daily life, civil laws determine what is just. Now, according to these laws, it is permissible for buyer and seller to deceive each other, and this occurs whenever a seller trades something for more than it is worth or when a buyer pays less than the thing is worth. Therefore it is lawful for anyone to sell a thing for more than it is worth.

Obj. 2. Moreover, whatever is common to all people would seem to be natural and not sinful. Now Augustine tells the story of a jester who made up a saying that became accepted by everybody: "Buy cheap and sell dear." That is similar to the story in Proverbs (20:14): "It is naught, it is naught, saith the buyer; but when he is gone his way, then he boasteth." Therefore it is lawful to sell a thing for more than it is worth.

Obj. 3. Furthermore, it does not seem unlawful if by mutual agreement the requirements of honesty are met. But according to the Philosopher [Aristotle], in any friendship based on utility, the recompense for a favor should depend on the utility received by the beneficiary. But this sometimes exceeds the value of the thing itself, as when a man needs something very badly, either to escape from danger or to obtain a particular advantage. Therefore, in contracts of buying and selling it is lawful to sell a thing for more than it is worth.

On the contrary, it is written in Matthew (7:12): "All things whatsoever ye would that men should do unto you, do ye even so to them." Now, no one wants to have a thing sold to him for more than it is worth. Therefore no one should sell a thing to another for more than it is worth.

I answer that it is altogether sinful to practice fraud for the purpose of selling something for more than its just price, inasmuch as a man deceives his neighbor to his hurt. As Cicero says, "All deception should be eliminated from contracts: the seller should not practice double-dealing nor the buyer deceive anyone bidding against him."

Aside from fraud, we may speak of buying and selling in two ways: first, considered in themselves, buying and selling seem to have been established for the mutual advantage of both parties, since one needs something that belongs to the other, and vice versa, as [Aristotle states in *Politics,* 2:3]. Now, what has been established for the common advantage should not be more burdensome for one than for another; hence, any contract between them ought to be based on the equality of thing with thing. The value of anything that is put to human use is measured by the price paid for it. For this purpose money was invented, as explained in the *Ethics* 5:5. Hence, if the price exceeds the value of the thing or, conversely, the thing exceeds the price, the equality of justice is lacking. Consequently, to sell for more, or to buy for less than a thing is worth is in itself unjust and unlawful.

We can also speak of buying and selling in another sense: in the case where it accidentally turns out to the advantage of one party and to the injury of the other, as for example, when one man has an urgent need for something, and another will be hurt if he is deprived of it. In such a case, the just price will take account of the thing sold, but also the loss incurred by the seller in parting with it. Thus a thing may lawfully be sold for more than it is worth in itself, though not more than it is worth to its owner. If, however, a man is greatly aided by something he has obtained from another, and the seller does not suffer any loss from doing without it, he ought not to charge more for it, since the other's gain was not due to the seller but only to the buyer's condition. No one has a right to sell what does not belong to him, though he may charge for any loss he suffers. However, anyone who derives great advantage from something obtained from another, may voluntarily pay the seller something extra. . . .

WHETHER IT IS SINFUL TO RECEIVE USURY FOR MONEY LENT

. . . To receive usury for money lent is in itself unjust, since it is selling what does not exist, thereby causing obvious inequality, which is contrary to justice.

In proof of this, it should be observed that there are some things whose use is also their consumption: e.g., we consume wine by using it for drink and wheat by using it for food. In such cases, therefore, the use cannot be reckoned apart from the thing itself, and when the use of the thing is granted, the thing is granted. The act of lending is in fact a transfer of ownership. Wherefore, if one were to sell wine and the use of the wine separately, he would be selling the same thing twice, or selling what does not exist; hence, he would obviously be guilty of the sin of injustice. Therefore, he commits injustice if he lends wine or wheat, expecting to receive two compensations, one being the return of an equal measure, and the other, payment for the use, which is called *usury*.

There are some things, however, the use of which is not the consumption of the thing itself. Thus, the use of a house is living in it, not destroying it. In such a case, both may be granted separately: for example, a man may transfer the ownership of a house to another, while keeping the use of it for a time; or conversely, a man may grant someone the use of a house, while retaining the ownership of it. Hence, one may lawfully receive payment for the use of his house and also expect to receive the house back afterwards, as in the case of renting or leasing.

Now money, according to the Philosopher (*Nichomachean Ethics,* 5:5; *Politics,*

1:3), was devised primarily for the purpose of effecting exchange; so the proper and principal use of money is its consumption or its alienation, whereby it is expended in making purchases. Therefore, by its very nature, it is unlawful to receive payment for the use of money lent, which is called usury: just as a man is bound to restore anything unjustly acquired, so he is bound to restore money received from usury. . . .

A man is not required to lend, . . . and it is a precept that he may not seek profit by lending, [but] . . . he may accept repayment for what he has lent, not more. Thus he is repaid according to the equality of justice. If, however, he exacts more for the use of a thing that has no use but consumption, he is seeking payment for something that does not exist, and therefore his exaction is unjust. . . .

BUSINESS PRACTICE

THE LIFE OF ST. GODRIC, A TWELFTH-CENTURY MERCHANT ADVENTURER

From Reginaldo, *De vita S. Godrici* (London, 1847), pp. 20, 24–25, 28–41 passim.

The following life of a successful merchant who also became a saint indicates the possible conflict between a life of trade and the social idealism expressed by St. Thomas.

This holy man's father was named Ailward, and his mother Edwenna; both of modest rank and wealth, but abundant in righteousness and virtue. They were born in Norfolk, and had long lived in the township called Walpole. . . .

After the boy had passed his childish years quietly at home, and as he grew to manhood, he began to follow more provident ways of life and to learn carefully and persistently the teachings of worldly forethought. Wherefore he chose not to follow the life of a farmer, but rather to study, learn, and exercise the rudiments of more subtle conceits. For this reason, aspiring to the merchant's trade, he began to follow the peddler's way of life, first learning how to gain in small bargains and things of insignificant price; and thence, while yet a youth, his mind advanced little by little to buy and sell and gain from things of greater expense. For, in his beginnings, he was wont to wander with small wares around the villages and farmsteads of his own district; but in the course of time, he gradually associated himself by compact with city merchants. Hence, in a short while, the youth who had trudged for many weary hours from village to village, from farm to farm, did so profit by his increase of age and wisdom as to travel with associates of his own age through towns and boroughs, fortresses and cities, to fairs and to all the various booths of the marketplace, in pursuit of his public trade. He went along the highway, neither puffed up by the good testimony of his conscience nor downcast in the nobler part of his soul by the reproach of poverty. . . .

Yet in all things he walked with simplicity; and in so far as he yet knew how, it was ever his pleasure to follow in the footsteps of truth. For, having learned the Lord's prayer and the creed from his very cradle, he oftentimes turned them over in his mind, even as he went alone on his longer journeys; and, in so far as the truth was revealed to his mind, he clung thereunto most devoutly in all his thoughts concerning God. At first, he lived as a peddler for four years in Lincolnshire, going on foot and carrying the smallest wares; then he traveled abroad, first to St. Andrews in Scotland and then for the first time to Rome.

On his return, having become close friends with some other young men who were interested in merchandise, he began to embark on bolder ventures, going frequently by sea to foreign lands that lay round about. Thus, sailing often to and fro between Scotland and Britain, he traded in many wares and, amid these occupations, learned much worldly wisdom. . . .

He underwent many perils of the sea, but by God's mercy he was never wrecked; for He who had upheld St. Peter as he walked upon the waves, by that same strong right arm kept this His chosen vessel from all misfortune amid these perils. Thus, having learned by frequent experience his wretchedness amid such dangers, he began to worship certain of the saints with more ardent zeal, venerating and calling upon their shrines, and giving himself up by wholehearted service to those holy names. In such invocations his prayers were often and anon answered by prompt consolation; some of which prayers he learned from the fellows with whom he shared these frequent perils; others he collected from faithful hearsay; others again from the custom of the site, for he frequently and zealously visited such holy places.

Thus aspiring ever higher, and always yearning upward with all his heart, at length his great labors and care bore much fruit of worldly gain. For he labored not only as a merchant but also as a seaman . . . to Denmark and Flanders and Scotland; in all which lands he found certain rare, and therefore valuable, wares, which he carried to other areas where he knew them to be less familiar and coveted by the inhabitants above the price of gold itself; wherefore he exchanged these wares for others coveted by men of other lands; and thus he traded most freely and assiduously. Hence he made great profit in all his bargains, and gathered much wealth, [selling] dear in one place wares he had bought at a low price elsewhere.

Then he purchased half of a merchant ship with some of his partners in the trade, and by his savings he bought the fourth part of another one. At length, because of his skill in navigation, excelling that of his fellows, he was promoted to helmsman. . . .

He was vigorous and keen of mind, whole of limb, and strong in body. He was of medium stature, broad-shouldered, deep-chested, with a long face, grey eyes clear and piercing, bushy brows, a broad forehead, long and open nostrils, a nose of comely curve, and a pointed chin. His beard was thick and longer than ordinary, his mouth well shaped, with lips of moderate thickness; in youth his hair was black, in age white as snow; his neck was short and thick, knotted with veins and sinews; his legs were somewhat slender, his instep high, his knees hardened and horny with frequent kneeling; his whole skin rough beyond the ordinary, until all this roughness was softened by old age. . . .

In labor he was strenuous, assiduous above all men; and, when by chance his bodily strength proved insufficient, he achieved his ends with great ease by the skill which his daily labors had given and by a prudence born of long experience. . . . He knew, from the aspect of the sea and stars, how to foretell fair weather or foul. In his voyages he visited many saints' shrines, to whose protection he was wont to commend himself most devoutly, especially the church of St. Andrew in Scotland, where he frequently made and paid his vows. On the way, he often touched at the island of Lindisfarne, where St. Cuthbert had been bishop, and at the Isle of Farne, where he had lived as an anchorite [hermit], and where St. Godric (as he himself would tell afterwards) would meditate with copious tears on the saint's life. Thence he began to yearn for solitude and to hold his merchandise in less esteem. . . .

Having lived 16 years as a merchant, he began to think of devoting to charity, to God's honor and service, the goods he had so laboriously acquired. He therefore took the cross as a pilgrim to Jerusalem, and having visited the Holy Sepulchre, returned to England by way of Santiago de Compostela.

Shortly afterward he became steward to a rich man of his own country, with the care of his whole house and household. Some of the younger servants, however, were sinful men who stole their neighbor's cattle in order to have luxurious feasts, at which Godric, in his ignorance, was sometimes present. Later, on learning the truth, he rebuked them and warned them to cease, but they paid no attention to him, . . . so he revealed the matter to the lord of the household, who, however, rejected his advice.

Wherefore he asked to be replaced and went on a pilgrimage, first to St. Gilles and thence to Rome, the abode of the Apostles, that he might thus pay the penalty for those misdeeds wherein he had ignorantly partaken. I have often seen him, even in his old age, weeping for this unconscious transgression. . . .

On his return from Rome, he lived a while in his father's house; until, inflamed again with holy zeal, he resolved to visit the abode of the Apostles and made his desire known to his parents. Not only did they approve, but his mother asked if she could bear him company, to which he gladly assented and willingly paid her every filial service he felt he owed her. They came therefore to London, and had scarcely departed from thence when his mother took off her shoes, thus going barefoot to Rome and back to London. Godric, humbly serving his parent, was wont to carry her on his shoulders. . . .

After having restored his mother safely to his father, Godric stayed a short while at home; for he was now already firmly resolved to give himself entirely to God's service. Wherefore, that he might follow Christ the more freely, he sold all his possessions, gave them to the poor, and went forth to no certain abode, but whither the Lord should lead him; for above all things he coveted the life of a hermit.

THE PEOPLE OF COLOGNE REBEL AGAINST THEIR ARCHBISHOP (1074)

From the *Annals of Lambert,* in Thatcher and McNeal, *Source Book,* pp. 585–586.

Another kind of conflict between mercantile and clerical interests is illustrated by the following document. Cologne was one of several German cities ruled by the Church, in this case by an archbishop, who apparently behaved like any other feudal magnate.

The archbishop spent Easter in Cologne with his friend the bishop of Münster, whom he had invited to celebrate this festival with him. When the bishop was ready to go home, the archbishop told his servants to get a suitable boat ready for him. After looking all about, they finally found a good boat belonging to a rich merchant of the city and demanded it for the use of the archbishop. They ordered it to be got ready at once and threw out all the merchandise it was loaded with. The merchant's servants in charge of the boat tried to resist, but the prelate's men threatened violence unless they obeyed at once.

Running to the merchant, his servants told him what had happened and asked what they should do. Now the merchant had a son who was bold as well as strong. He was related to the great families of the city and, because of his character, very popular. He hastily collected his servants and as many of the young men of the city as he could, rushed to the boat, ordered the servants of the archbishop to get out of it, and violently ejected them from it. The advocate of the city was called in, but his arrival only increased the tumult, and the merchant's son . . . put him to flight. Friends on both sides took up arms and came to their aid, and it looked as if there would be a great battle fought in the city.

News of the struggle was relayed to the archbishop, who sent men to stop the riot. Being very angry, however, he threatened the rebellious young men with dire punishment in the next session of the court. Now, the archbishop was gifted with all virtues and his uprightness in matters both of church and state had often been proved. But he had one vice. When he got angry he could not control his tongue, but overwhelmed all and sundry with bitter upbraiding and vituperation. Afterwards, he regretted his fault and reproached himself for it.

The riot in the city was finally quieted a little, but the young man, who was both angry and elated over his first success, kept on making all the disturbance he could. He made speeches to the people about the harsh government of the archbishop, accusing him of laying unjust burdens on the people, depriving innocent persons of their property, and insulting honorable citizens with his violent and offensive words. . . . It was not difficult for him to raise a mob. . . . Besides, they all thought it a glorious deed that the people of Worms had driven out their bishop because he was governing them too rigidly. And since they were more numerous and wealthy than the people of Worms, and had arms, they disliked having it thought that they were not equal to the people of Worms in courage, and it seemed to them a disgrace to submit like women to the rule of the archbishop, who was governing them in a tyrannical manner. . . .

THE HANSEATIC LEAGUE

From Thatcher and McNeal, *Source Book*, pp. 610–612.

Although the German maritime cities had cooperated for mutual protection as early as the eleventh century, it was only with the conclusion of the following treaty between Lübeck and Hamburg in 1241 that the foundation was laid for the development of the powerful Hanseatic League that eventually numbered between 100 and 160 towns, with outposts as far away as London and Novgorod. The first known meeting of League representatives was in 1256. Some of their decrees from that early period follow.

Agreement for Mutual Protection between Lübeck and Hamburg

The Advocate, Council and Commune of Lübeck . . . have made the following agreement with our dear friends, the citizens of Hamburg.

1. If robbers or other depredators attack citizens of either city anywhere from the mouth of the Trave river to Hamburg, or anywhere on the Elbe river, the two cities shall bear the expense equally in destroying and extirpating them.

2. If anyone who lives outside the city, kills, wounds, beats, or mishandles, without cause, a citizen of either city, the two cities shall bear the expenses equally in punishing the offender. We furthermore agree to share the expenses equally in punishing those who injure their citizens in the neighborhood of their city and those who injure our citizens in the neighborhood of our city.

3. If any of their citizens are injured near [Lübeck], they shall ask our officials to punish the offender, and if any of our citizens are injured near [Hamburg], they shall ask their officials to punish the offender.

Decrees of the Hanseatic League, 1260–1264

We wish to inform you of the action taken in support of all merchants who are governed by the law of Lübeck.

1. Each city shall, to the best of her ability, keep the sea clear of pirates, so that merchants may freely carry on their business by sea.

2. Whoever is expelled from one city because of a crime shall not be received in another.

3. If a citizen is seized [by pirates or bandits] he shall not be ransomed, but his sword-belt and knife shall be sent to him [as a threat to his captors].

4. Any merchant ransoming him shall lose all his possessions in all the cities which have the law of Lübeck.

5. Whoever is proscribed in one city for robbery or theft shall be proscribed in all.

6. If a lord besiege a city, no one shall aid him in any way to the detriment of the besieged city, unless the besieger is his lord.

7. If there is a war in the country, no city shall on that account injure a citizen from the other cities, either in his person or goods, but shall give him protection.

8. If any man marries a woman in one city, and another woman from some other city comes and proves that he is her lawful husband, he shall be beheaded.

9. If a citizen gives his daughter or niece in marriage to a man [from another city], and another man comes and says that she is his lawful wife, but cannot prove it, he shall be beheaded.

This law shall be binding for a year, and after that the cities shall inform each other by letter of what decisions they make.

STATUTE OF LABORERS

Statutes of the Realm, 1:307.

This first statute of laborers—similar acts were adopted throughout the later Middle Ages—was a response to the ravages of the Hundred Years' War and the bubonic plague or Black Death, which created an acute shortage of goods and services. The population of England was reduced by as much as one third and many towns were completely wiped out. The king and Parliament tried, by these statutes, to help the communities rather than the individuals. But the fact that similar statutes had to be passed in 1360, 1368, and 1388—plus a half a dozen more in the fifteenth century—indicates that enforcement was difficult and the results unsatisfactory.

Edward [III] by the grace of God etc. to the reverend father in Christ William, by the same grace archbishop of Canterbury, primate of all England, greeting. Because a great part of the people and especially of the workmen and servants has now died in that pestilence, some, seeing the straights of the masters and the scarcity of servants, are not willing to serve unless they receive excessive wages; and others, rather than through labor to gain their living, prefer to beg in idleness: We, considering the grave in-conveniences which might come from the lack especially of ploughmen and such laborers, have held deliberation and treaty concerning this with the prelates and other learned men sitting by us; by whose . . . counsel we have seen fit to ordain: that every man and woman of our kingdom of England, of whatever condition, whether bond or free, who is able-bodied and below the age of sixty years, not living from trade nor carrying on a fixed craft, nor having of his own the means of living, or land of his own with regard to the cultivation of which he might occupy himself, and not serving another,—if he, considering his station, be sought after to serve in a suitable service, he shall be bound to serve him who has seen fit to seek after him; and he shall take only the wages, liveries, meed or salary which, in the places where he sought to serve, were accustomed to be paid in the twentieth year of our reign of England, or the five or six common years next preceding. Provided, that in thus retaining their service, the lords are preferred before others of their bondsmen or their land tenants: so, nevertheless that such lords thus retain as many as shall be necessary and not more; and if any man or woman, being thus sought after in service, will not do this, the fact being proven by two faithful men before the sheriffs or the bailiffs of our lord the king, or the constables of the town where this happens to be done—. . . he shall be taken and sent to the next jail, and there he shall remain in strict custody until he shall find surety for serving in the aforesaid form.

And if a reaper or mower, or other workman or servant, . . . who is retained in the service of anyone, do depart from the said service before the end of the term agreed, without permission or reasonable cause, he shall undergo the penalty of imprisonment. . . . Let no one, moreover, pay or permit to be paid to anyone more wages . . . than was customary as has been said. . . .

Likewise saddlers, skinners, white-tawers, cordwainers, tailors, smiths, carpenters, masons, tilers, shipwrights, carters and all other artisans and laborers shall not take for their labor and handiwork more than what, in the places where they happen to labor, was customarily paid to such persons, . . . as has been said; and if any man take more, he shall be committed to the nearest jail in the manner aforesaid.

Likewise let butchers, fishmongers, hostlers, brewers, bakers, pulters and all other vendors of any victuals, be bound to sell such victuals for a reasonable price, having regard for the price at which such victuals are sold in the adjoining places; . . . and if anyone sell such victuals in another manner, and be convicted of it, . . . he shall pay the double of that which he received to the party injured. . . .

And because many sound beggars do refuse to labor so long as they can live from begging alms, giving themselves up to idleness and sins, and at times to robbery and other crimes—let no one, under the aforesaid pain of imprisonment presume, under color of piety or alms to give anything to such as can very well labor, or to cherish them in their sloth,—so that thus they may be compelled to labor for the necessaries of life.

CHAPTER 10

THE ITALIAN RENAISSANCE: BIRTH OR REBIRTH?

To American students, the Renaissance is probably the most familiar event of European history; it is also the most widely misunderstood. The following documents may offer some correctives, but let us begin with a few questions:

1. Was the so-called *Renaissance* a rebirth of Antiquity, as the name suggests? Or was it the birth of the Modern? Were painters like Michelangelo and Raphaël merely imitating Classical forms and methods? Was Machiavelli simply reviving the politics of the Augustan Principate?
2. Was the Renaissance the most important event in Europe at the time (1350–1550)?
3. Did it advance the cause of modern science?
4. How did it affect the subsequent course of events?
5. Did it help our appreciation of Gothic art and architecture?
6. Who benefited from it? What was its effect on the common people?

Some of these questions go beyond the limits of the present chapter; the list of contemporary events, for example, would include:

The Hundred Years' War between France and England, 1337–1453
The capture of Constantinople by the Turks, 1453
The voyages of Columbus and da Gama, 1492ff
The Protestant Reformation, 1517ff
The invention of printing, ca. 1450

For years scholars have been trying to find a better name than *Renaissance;* maybe you can think of one and win an autographed copy of the text, bound in scarlet and silver! Names are very important, after all: if you changed the word Renaissance to *Decadence,* for example, would that change your attitude? And some scholars do think it was more decay than birth, especially in the *quattrocento* or fifteenth century. Others think that every major cultural movement has its period of nascence, maturity, and decline, "and God fulfills himself in many ways, lest one good custom should corrupt the world."

PETRARCH AND THE CULT OF THE CLASSICS (ca. 1365)

From his *Epistolae,* trans. J. Robinson and H. Rolfe, in *Petrarch, the First Modern Scholar and Man of Letters* (New York, 1898), pp. 275–278.

Petrarch (1304–1374) was one of the first modern humanists. An Italian patriot, poet, and critic, he taught himself to speak and write Latin. The following letter shows his reverence for the human mind, as well as some of his difficulties in that age of transition called *Renaissance.*

[Dear] Lapo: Your Cicero has been in my possession for four years, but there is a reason for such delay; namely, the scarcity of copyists who understand such work. This state of affairs results in an incredible loss to scholarship. Books that . . . are a little hard to understand are no longer multiplied; . . . so they have sunk into neglect and in the end perished. Hence, our age has let fall some of the richest and sweetest fruits of the tree of knowledge; has thrown away the results of the labors of the greatest men of genius—things of more value, I am almost tempted to say, than anything else in the world. . . .

But to come back to your Cicero. I could not do without it, but the incompetence of the copyists kept me from having my own copy. What was left for me but . . . to press these weary fingers and ragged pen into service? . . . Not a word did I read except as I wrote. . . . Knowing it was a work of Tullius [Cicero] was enough: I found at every step so much sweetness and charm and I felt such a strong desire to advance, that the only difficulty I experienced was that my pen could not go as fast as I wished. . . .

I finally reached a point in my copying where I was overcome by fatigue; not mental, for that is unlikely where Cicero is concerned, but the kind of fatigue that comes from excessive manual labor. I began to regret having undertaken a task for which I was not trained, when suddenly I came across a place where Cicero tells how he himself copied the orations of—someone or other. . . . These are his words: "You say you have been in the habit of reading the orations of Cassius in your idle moments. But I," he jokingly adds, with his customary disregard of his adversary's feelings, "have made a practice of *copying* them, so that I might *have* no idle moments." As I read this, I grew hot with shame, saying to myself, "So Cicero copied orations another wrote, and you are not ready to copy his? What ardor! What scholarly devotion! . . ." These thoughts were a spur to me and I pushed on with all my doubts dispelled. If ever from my darkness there shall come a single ray that enhances the splendor of the reputation which his heavenly eloquence has won for him, it will proceed in no slight measure from the fact that I was so captivated by his ineffable sweetness that I did a thing in itself most irksome with such delight and eagerness that I scarcely knew that I was doing it at all.

So at last your Cicero has the pleasure of returning to you, with my thanks. And yet he also stays, very willingly, with me; a dear friend, whom I credit with being almost the only man of letters for whose sake I would go to such lengths in spending my time [when] the years are closing in upon me. . . . But Cicero! he assuredly is worthy of a part of even the little I still have left. Farewell.

CELLINI: AUTOBIOGRAPHY

J.A. Symonds, *The Life of Benvenuto Cellini Written by Himself* (2 vols., London, 1888), 2:182–264 passim, revised.

Sculptor and metalsmith, Benvenuto Cellini (1500–1571) is best known for his autobiography, an important Renaissance document. His ingenious sculpture, *Perseus and Medusa,* stands opposite Michelangelo's *David* on the Piazza Signorina in Florence, and two of his gold cups are in the Metropolitan Museum of Art in New York.

In August 1545, the Duke Cosimo de' Medici was staying at Poggio a Cajano, about 10 miles from Florence. I went there to pay him my respects, . . . first because I was a Florentine, and secondly, because my forefathers had always supported the Medici party, and I yielded to none of them in my affection for this Duke Cosimo. . . .

Upon my being introduced, the Duke received me very kindly. Then he and the Duchess questioned me about the works I had done for the King of France [Francis I]. I replied enthusiastically and in considerable detail. He said he had heard as much and that I spoke the truth, adding in a tone of commiseration: "Small recompense for such great and noble works! Friend Benvenuto, if you would be willing to execute something for me also, I am prepared to pay you far more than that king of yours, of whom your kind nature prompts you to speak so graciously."

Sensing his implications, I described my profound obligations to the king for having obtained my release from . . . prison and for giving me the means to carry out more admirable works than any other artist of my quality. . . .

"If you are disposed to work for me," he replied, "I will treat you in a way that will astonish you, provided the results of your labor give me satisfaction, which I do not doubt."

I, poor unhappy mortal, burning with the desire to show the noble school of Florence that, having left her in my youth, I had practiced other branches of the art than [goldsmithing], I told the Duke that I would gladly execute for him a mighty statue in marble or bronze for his fine piazza. For a first essay, he said he would like me to produce a Perseus; he had long set his heart on such a monument and asked me to begin a model for it. Eagerly setting myself to the task, in a few weeks I had finished the model, which was about a cubit [18″] high, in yellow wax, delicately wrought in all its details. . . .

Several days passed before I had a chance to show my model to the Duke. Then it seemed as though he had never set eyes on me before, . . . an ill omen for my future dealings with his Excellency. Later on, however, one day after dinner I took it to his antechamber, where he came to inspect it with the Duchess and some of his courtiers. As soon as he saw it, he expressed his pleasure and praised it to the skies, which gave me some hope that he might really be a connoisseur of art. After having examined it carefully for some time, with ever increasing delight, he said, "If only you could execute this model on a larger scale with the same perfection, it would be the finest work on the piazza."

"Most excellent my Lord," I cried, "there are now on the piazza works by the great Donatello and the incomparable Michelangelo, the two greatest men since the Ancients! But because your Excellency compliments my model with such praise, I am encouraged to execute it three times as well in bronze." . . . I was sure of being able to do more than I had promised his Excellency, but [I said] that he should give me the means to carry out my work. . . . [He] bade me formulate my needs in a petition [and] he would see them liberally attended to.

If I had been shrewd enough to obtain by contract all I needed for my work, I would not have had the great troubles that came to me by my own fault. But he showed such a strong desire to have the work done and so great a willingness to arrange the preliminaries, that I, unaware that he was more merchant than duke, had dealt very frankly with his Excellency, as if I had to do with a prince and not a bourgeois. So I sent in my petition: . . . "Most rare and excellent patron, petitions of any validity and compacts between us do not depend on words and writing; the whole point is that I should succeed in my work according to my promise; if I do succeed, I am sure your illustrious Excellency will well remember what you have engaged to do for me." This is so charmed the Duke, both by way of acting and of speaking, that he and the Duchess began treating me with extraordinary marks of favor.

Now imbued with a great desire to set to work, I told his Excellency that I needed a house where I could install myself and build furnaces in order to begin working in clay and bronze, and also, after their separate requirements, in gold and silver. . . . I had already chosen a convenient house in a quarter much to my liking. As I did not wish to impose on his Excellency for money or anything of the sort, I had brought with me from France two jewels, with which I asked him to buy me the house and keep them until I had earned it with my labor. The jewels, after my own design, were excellently crafted by my own workmen. Having minutely inspected them, he uttered these enthusiastic words, which fed my spirit with false hope: "Take back your jewels, Benvenuto, I want you, not them! You shall have your house free of charge."

Then he signed a rescript under my petition, which I have always kept among my papers: "Let the house be seen to, who is the vendor and at what price, for we wish to comply with Benvenuto's request." . . . His Excellency gave the execution of these orders to his majordomo, Ser Pier Francesco Riccio, who . . . had been the Duke's tutor. So I talked to this jackass and described my requirements; beside the house was a garden, in which I wanted to build a workshop. He then turned the matter over to a dry little paymaster named Lattanzio Gorini. This skinny chap, with his spidery little hands and tiny insect's voice, went about the business at a maddeningly slow pace. Finally, he sent me enough stone, sand, and lime to build a pigeoncoop, if carefully planned.

Seeing how sluggishly things were moving, I began to be disheartened, but said to myself, "Great oaks from little acorns grow." I also took heart from the thousands of ducats squandered on the ugly sculptures by that great ox of a blockhead Bandinelli. So I rallied my spirits and kept on prodding Lattanzio Gorini, which was like shouting at a team of lame donkeys driven by a blind dwarf. Faced with these difficulties, I used my own money to mark out the foundations of the workshop and clear the ground of trees and vines, working with ardor and some impatience, perhaps, as was my wont. . . .

I was making vigorous preparations for my great undertaking—indeed a portion of lime had already been used—when I suddenly received notice to appear before the majordomo. . . . On entering, I paid him marked respect, while he received me with great stiffness. He asked who had let me in the house and by what authority I had begun building there. . . .

I replied that I had been installed in the house by his Excellency, who had given the orders to Lattanzio Gorini. "Lattanzio brought stone, sand, and lime, and provided what I wanted, saying he did so at your Lordship's orders." The brute turned on me with still greater tartness, vowing that neither I nor those I had mentioned spoke the truth.

Stung to the quick, I replied, "O Majordomo, so long as your Lordship uses language becoming the high office you hold, I shall honor you and speak as respectfully as I do to the Duke, but if you take another line with me, I shall address you as merely Ser Pier Francesco Riccio."

He flew into such a rage that I thought he would go mad on the spot. . . . Uttering a torrent of abuse, he roared that he was surprised at himself for having let me speak to a man of his quality, to which, my blood being up, I exclaimed, "Listen here, Ser Pier Francesco Riccio, I will tell you what sort of men are my equals, and what yours—yours are merely alphabet-tutors to children!"

His face contracted in a spasm, he raised his voice and shouted the same words in a still more insulting tone. Matching his arrogance with more of the same, I told him bluntly that men of my sort were worthy of talking with popes and emperors and great kings, while ten of his sort might be found in every doorway. . . . I added that I no longer cared to serve the Duke but would return to France, where I was always welcome. . . .

I think the Duke must not have been informed of this diabolical scene, for I waited several days before hearing from him. Giving up all thoughts of Florence, I made preparations to return to France. . . . I had no intention of asking leave of the Duke or anybody else, when one morning the majordomo sent very humbly to entreat my presence. He started in on a long pedantic oration in which I could discover neither head nor tail. I could only gather that he was asking me in the Duke's name what salary I would be willing to accept. . . .

When he saw that I did not intend to reply, he was clever enough to put it: "Benvenuto, dukes expect to be answered, and what I am saying to you, I say from his Excellency's lips." I said if the message came from the Duke, . . . to report to him that I could not accept any position inferior to that of anyone else employed as an artist by his Excellency. The majordomo replied, "Bandinelli gets 200 crowns a year; if you are satisfied with that, then your salary is settled." And I agreed to those terms. . . .

While the workshop for my Perseus was being built, . . . I modeled the statue [full scale] in plaster, intending to cast it from this mold. But finding that it would take rather long to carry out in this way, I resolved upon another expedient: . . . I began the figure of Medusa and built the skeleton of iron. Afterwards I put on the clay and when it was modelled, baked it. . . .

Suffering slightly in the loins at this time and being unable to work hard, I was glad to pass my time in the Duke's antechamber with two young goldsmiths, . . . who made a little cup under my direction. It was chased in bas-relief with figures and other pretty ornaments; his Excellency meant it for the Duchess to drink water from. He also commissioned me to make a gold belt, which I enriched with gems, delicate masks, and other fancies. The Duke came by frequently and took pleasure in watching me work and talking to me. When my health improved, I had clay brought and made a portrait of his Excellency, larger than life, which I modelled while he posed for me. He was highly delighted with this piece and took such a liking to me that he urged me to take up working quarters in the palace. . . . I replied that that was impossible; I should not finish my undertakings in a hundred years. . . .

Meanwhile, I was proceeding with my great statue of Medusa. I had covered the iron skeleton with clay, which I modelled like an anatomical subject, about half an inch thinner than the bronze would be. This I baked well and then began spreading on the wax surface, in order to complete the figure to my liking. The Duke, who often came to inspect it, was so worried that I might not succeed with the bronze that he wanted me to call in some master to cast it for me. . . .

The first piece I cast in bronze was that great bust, the portrait of his Excellency. . . . It gave me pleasure when completed, though my only object was to gain the experience of clays suitable for bronze-casting. I was aware, of course, that . . . Donatello had cast his bronzes with Florentine clay; yet it seemed to me that he had had great difficulty with their execution. . . .

When I found that this bust came out sharp and clean, I at once built a furnace in the workshop the Duke had set up for me. [Then] I went to work in earnest on the casting of the Medusa—the woman twisted in a heap beneath the feet of Perseus. . . . The first cast I took in my furnace succeeded to a superlative degree and was so clean that my friends thought I need not retouch it, . . . but any bronze when first cast ought to be worked over and beaten with hammers and chisels, according to the manner of the Ancients, and the moderns, too—such moderns, I mean, as have known how to work in bronze. . . .

One feast-day I went to the palace after dinner and was [admiring] an ancient Greek statue, . . . while explaining the beauty of the workmanship, the consummate science, and the rare technique displayed in the fragment. As I was thus pleasantly engaged in entertaining the Duke, . . . Bandinelli came in. Casting a glance at the . . . statue, he turned to the Duke and said, "My Lord, this illustrates the truth of what I have so often told your Excellency . . . that the Ancients were wholly ignorant of anatomy. . . ."

"Benvenuto," said the Duke, "That is the opposite of what you were just saying. . . . Say something in defense of the statue."

. . . "My Lord, your most illustrious Excellency must of course know that Baccio Bandinelli is made up of everything bad. So whatever he looks at . . . becomes in his

Bandinelli's Hercules and Cacus, *for which Cellini had few kind words, and rightly so. (Alinari/Editorial Photocolor Archives.)*

ungracious eyes as bad as can be. I myself, inclining only to the good, discern the truth in its purer sense. . . ."

[Later on] Bandinelli again began chattering: "Prince," he said, "when I unveiled my Hercules and Cacus, I do believe there were a hundred sonnets written against me, full of the worst abuse that could be invented by the ignorant rabble."

"Prince," I countered, "when Michelangelo Buonarroti displayed his Sacristy [of S. Lorenzo], with so many fine statues in it, our men of talent . . . published over a hundred sonnets . . . praising those masterpieces to the skies." . . . These words made Bandinelli very angry and, turning to me, he cried, "Well, what have *you* to say against my work?"

"If you have the patience to hear me out, I will tell you. . . . It pains me to indicate the faults in your statue, so I shall not express my own feelings, but [only] what our most eminent School of Florence says about it. . . . [They say] that if you were to shave the head of your Hercules, there would not be enough skull left for his brains; that it is impossible to tell whether his features are those of a man or some cross between a lion and an ox; also, the head is facing away from the action and is so badly set on the neck, with such lack of art and grace that nothing worse was ever seen; that his sprawling shoulders are like the two pummels of a donkey packsaddle. His chest and all the muscles of the body are not modelled after a man but after a sack of melons set up against a wall. The loins seem modelled after a bag of skinny squash, and no one can tell how the legs are attached to that ugly body. It is impossible to say which leg he is standing on or which one he is using to apply his strength, nor does he seem to be resting on both, as some knowledgeable sculptors have occasionally posed their figures. It is obvious that the body is leaning forward more than one third of a cubit, which is the single most unpardonable fault committed by ordinary vulgar hacks. As for the arms, they say they are both extended with no touch of grace nor any spark of artistic talent—as if you had never seen a nude model. Furthermore, the right legs of Hercules and Cacus have only one quantity of flesh between them, so that if they were to be separated, neither one would be left with a calf at the point where they are touching. They say, too, that Hercules has one of his feet under the ground, while the other seems to be resting on hot coals."

. . . When Bandinelli saw the amused expression on the Duke's face, . . . he let his insolence get the better of him. Turning to me with that hideous face of his, he cried, "Oh, hold your tongue, you vile s———!"

Having succeeded so well with the cast of the Medusa, I had high hopes of bringing my Perseus through. . . . The wax model produced so fine an effect that when the Duke saw it, he was struck with its beauty. . . . He came to visit me more frequently than usual and on one occasion said, "Benvenuto, this figure cannot succeed in bronze; the laws of art will not allow it."

Stung, I replied, "My Lord, I know how little confidence you have in me and I believe that it is because your Excellency listens too readily to my detractors or else you do not understand my art."

"I hold myself a connoisseur and understand it very well indeed."

"Yes, as a prince, not as an artist," I replied, "for if your Excellency understood my trade as well as you think, you would trust me on the proofs I have already given: First, the colossal bronze bust of your Excellency, which is now in Elba; secondly, the restoration of the Ganymede in marble; . . . thirdly, the Medusa, cast by me in bronze, now here before your eyes, the execution of which was a still greater triumph of strength and skill than any of my predecessors . . . have achieved. Look you, my Lord! I constructed that furnace on principles quite different from those of other founders; besides many technical improvements and ingenious devices, I provided it with two issues for the metal; otherwise this difficult and twisted figure could not have come out perfect. . . . I should also like you to know, my Lord, that the only reason why I succeeded with all those great and arduous works in France under his most admirable Majesty King Francis, was the high courage [he] put into my heart by the

Florence: entrance to the Palazzo Vecchio. *Cellini's Perseus and Medusa is in the foreground. (Alinari/Editorial Photocolor Archives.)*

liberal allowances he made me and the great number of workers he put at my disposal. I could have as many as I asked for, employing above forty at a time, all chosen by myself. Those were the reasons why I produced so many masterpieces in so short a time. Now, my Lord, trust me, give me the help I need, and I am confident of being able to complete a work that will delight your spirit. But if your Excellency keep at me and does not give me the assistance I must have, neither I nor any man on earth can hope to achieve anything worth while."

It was all the Duke could do to stand by and listen to my pleadings. . . . Suddenly he cried, "Come now, tell me, Benvenuto, how is it possible for yonder fine head of Medusa, so high up there in Perseus's grasp, to come out perfect?"

"If your Excellency understood my craft as you claim, you would not fear for the fine head you speak of. But on the other hand, there is every reason to feel worried about this right foot, so far down and away from the rest." . . .

"I will listen patiently," he said, "to any argument you can possibly give in explanation of your statement." . . .

"You must know, my Lord," I began, "that it is the nature of fire to rise, and therefore I promise you the head of Medusa will come out famously; but since it is not the nature of fire to descend, I must force it down six cubits by artificial means. I assure your Excellency, on this ground of proof, that the foot cannot possibly come out. It will be quite easy, however, for me to restore it." After I had made these arguments and others too tedious to set down here, the Duke shook his head and left. . . .

Accordingly, . . . I clothed my Perseus with the clay I had prepared many months before. . . . After making its clay tunic (that is the term used in this art) and properly arming and fencing it with iron girders, I began drawing out the wax with a slow fire. It melted and issued from the numerous air vents I had made, the more of which there are, the better will the mould fill. When I had drawn off the wax, I built a funnel-shaped furnace all round the Perseus. It was built of bricks so interlaced that many openings were left for the fire to exhale. Then I began laying on wood by degrees and kept it burning for two days and nights. When the wax was gone and the mould well baked, I set to work digging the pit in which to sink it. . . . Then I raised the mould by stout ropes and windlasses to a perpendicular position with the greatest care, one cubit above the level of the furnace. . . . I next lowered it gently to the very bottom of the furnace and had it firmly placed with every possible precaution. . . . I began to bank it up with the earth I had excavated and as the earth grew higher, I introduced its proper air vents, little tubes of earthenware. . . . I saw that my workmen understood my method, [so] feeling confident I could rely on them, I next turned to my furnace, which I had filled with pigs of copper and other bronze stuff. The pieces were piled . . . so that the flames could play freely through them and melt the metal quickly. Then I called heartily to set the furnace going. The pine logs were heaped in and, what with the unctuous resin of the wood and the good draught I had given, my furnace worked so well that . . . the workshop took fire and we were afraid the roof would fall in on our heads; while from the garden such a wind and rain storm kept blowing in that it markedly cooled the furnace.

Battling against all these untoward circumstances for several hours, . . . at last I could bear up no longer and a sudden fever of the greatest intensity attacked me. I absolutely had to go to bed. . . . Turning to my assistants, about ten or more, including Bernardino, . . . my apprentice through several years, I spoke to him in particular: "Look, my dear Bernardino, observe the rules I have taught you; do your best with all dispatch, for the metal will soon be fused. You cannot go wrong; these worthy men will get the channels ready; you can easily drive back the two plugs with this pair of iron crooks and I am sure my mould will fill miraculously. I feel sicker than I have ever felt in my life and verily believe it will kill me in a few hours." . . .

I spent two hours battling the fever, crying out repeatedly, "I think I am dying." My housekeeper, a very capable manager and equally warmhearted, kept chiding me for my despair, while at the same time paying me every possible kind attention. . . . As I was thus terribly afflicted, I beheld the misshapen figure of a man enter my chamber to announce in a doleful voice, . . ."O Benvenuto! Your statue is ruined; there is no hope of saving it." . . .

When I had got my clothes on, I strode to the workshop, bent on mischief. . . . "Up with you," I cried, "Attend to me! Since you have not obeyed my instructions, obey me now that I am with you in person. Let no one contradict me, for we don't need advice, we need hands and ears."

. . . "On then, give orders!" they cried, "We will obey your every command so long as life is in us." I think they thought I might fall dead on the spot. I went at once to inspect the furnace and found the metal was all curdled—"caked," as we call it. I sent two of the lads across the street to fetch a load of young oak wood from the butcher's. That kind of wood heats more than any other kind. . . . Accordingly, when the logs caught fire, oh! how the cake began to stir beneath that awful heat. . . . I kept stirring up the channels and sent up on the roof to stop the conflagration. . . . I also had boards, carpets, and other hangings set up against the garden to protect us from the violence of the rain.

Having guarded against these several disasters, I roared to one man and then another: "Bring this here! Take that there!" In this crisis, when they all saw the cake was on the point of melting, they did my bidding, each one working with the strength of three. Then I ordered half a pig of pewter, weighing about 60 pounds, to be brought and flung into the middle of the cake in the furnace. By this means and by piling on wood and stirring now with pokers, now with iron rods, the curdled mass rapidly began to liquify. . . .

All of a sudden an explosion occurred, attended by an enormous flash of flame, as though a thunderbolt had been discharged among us. Terror seized everyone, myself even more than the others. When the din was over, . . . I discovered that the cap of the furnace had blown off, and the bronze was bubbling over from its source beneath. So I immediately had the mouths of my mould opened, at the same time driving in the two plugs that kept back the molten metal. But I saw that it did not flow as rapidly as usual, the reason probably being that the fierce heat of the fire had consumed its base alloy. So I sent for all my pewter platters, porringers, and dishes, some 200 pieces, and had them cast one by one into the channels and others into the furnace. This expedient succeeded, everyone perceiving that my bronze was in perfect liquification and my mould filling. . . .

"O God!" I cried, "Thou that by Thy immeasurable power didst rise from the dead and in Thy glory didst ascend into heaven!" . . . Even thus in a moment my mould was filled and, seeing my work finished, I fell on my knees and gave thanks to God with all my heart. . . .

After letting my statue cool for two full days, I began to uncover it by slow degrees. The first thing I found was that the head of Medusa had come out most admirably, thanks to the air vents; for as I had told the Duke, it is the nature of fire to ascend. Advancing further, I discovered that the other head, Perseus's, had succeeded no less admirably, and this astonished me the more because it is at a considerably lower level than Medusa's. . . . Nothing was lacking on the statue. In my great astonishment I seemed to see in this the hand of God arranging and controlling all.

I went on uncovering the statue with success, and ascertained that everything had come out in perfect order, until I reached the foot of the right leg on which the statue rests. There the heel itself was formed, and going farther, I found the foot apparently complete. This gave me great joy, on the one hand, but was unwelcome, on the other, simply because I had told the Duke that it could not come out. But when I reached the end, it appeared that the toes and a little bit above them were unfinished, so that about half the foot was missing. Though I knew this would add to my labor, I was well pleased because I could now prove to the Duke how well I knew my business. True, more of the foot than I had expected was perfectly formed, the reason being that . . . the bronze was hotter than our rules of art prescribe; also because I had been obliged to supplement the alloy with my pewter cups and plates, which no one, I think, had ever done before. . . .

When the Duke was informed that the whole of my work for the Perseus could be exhibited as finished, he came one day to look at it. His manner clearly showed that it gave him great satisfaction; but afterwards he turned to his courtiers and said, "Although this statue seems in our eyes a very fine piece, it still has to win the favor of the people. Therefore, my Benvenuto, before you put the finishing touches on it, I should like you to remove a part of the scaffolding on the side of the piazza some day around noontime in order that we may learn what folks think of it. There is no doubt that when it is thrown open to space and light it will look quite different from what it does in this enclosure." . . .

When the Duke left, I gave orders to have the screen removed. Some trifles of gold, varnish, and little finishings were still wanting, wherefore I began to murmur and complain angrily, cursing the unhappy day that brought me to Florence. Too well I knew the great, irreparable sacrifice I made when I left France. . . . From the beginning to the middle to the end, everything I had done had been to my great disadvantage. So it was with profound ill-humor that I disclosed my statue on the following day.

Now it pleased God that, on the instant of its exposure, a shout of boundless enthusiasm went up in praise of my work, which consoled me not a little. Folks kept attaching sonnets to the doorposts, which were protected by a curtain while I gave the finishing touches to the statue. On the day I opened it to the public for a few hours, I believe that more than twenty were posted, all of them overflowing with the highest panegyrics. Afterwards, when I again shut it off from view, every day brought sonnets with Latin and Greek verses.

MACHIAVELLI: THE PRINCE (1513)

Il principe (Florence, 1927), pp. 11–14, 88–106, 141–146.

When Machiavelli was thirty years old, he entered the diplomatic service of the Florentine Republic and was promoted to become Defense Secretary in a very short time. In this position he met many figures of importance in the power politics of that era: Cesare Borgia, Pope Julius II, Louis XII of France, and Holy Roman Emperor Maximilian I. However, the return of the Medici in 1512 led to Machiavelli's dismissal. After a stint in prison for allegedly having plotted against the Medici, he retired to his country estate.

Niccolò Machiavelli, *from a portrait by Santi di Tito, showing something of the philosphical side of the first modern political scientist. (Scala/Editorial Photocolor Archives.)*

There he wrote many famous works, including *The History of Florence,* besides *The Prince,* which was also a job application to Lorenzo, and apparently never acknowledged. Machiavelli died in 1527, deeply disappointed and embittered.

Niccolò Machiavelli to the Magnificent Lorenzo de' Medici: Those who court the favor of a prince frequently offer him things they themselves value or things they think he will prize, such as horses, armor, cloth of gold, and precious stones, worthy of his greatness. For my part, wishing to commend myself to your Highness, with the best proof of my devotion, has not enabled me to discover, amongst all I possess, anything I esteem more highly than a knowledge of the actions of famous men, acquired by long experience of modern times and diligent perusal of ancient writers. . . .

I am therefore bold enough to hope that you will accept this feeble tribute in the spirit in which it is offered; and if you condescend to read it with attention, you will find evidence of my ardent desire to see you achieve the greatness to which destiny and your own qualities have called you. If from that elevated position you should condescend to look down on a person in my lowly station, you will see how unjustly I have been persecuted by the extreme and continuous malevolence of fortune. . . .

Chapter 14. Duties of a Prince Regarding His Army

Princes . . . should make the art of war their sole study and occupation, for it is peculiarly the science of those who govern. . . . By this means princes can keep possession of their dominions, . . . while on the other hand, we frequently see princes shamefully reduced to nothing . . . by lazy inactivity. . . .

By keeping an army at his disposal, Francesco Sforza rose from the rank of a private citizen to become the Duke of Milan; and his successors, by deviating from this rule, were reduced to the rank of private citizen again. . . . Nothing is more likely to injure

Lorenzo de' Medici. *A fine figure of a Renaissance despot and patron of the arts. (Scala/Editorial Photocolor Archives.)*

our esteem for the character of a prince than to see him destitute of military force. . . . It is therefore necessary for princes to give their undivided attention to the art of war, which includes intellectual work and study as well as military exercise. . . .

Chapter 15. The Things for which Men, and Especially Princes, are Praised or Blamed

. . . A prince who wants to keep his power should learn that he ought not always to be good. . . . All men, and especially princes, are noted for some characteristics deserving of either praise or blame. For instance, men are accounted liberal or stingy, . . . honorable or dishonorable, . . . effeminate and pusillanimous or wild and spirited; humane or cruel, even-tempered or surly, affable or haughty, wise or debauched, tough or pliant, serious or frivolous, religious or skeptical, and so forth.

It would doubtless be good if a prince united in himself every species of good quality, but since our natures do not allow so great a perfection, a prince should have the prudence to avoid those defects and vices that might occasion his ruin; as for the others, he should guard against those that might compromise his safety. . . . But he should not shrink from blame for vices that are essential to the preservation of his state. Some ostensible virtues would prove the ruin of a prince if he put them into practice, while others, seemingly bad and vicious, may be vital to his welfare and security.

Chapter 16. Generosity and Selfishness

It is to a prince's interest to be considered generous, but dangerous to practice that generosity so that he is neither feared nor respected. . . . If a prince is liberal only so far as it suits his purposes, he will please few and be called selfish. Any prince who wants to earn a reputation for generosity must disregard all expenses; and to support such a reputation he will often be forced to increase the taxes on his subjects, which cannot fail to make him odious. Besides exhausting the public treasury, . . . he will destroy his credit and risk the loss of his dominions at the first reversal of fortune—his generosity having won him more enemies than friends. . . . What is worse, he cannot avoid the charge of avarice if he tries to reverse himself and replenish his finances.

A prince therefore . . . should not bother about being called a miser, for he will be considered liberal when people see that by his parsimony he has increased revenues, defended his dominions, and even undertaken useful enterprises without the need for new taxes. Then the many from whom he took nothing will term him liberal, . . . and only the few from whom he withheld his gifts will call him a miser. . . .

Chapter 17. On Cruelty and Clemency, and Whether It Is Better To Be Loved than Feared

It has sometimes been asked whether it is better to be loved than feared, to which I answer that one should wish to be both. But since that is difficult and if one must choose, I think it is safer to be feared than loved. For it may be truly said of mankind that they are ungrateful, fickle, timid, dissembling, and self-centered; so long as you can be useful to them, they are entirely devoted to you: their wealth, their blood, their lives, even their children's lives are all yours—when you have no need of them—but when your need arises, they turn their backs on you. . . . And the reason is clear: this kind of friendship, involving a simple obligation resulting from a benefit, cannot hold against the calculations of interest; but fear includes the dread of possible punishment, from which they cannot escape.

However, a prince should make himself feared in such a way that, if he cannot win their love, he at least avoids their hatred: this he may do by respecting his subjects' property and the honor of their wives. When he does have to shed blood, he should have good and sufficient reasons and *never* touch the condemned's property, because men will sooner forget their father's death than the loss of their patrimony. Besides, a prince who starts taking his subjects' property can always find reasons for robbing others, whereas excuses for shedding blood are harder to come by.

A prince at the head of his troops, however, should pay no attention to being called cruel, for without it he could not keep his men in line and ready for action. . . .

Chapter 18. How Princes Should Keep their Word

Everyone agrees that it is praiseworthy for princes to keep their word and live with integrity rather than cunning; but from recent experience we see that those who have distinguished themselves the most have paid little attention to keeping their promises, but have, instead, deceived others who acted in good faith.

You should consider, then, that there are two ways of fighting, one with laws, the other with force. The first is peculiar to man, the second to animals. But when laws are not sufficient, you may have to resort to force. So a prince must know how to use each method, . . . making the fox and the lion both his models. . . . From the fox he will learn how to avoid traps, from the lion how to keep the wolves in awe. Those who rely wholly on the lion's strength do not always succeed. Thus a wise prince cannot and should not keep his word when to do so would go against his interest or when the reason he pledged it no longer holds. If all men were good, this rule would not apply, but since most are bad, ever ready to go back on their word, there is no reason for a prince to keep his. Modern history offers many examples of this behavior, showing numberless engagements and treaties broken by the treachery of princes, and how those who played the fox succeeded best. But you must conceal your craft and thoroughly understand the art of feigning and dissembling; for men are generally so simple and weak that the deceiver easily finds dupes.

One example from our own time will suffice: Pope Alexander VI played the game of deception the whole of his life and, even though his behavior was well known, his artifices always succeeded. Promises and oaths cost him nothing; never did a prince so often break his word or go back on his promises, because he well understood this chapter in the art of governing.

A prince need not have all the good qualities I have listed so long as he *seems* to have them. . . . A prince should try to gain a reputation for kindness, mercy, piety, justice, and sincerity. And it is good to possess all these qualities, but you must be prepared to exhibit the exact opposites, when necessary. A prince, especially a new one, cannot possibly exercise all these virtues, because the preservation of the state frequently requires him to go against his word, and violate the rules of charity, humanity, and religion. He should know how to bend easily before the force of circumstance and fortune and, while holding to the good, still . . . know how to enter into evil, when necessary.

The prince must take care never to utter a word that does not . . . breathe of kindness, justice, humanity, and piety. The last is most important, since men judge more by appearances than substance. . . . Few can discern your inner being and they dare not oppose the masses, who have the majesty of State with them.

Chapter 26. An Exhortation to Liberate Italy from the Barbarians

In view of the things discussed above, I ask myself whether the time is ripe for the coming of a new prince to Italy, if there is material here that a capable leader might mold into a new form for the benefit of all men. And I can think of no time more propitious. . . .

Our country, almost lifeless, awaits a leader who will heal her wounds, stop the ravaging in Lombardy, end the looting of [Naples] and Tuscany and minister to her sores that have been festering for so long. See how eager she is to follow a banner if only someone will raise one up. . . .

On whom but your illustrious house can Italy now cast her eyes? Favored by God and the Church, now headed by your family, you possess the power and the merit for so glorious an enterprise. . . . Reflect on the deeds of the heroes described above. . . .

Their cause was not more lawful than yours, and God's blessing will attend you no less than them. "Every necessary war is a just war."

PETITION OF THE CIOMPI (22 July 1378)

L.A. Muratori, *Rerum italicarum scriptores,* ed. G. Scaranella (Bologna, 1902), 3:146–147.

The soft underbelly of the Italian Renaissance is illustrated by the revolt of the linen workers *(Ciompi)* in the late fourteenth century. For two hundred years the economy of Florence had been based on the production of woolen goods. *The Arte della Lana,* or merchant guild, bought raw wool in England, processed it with the help of various artisans in Florence, and then sold the finished product all over Europe and the Mediterranean seacoast.

In the course of time the gap between the merchants, called the *popolo grasso* ("Fat Ones") and the *popolo minuto,* or artisans, had widened, with the former not only reaping all the profits but also controlling the politics of the city.

Then there was a bottom group, represented by nobody and with no guild organization, called the *minutissimi* ("The Littlest People"). They were the most numerous class of Florentine citizens. The following petition speaks for both the minuti and the minutissimi.

In the end the revolt failed, but did not fail completely until the Medici family took power beginning in 1434.

Only citizens of the Commune of Florence shall be officers in the *Arte della Lana.*

That those who card, wash, dye, or in any way prepare the wool, shall no longer be under the jurisdiction of the Arte della Lana, but shall have their own guild. The same shall be true for those who are cutters and tailors of woolen cloth. . . .

That the executive body of the Commune shall comprise two delegates from the minutissimi, two from craft guilds, and the remaining two positions to be filled by representatives of the Arte della Lana.

That three of the 12 Elders of the Commune shall be chosen from the workers. . . .

The Gonfalonier of Justice shall represent the whole Commune and even the least of the state shall be eligible for election. . . .

That the said minutissimi must have a building, supplied by the Commune and worth 500 florins, where they can meet.

That all associations which have been disbanded be restored and that all those who have been declared rebels or falsely accused in any way may be members of the reorganized societies. . . .

That the Office for the Regulation of the Meat Supply in the city shall be closed and never again reopened.

That whoever has committed a misdemeanor shall not be mutilated but shall be punished in the normal manner.

That the minutissimi shall have 40 seats on the Council of the Eighty.

That the minutissimi shall have 10 seats on the Council of the Commune.

That no one whose house was destroyed by the wrath of the people shall ever again hold office. . . .

That the leader of the People's Party shall have an office in the city hall and never be arrested on any pretext whatever.

That those men and women who have been put on probation and blacklisted shall be removed from the list and never again be blacklisted. . . .

That none of the popolo grasso shall be members of the Council of the Commune, but their places shall be taken by 10 of the popolo minuto.

These are the reasons why we demonstrated on July 20th.

CHAPTER 11

AGE OF DISCOVERY

Imagine that you are a native European in 1500, believing that your continent is the center of the universe, when one day you awaken from your wool-gathering to discover that your world has been pushed out in all directions, first by Columbus sailing West, and then by da Gama sailing East, all the way to India via the Cape of Good Hope, and all this in less than a decade, between 1492 and 1499.

Then imagine, if you will, that a few years later you read a book by a Polish astronomer, Copernicus, arguing that the earth is not even the center of the universe but only one of the lesser planets circling the sun. If you should then live to be a hundred, you will read in Galileo that nothing in the heavens that you see with the naked eye is what it appears to be.

Next, a century after Copernicus, the Frenchman Descartes will tell your descendants that the way to discover truth is by skepticism: clear your mind of all received ideas and doubt everything, even that you exist. Can you then doubt that you are doubting?

But it all comes together again in Sir Isaac Newton's formula of universal gravitation:

$$f = \frac{M_1 M_2}{d^2}$$

where f = the force of attraction, or gravity
M_1 and M_2 = the masses of any two bodies in the universe
d = the distance between their centers

As Newton saw it, the world was a wonderful machine, like an enormous clock, originally invented by God and kept running all these ages by His perfect laws; and man had only to discover these laws in order to find happiness on earth.

Some questions for discussion: Do you think Columbus's motives in going overseas were typical of most conquistadores?

To what extent might Copernicus have been indebted to Columbus for his ideas?

Considering Galileo's use of the telescope, can you draw any conclusions about the relationship between science and technology?

How would you characterize Francis Bacon's role in the Age of Discovery?

Compare the contributions of Descartes and Newton.

JOURNAL OF THE FIRST VOYAGE OF COLUMBUS (1492)

The Journal of Christopher Columbus, trans. C. Markham, in *Works Issued by the Hakluyt Society*, v. 56 (London, 1893).

Columbus (b. Genoa, 1451) was by no means the first to think of sailing west to reach the Indies. The idea that there were islands in the Atlantic went back to the Middle Ages and classical antiquity. But Columbus's greatness, aside from his being one of the best sailors in modern times, came from his dogged determination in the achievement of his "Enterprise of the Indies." After having been rebuffed by the Portuguese, he spent eight years pleading with Ferdinand and Isabella. Finally the Queen granted him three ships and he set sail on August 3, 1492, returning eight months later. In all, he made four voyages to the islands, discovering Haiti, Cuba, Puerto Rico, Guadeloupe, Jamaica, Trinidad, and the coasts of Central and South America. Proclaimed "Admiral of the Ocean Sea," Columbus eventually fell from favor and died in poverty and disgrace in 1506.

In the name of our Lord Jesus Christ.

Because, O most Christian, and very high, very excellent and puissant Princes, King and Queen of the Spains and of the islands of the Sea, our Lords, in this present year of 1492, after your Highnesses had given an end to the war with the Moors who reigned in Europe, and had finished it in the very great city of Granada, where in this present year, on the second day of the month of January, by force of arms, I saw the royal banners of your Highnesses placed on the towers of Alhambra, which is the fortress of that city, and I saw the Moorish King come forth from the gates of the city and kiss the hands of your Highnesses, and of the Prince my Lord, and presently in that same month, acting on the information that I had given to your Highnesses touching the lands of India, and respecting a Prince who is called *Gran Can,* which means in our language King of Kings, how he and his ancestors had sent to Rome many times to ask for learned men of our holy faith to teach him, and how the Holy Father had never complied, insomuch that many people believing in idolatries were lost by receiving doctrine of perdition: YOUR HIGHNESSES, as Catholic Christians and Princes who love the holy Christian faith, and the propagation of it, and who are enemies to the sect of Mahomet and to all idolatries and heresies, resolved to send me, Cristobal Colon, to the said parts of India to see the said princes, and the cities and lands, and their disposition, with a view that they might be converted to our holy faith; and ordered that I should not go by land to the eastward, as had been customary, but that I should gó by way of the west, whither up to this day we do not know for certain that anyone has gone.

Thus, after having turned out all the Jews from all your kingdoms and lordships, in the same month of January, your Highnesses gave orders to me that with a sufficient fleet I should go to the said parts of India. . . .

Land was sighted at two hours after midnight [on October 12, 1492] at a distance of two leagues. They shortened sail and lay by under the mainsail without the bonnets.

The vessels were hove to, waiting for daylight, and on Friday they arrived at a small island of the Lucayos [renamed San Salvador by Columbus; now Watling Island]. Presently they saw naked people. The Admiral went on shore in the armed boat, and Martin Alonzo Pinzon and Vicente Yañez, his brother, who was captain of the *Nina*. The Admiral took the royal standard, and the captains went with two banners of the green cross, which the Admiral took in all the ships as a sign, with an F and a Y and a crown over each letter, one on one side of the cross and the other on the other. Having landed, they saw trees very green, and much water, and fruits of diverse kinds. The Admiral called to the two captains and to the others who leaped on shore . . . and said that they should bear faithful testimony that he, in the presence of all, had taken, as he now took, possession of the said island for the King and for the Queen, his Lords making the declarations that are required. . . .

Presently many inhabitants of the island assembled. . . . I saw and knew (says the Admiral) that these people are without any religion, not idolaters but very gentle, not knowing what is evil, nor the sins of murder and theft, being without arms, and so timid that a hundred would fly before one Spaniard, although they joke with them. They, however, believe and know that there is a God in heaven, and say that we have come from heaven. At any prayer that we say, they repeat, and make the sign of the cross. Thus your Highnesses should resolve to make them Christians, for I believe that if the work was begun, in a little time the multitude of nations would be converted to our faith, with the acquisition of great lordships, peoples, and riches for Spain. Without doubt there is in this land a vast quantity of gold, and the Indians . . . do not speak without reason when they say that in these islands there are places where they dig out gold, and wear it on their necks, ears, arms, and legs, the rings being very large. There are also precious stones, pearls, and an infinity of spices. . . . Here also there is a great quantity of cotton, and I believe it would have a good sale here without sending it to Spain, but to the cities of the Gran Can, which will be discovered without doubt, and many others ruled over by other lords, who will be pleased to serve your Highnesses, and whither will be brought other commodities of Spain and of the Eastern lands; but these are to the West as regards us. . . .

COPERNICUS: ON HEAVENLY MOTIONS (1520s)

From "Commentariolus" (MS), in L. Prowe, *Nicolaus Coppernicus* (2 vols., Berlin, 1883–1884), 2:184–190.

Nicholas Copernicus (1473–1543), Polish M.D., mathematician, and astronomer, wrote a book that literally turned the world upside down: *De revolutionibus orbium coelestium* ("On the Revolution of the Heavenly Bodies") replaced the Aristotelian-Ptolemaic model of a geocentric universe with a hypothesis that put the sun at the center and demoted the earth to being one planet among many. Although Copernicus's book was not published until the year of his death, he had completed it by 1530 and outlined the principles of it in the following letter written sometime in the 1520s.

NICOLAI COPERNICI

net, in quo terram cum orbe lunari tanquam epicyclo contineri diximus. Quinto loco Venus nono menſe reducitur. Sextum deniq; locum Mercurius tenet, octuaginta dierum ſpacio circū currens. In medio uero omnium reſidet Sol. Quis enim in hoc

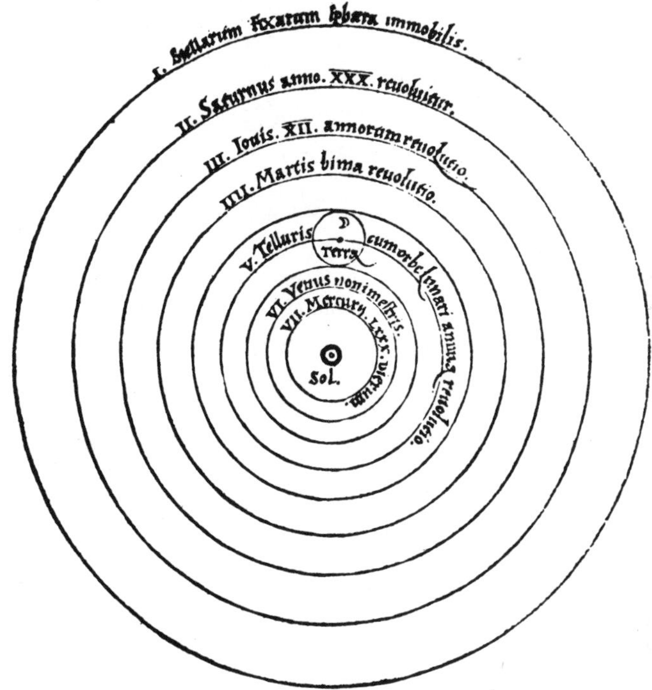

Copernican Planetary System. *Diagram from De revolutionibus orbium coelestium, published in 1543. Note the sun in the center and the earth (Terra) "demoted" to the third orbit around the sun. (The British Library, London.)*

Our ancestors posited . . . a large number of celestial spheres . . . in order to explain the apparent motion of the planets according to the principle of "regularity," since they thought it quite absurd that a heavenly body—a perfect sphere—should not move uniformly at all times. By connecting and combining regular motions in various ways, they saw that they could make a heavenly body move to any given position.

[Those] . . . who tried to solve the problem by the use of concentric spheres still could not account for all the movements of the planets; they had to explain not only their apparent revolutions but also the fact that these bodies sometimes appear to rise higher in the heavens, and sometimes to descend, which behavior is incompatible with the principle of concentricity. It seemed better, therefore, to use eccentrics and epicycles, a system finally adopted by most scholars. But the planetary theories of

Ptolemy and most other astronomers, while consistent with the numerical facts, seemed likewise to present considerable difficulty. . . .

Once I had become aware of these defects, I often wondered if there could possibly be found a more reasonable arrangement of circles, one from which every apparent inequality would be derived, and in which everything would move uniformly about its proper center, according to the rule of absolute motion. After I had addressed myself to this difficult and almost insoluble problem, the idea finally came to me how it could be solved with fewer and much simpler constructions, provided certain assumptions called *axioms,* were granted me in the following order:

1. There is no one center of all celestial circles or spheres.
2. The center of the earth is not the center of the universe, but only a center of gravity and of the moon's sphere.
3. All the spheres rotate around the sun as their midpoint, and the sun is therefore the center of the universe.
4. The ratio of the earth's distance from the sun to the height of the firmament is so much smaller than the ratio of the earth's radius to its distance from the sun that the distance from the earth to the sun is imperceptible in comparison with the height of the firmament.
5. Whatever motion appears in the firmament arises not from any motion of the firmament but from the earth's motion. The earth together with its surrounding elements performs a complete rotation on its fixed poles in a daily motion, while the firmament and highest heaven remain unchanged.
6. What appears to us as motions of the sun arise not from its motion but from the motion of the earth and our sphere, with which we revolve about the sun like any other planet. Thus, the earth has more than one motion.
7. The apparent retrograde and direct motion of the planets arises not from their motion but from the earth's. And so the motion of the earth alone suffices to explain so many apparent irregularities in the heavens.

Having set forth these assumptions, I shall try to show briefly how uniformity of the motions can be saved in a systematic way. For the sake of brevity, however, I have thought it best to omit here any mathematical demonstrations, keeping those for my larger work. But in the explanation of the circles I shall set down the lengths of the radii, from which the reader not acquainted with mathematics may readily see how closely this arrangement of circles agrees with the numerical data and the observations.

Let no one suppose, however, that I have gratuitously asserted, with the Pythagoreans, the motions of the earth, strong proof of which will be found in my exposition of the circles. For the principal arguments by which natural philosophers try to establish the immobility of the earth are based mainly on appearances, and it is those arguments, in particular, that collapse here, since I treat the earth's immobility as resulting from appearances.

The Order of the Spheres

The celestial spheres are arranged in the following order: the highest is the immovable sphere of the fixed stars, which contains and gives position to all things; beneath it is

Saturn, followed by Jupiter and then Mars; below Mars is the sphere on which we revolve, then Venus, and lastly, Mercury. The lunar sphere revolves about the center of the earth and moves with the earth like an epicycle. In the same order also, one planet surpasses another in speed of revolution, according as they trace larger or smaller circles: thus, Saturn completes its revolution in thirty years, Jupiter in twelve, Mars in two and a half, the earth in one year, Venus in nine months and Mercury in three.

Apparent Motions of the Sun

The earth . . . revolves annually in a great circle around the sun in the order of the signs, always describing equal arcs in equal times. The distance from the center of the circle to the center of the sun is 1/25th the radius of the circle. It is assumed that the length of the radius is imperceptible in comparison to the height of the firmament. Consequently, the sun appears to revolve with this motion as if the earth lay in the center of the universe. But this appearance is caused not by the motion of the sun but by that of the earth, so that, when the earth is in the sign of Capricorn, for example, the sun is seen diametrically opposite in Cancer, and so forth. Because of the above-mentioned distance of the sun from the center of the circle, this apparent motion of the sun is not uniform, the maximum irregularity being 2–1/6 degrees.

The second motion, which is peculiar to the earth, is its daily rotation on the poles in the order of the signs, that is, from west to east. As a result of this rotation, the entire universe appears to revolve with enormous speed. Thus does the earth rotate together with its surrounding waters and encircling atmosphere.

GALILEO: THE SIDEREAL MESSENGER (1610)

Trans. E. S. Carlos (London, 1880), pp. 10–12, 14–15, 40–41, revised.

Italian astronomer, mathematician, and physicist, Galileo (1564–1642) is to science what Columbus is to exploration. While others were still quoting ancient Greek science, Galileo tested Aristotle's laws of physics and disproved them. He is supposed, for example, to have dropped objects from the tower in Pisa, where he was professor of mathematics, finding that heavy bodies fell no faster than light ones; in fact, they fell at the same rate, with uniform acceleration. The intellectual community was both shocked and outraged.

Later, when he accepted and defended the Copernician theory of a heliocentric universe, he was tried by the Inquisition (1633) and imprisoned, briefly. The last ten years of his life were spent in seclusion near Florence, but he continued an active pursuit of scientific truths. The following excerpt from his "newsletter" describes how he built the first astronomical telescope and helped pave the way for the future exploration of space.

About ten months ago a report reached me that a Dutchman had constructed a telescope by the aid of which visible objects, although at a great distance from the eye of the

Cathedral and leaning tower of Pisa. *Although the cathedral was not built until the seventeenth century, the famous tower was started in 1174, then abandoned at the third tier when the tower began to lean because of weaknesses in the subsoil. A century later, however, it was completed with a list of fourteen feet off the perpendicular. This made it ideal for Galileo to test the rate of acceleration of falling bodies. Incidentally, the tower continues to lean at the rate of one millimeter per year or four inches per century. (Courtesy of the Italian Cultural Institute.)*

observer, were seen distinctly as if near; and proofs of its wonderful performances were reported, which some gave credence to but others contradicted. A few days after, I received confirmation of the report in a letter from a Parisian nobleman, Jacques Badovère, which finally determined me to inquire into the principle of the telescope and to consider the means by which I might invent a similar instrument, which I shortly succeeded in doing, by intensive study of the theory of refraction. I prepared a tube, at first of lead, in the ends of which I fitted two glass lenses, both plane on one side, but on the other side: one spherically convex, the other concave. Then, bringing my eye to the concave lens, I saw objects satisfactorily large and near, for they appeared one-third of the distance off and nine times larger than when they are seen with the naked eye alone. Shortly afterward, I constructed another telescope with greater refinement, which magnified objects more than sixty times. At length, by sparing neither labor nor expense, I succeeded in constructing an instrument so superior that objects seen through it appeared magnified nearly a thousand times, and more than thirty times nearer than if viewed by the natural powers of sight alone.

It would be a waste of time to enumerate the number and importance of the benefits of this instrument when used by land or sea. But without considering its use for terrestrial objects, I betook myself to the observation of the heavenly bodies. First of all I viewed the moon as near as if it was scarcely two semidiameters of the earth distant. After the moon, I frequently observed other heavenly bodies, both fixed stars and planets, with incredible delight. When I saw their very great number, I began to consider a method by which I might be able to measure their distances apart, and at length I found one. And here it is fitting that all who intend to make observations of this kind should be cautioned: first, it is absolutely essential for them to prepare a most perfect telescope, one which will show very bright objects distinct and free from mistiness, and will magnify them at least 400 times, for then it will show them as if only one-twentieth of their distance off. For unless the instrument be of such power, it will be useless to attempt to view all the things which I have seen in the heavens, or which will be enumerated hereafter. . . .

Let me first speak of the moon's surface which is turned toward us. To be understood more easily, I distinguish two parts in it, which I call respectively the brighter and the darker. The brighter part seems to surround and pervade the whole hemisphere; but the darker part, like a sort of cloud, discolors the moon's surface and makes it appear covered with spots. Now these spots, as they are somewhat dark and of considerable size, are plain to everyone, and every age has seen them, wherefore I shall call them *great* or *ancient* spots, to distinguish them from other spots, smaller in size but so thickly scattered that they sprinkle the whole surface of the moon, especially the brighter portion of it. These spots have never been observed by anyone before me; and from my observation of them, often repeated, I have been led to that opinion which I have expressed, namely, that I feel sure that the surface of the moon is not perfectly smooth, free from inequalities, and exactly spherical, as a large school of philosphers considers with regard to the moon and the other heavenly bodies, but that, on the contrary, it is full of inequalities, uneven, full of hollows and protuberances, just like the surface of the earth itself, which is varied everywhere by lofty mountains and deep valleys. . . .

The difference between the appearance of the planets and the fixed stars seems also worth noting. The planets present their disks perfectly round, as if described with a compass, and appear as so many little moons, completely illuminated and globular in shape; but the fixed stars do not look to the naked eye bounded by a circular circumference, but rather like blazes of light, shooting out beams on all sides, and very sparkling, and with a telescope they appear of the same shape as when they are viewed by simply looking at them, but so much larger that a star of the fifth or sixth magnitude seems to equal Sirius, the largest of all the fixed stars.

But beyond the stars of the sixth magnitude you will behold through the telescope a host of other stars, which escape the unassisted sight, so numerous as to be almost beyond belief. . . .

THE NEW METHOD

FRANCIS BACON: NOVUM ORGANUM (NEW METHOD), 1620

Trans. Ellis-Spedding, in *The Philosophical Works of Francis Bacon,* ed. J. M. Robertson (London, 1905), pp. 259–270, revised.

Though not himself a scientist, Francis Bacon (1561–1626) was the prophet and propagandist for the new learning. He was one of the first to see the immense possibilities for mankind of a science free from superstition and dogmatic restrictions. By studying natural laws and learning to obey them, people, he felt, could exercise untold power over nature. His writings filled his contemporaries and their descendants with immense hope for the future and also gave them courage for the coming struggle against tradition and willful ignorance.

Aphorisms

1. Man, as the minister and interpreter of nature, does and understands as much as his observations on the order of nature . . . permit him, and neither knows nor is capable of more.

2. The unassisted hand and the understanding left to itself possess but little power. Effects are produced by . . . means of instruments and helps, which the understanding requires no less than the hand; and as instruments either promote or regulate the motion of the hand, so . . . those that are applied to the mind prompt or protect the understanding.

3. Knowledge and human power are synonymous, since . . . ignorance of the cause frustrates the effect; for nature is only subdued by submission, and that which in contemplative philosophy corresponds with the cause in practical science becomes the rule.

9. The sole cause . . . of almost every defect in the sciences is this, that while we falsely admire and extol the powers of the human mind, we do not search for its real helps.

11. As the present sciences are useless for the discovery of effects, so the present system of logic is useless for the discovery of the sciences.

12. The present system of logic rather assists in confirming . . . the errors founded on vulgar notions than in searching after truth, and is therefore more hurtful than useful.

13. The syllogism is not applied to the principles of the sciences, and is of no avail in intermediate axioms, as being very unequal to the subtility of nature. It forces assent, therefore, and not things.

19. There are and can exist but two ways of investigating and discovering truth. The one hurries on rapidly from the senses and particulars to the most general axioms. This is the way now in use. The other constructs its axioms from the senses and particulars, by ascending continually and gradually, till it finally arrives at the most general axioms, which is the true but unattempted way.

39. Four species of idols beset the human mind, to which . . . we have assigned names, calling the first Idols of the Tribe, the second Idols of the Den, the third Idols of the Market, and fourth Idols of the Theatre.

40. The formation of notions and axioms on the foundation of true induction is the only fitting remedy by which we can ward off and expel these idols. It is, however, of great service to point them out; for the doctrine of idols bears the same relation to the interpretation of nature as that of the confutation of sophisms does to common logic.

41. The idols of the tribe are inherent in human nature, . . . for man's sense is falsely asserted to be the standard of things; on the contrary, all the perceptions both of the senses and the mind bear reference to man and not to the universe, and the human mind resembles those uneven mirrors which impart their own properties to different objects, from which rays are emitted and distort and disfigure them.

42. The idols of the den are those of each individual; for everybody (in addition to the errors common to the race of man) has his own individual den or cavern, which intercepts and corrupts the light of nature, either from his own peculiar and singular disposition, or from his education and intercourse with others, or from his reading, and the authority acquired by those whom he reverences and admires, or from the different impressions produced on the mind, as it happens to be preoccupied and predisposed, or equable and tranquil, and the like; so that the spirit of man . . . is variable, confused, and as it were actuated by chance; and Heraclitus said well that men search for knowledge in lesser worlds, and not in the greater or common world.

43. There are also idols formed by the reciprocal intercourse and society of man with man, which we call idols of the market, from the commerce and association of men with each other; for men converse by means of language, but words are formed at the will of the generality, and there arises from a bad and unapt formation of words a wonderful obstruction to the mind. Nor can the definitions and explanations with which learned men are wont to guard and protect themselves in some instances afford a complete remedy,—words still manifestly force the understanding, throw everything into confusion, and lead mankind into vain and innumerable controversies and fallacies.

59. The idols of the market are the most troublesome of all, those namely which have entwined themselves round the understanding from the associations of words and names. For men imagine that their reason governs words, whilst, in fact, words react upon the understanding; and this has rendered philosophy and the sciences sophistical and inactive. Words are generally formed in a popular sense, and define things by those broad lines which are most obvious to the vulgar mind; but when a more acute understanding, or more diligent observation is anxious to vary those lines, and to adapt them more accurately to nature, words oppose it. Hence the great and solemn disputes of learned men often terminate in controversies about words and names, in regard to which it would be better (imitating the caution of mathematics) to proceed more advisedly in the first instance, and to bring such disputes to a regular issue by definitions. Such definitions, however, cannot remedy the evil in natural and material objects, because they consist themselves of words, and these words produce others; so that we must necessarily have recourse to particular instances, and their regular series and arrangement. . . .

60. The idols imposed upon the understanding by words are of two kinds. They are either the names of things which have no existence . . . or they are the names of actual objects, but confused, badly defined, and hastily and irregularly abstracted from things. Fortune, the *primum mobile,** the planetary orbits, the elements of fire, and the like fictions, which owe their birth to futile and false theories, are instances of the first kind. And this species of idols is removed with greater facility, because it can be exterminated by the constant refutation or the desuetude of the theories themselves. The others, which are created by vicious and unskilful abstraction, are intricate and deeply rooted. Take some word for instance, as *moist,* and let us examine how far the different significations of this word are consistent. It will be found that the word moist is nothing but a confused sign of different actions admitting of no settled and defined uniformity. For it means that which easily diffuses itself over another body; that which is indeterminable and cannot be brought to a consistency; that which yields easily in every direction; that which is easily divided and dispersed; that which is easily united and collected; that which easily flows and is put in motion; that which easily adheres to, and wets another body; that which is easily reduced to a liquid state though previously solid. . . .

61. The idols of the theatre are not innate, nor do they introduce themselves secretly into the understanding, but they are manifestly instilled and cherished by the fictions of theories and depraved rules of demonstration. To attempt, however, . . . their confutation would not be consistent with our declarations. For since we neither agree in our principles nor our demonstrations, all argument is out of the question. . . .

Our method of discovering the sciences is such as to leave little to the acuteness and strength of wit . . . and intellect. For as the drawing of a straight line, or accurate circle by . . . hand, much depends on its steadiness and practice, but if a ruler or compass be employed there is little occasion for either; so it is with our method. Although, however, we enter into no individual confutations, yet a little must be said, first, of the sects and general divisions of these species of theories; secondly, something further to show that there are external signs of their weakness; and, lastly, we must consider the causes of so great a misfortune, and so long and general a unanimity in error, that we may thus render the access to truth less difficult, and that the human understanding may the more readily be purified, and brought to dismiss its idols.

62. The idols of the theatre, or of theories are numerous, and may, and perhaps will, be still more so. For [if] men's minds had [not] been occupied for many ages in religious and theological considerations, and civil governments (especially monarchies), had [not] been averse to novelties of that nature even in theory (so that men must apply to them with some risk and injury to their own fortunes, and not only without reward, but subject to contumely and envy), there is no doubt that many other sects of philosophers and theorists would have been introduced, like those which formerly flourished in such diversified abundance amongst the Greeks. For as many imaginary theories of the heavens can be deduced from the phenomena of the sky, so it is even more easy to found many dogmas upon the phenomena of philosophy—and the plot of this our theatre resembles those of the poetical, where the plots which are

*In Ptolemaic astronomy the tenth sphere, carrying the fixed stars.—Ed.

invented for the stage are more consistent, elegant, and pleasurable than those taken from real history. . . .

DESCARTES: DISCOURSE ON METHOD (1637)

From *Oeuvres et lettres* (Paris, 1953), pp. 126, 130, 135, 147–148; trans. John Veitch (1850), revised.

Cogito, ergo sum (I think, therefore I am). René Descartes (1596–1650), unlike the scholastic philosophers, rejected all received ideas and started his philosophy from scratch. He proceeded to doubt everything. But there was one thing he could not doubt—his own doubting. From there he went on to prove his existence as well as that of God Himself. That is how he developed his method of testing all thinking and knowledge. Immediately, he became both popular and controversial. (His books are still on the Index). But he influenced such diverse figures as Spinoza, Pascal, Locke, and Leibniz. Descartes's method, however, based on logic, was not destined to be the scientific method of the future; that would be the method of observation, hypothesis, and experiment currently being developed by Bacon, Galileo, *et al.* But Cartesian skepticism has continued to play an important role in the rise of modern science up to the present day.

Good sense is, of all things among men, the most equally distributed; for everyone thinks himself so abundantly provided with it that even those who are most difficult to satisfy in everything else do not usually desire a larger measure of this quality than they already have. And in this it is not likely that all are mistaken: the conviction is rather to be held as testifying that the power of judging aright and of distinguishing Truth from Error, which is properly called Good Sense or Reason, is by nature equal in all men; and that the diversity of our opinions does not arise from some being endowed with a larger share of Reason than others, but solely from this, that we conduct our thoughts along different lines and do not fix our attention on the same objects. For to be possessed of a vigorous mind is not enough; the prime requisite is rightly to apply it. The greatest minds, as they are capable of the highest excellencies, are open likewise to the greatest aberrations; and those who travel very slowly may yet make far greater progress, provided they keep always to the straight road, than those who, while they run, forsake it.

For myself, I have never fancied my mind to be in any respect more perfect than those of others; on the contrary, I have often wished that I were equal to some others in quickness of thought, or in clearness and distinctness of imagination, or in extent and readiness of memory. And besides these, I know of no other qualities that contribute to the perfection of the mind; for as to Reason or Sense, inasmuch as it is that alone which makes us human and distinguishes us from the animals, I am disposed to believe that it is to be found complete in each individual; and on this point to adopt the common opinion of philosophers, who say that the difference of greater and less holds only among the *accidents,* and not among the *forms* or *natures* of *individuals* of the same *species*. . . .

I was especially delighted with Mathematics, on account of the certainty and clarity of their reasonings; but I had not as yet a precise knowledge of their true use; and thinking that they but contributed to the advancement of the mechanical arts, I was astonished that foundations, so strong and solid, should have had no loftier superstructure reared on them. On the other hand, I compared the disquisitions of the ancient Moralists to very towering and magnificient palaces with no better foundation than quicksand: they laud the virtues very highly and exhibit them as estimable far above anything on earth; but they give no adequate criterion of virtue, and frequently what they designate with so fine a name is but apathy, or pride, or despair, or parricide. . . .

[Neither] could I approve in any degree of those restless and busy meddlers who, unqualified either by birth or fortune to take part in the management of public affairs, are yet always projecting reforms; and if I thought that this Tract contained aught which might justify the suspicion that I was a victim of such folly, I would by no means permit its publication. I have never dreamed of anything more than the reformation of my own opinions and basing them on a foundation wholly my own. Although satisfaction with my work has led me to present here a draft of it, I do not by any means therefore recommend to everyone else to make a similar attempt. Those whom God has endowed with a large measure of genius will entertain, perhaps, designs still more exalted; but for the many I am much afraid lest even the present undertaking be more than they can safely venture to imitate. The single design to strip one's self of all past beliefs is one that ought not to be taken by everyone. The majority of people is composed of two kinds, for neither of which would this be an appropriate undertaking: in the first place, for those who think themselves cleverer than they are, cannot refrain from jumping to conclusions, and lack the necessary patience for orderly and circumspect thinking; whence it happens that if these people once take the liberty to doubt of their accustomed opinions, and leave the beaten track, they will never find the right path but remain lost all their lives; in the second place, of those who, possessed of sufficient sense or modesty to decide that there are others who excel them in the power of discriminating between truth and error, and by whom they may be instructed, ought rather to content themselves with the opinions of such than trust for more correct opinions to their own reason. . . .

I am not sure if I should discuss my earlier meditations, since they are so metaphysical and uncommon as not to be to everyone's taste. But in order to determine whether the foundations I have laid are solid, I feel obliged . . . to speak of them. In practice, I have found that it is sometimes necessary to accept ideas that are highly dubious . . . Now, because I wanted to devote myself entirely to the search for truth, I felt that I should follow the exact opposite procedure and reject completely everything in which I could conceive the slightest doubt, in order to see if anything remained that was absolutely indubitable. Because the senses sometimes mislead us, I was willing to assume that nothing is really the way our senses represent it. And because some people err in reasoning even in the simplest matters, . . . I rejected as false all the reasonings I had previously taken as proven. Then, realizing that all the thoughts that occur to us when awake may also come to us in our sleep—and none of them true—I supposed that everything entering my mind was no truer than my dreams. I immediately discovered, however, that while I thus tried to think everything false, I who was doing the thinking must of necessity exist. *I think, therefore I am*—this truth was so certain and obvious that no skeptic could ever find grounds, however absurd, for shaking it. And I concluded that this was the first principle of the philosophy I was looking for.

Next, examining carefully what I was and seeing that I could assume that I had no body and that I was nowhere, I nevertheless could not assume that I did not exist; on the contrary, from the fact that I could doubt the truth of other things, it clearly and certainly followed that I *was*. While, on the other hand, if I had simply stopped thinking, although all the other things I had ever imagined really existed, I should have had no reason to believe that I was existing. I thence concluded that I was a substance whose essence consists only in thinking, and which, in order to be, has no need of any place nor any material thing. So that "I," meaning the mind by which I am what I am, is entirely distinct from the body and is even easier to know than the body, and is such that, even if the latter were not, it would continue to be all that it is.

After that, I considered what is generally necessary to make a proposition true and certain; for since I had just found one I knew to be so, I thought that I ought also to know in what this certainty consisted. And I discovered that there is nothing in this *I think, therefore I am* to insure that I speak the truth except that I see clearly that in order to think I have to exist. Therefore I concluded that I might take it as a general rule that the things which we conceive very clearly and distinctly are all true, and that the only difficulty is in seeing plainly which things are so conceived by us.

NEWTON: PRINCIPIA MATHEMATICA (1687)

Trans. A. Motte (New York, 1848), pp. lxvii–lxviii, 83–84, 384–385.

Sir Isaac Newton (1642–1727) took the works of Copernicus, Bacon, Galileo, *et al.*, and combined them with his own extensive research to form a synthesis which he called "The Mathematical Principles of Natural Philosophy," or *Principia,* for short. This work not only sparked the Enlightenment of the eighteenth century, but it established a model that went unchallenged until the Age of Einstein. As a poet of the Enlightenment saw it,

Nature and Nature's law
Lay hid in night;
God said, "Let Newton be,"
And all was light.

Newton was more modest: "I seem to have been only like a boy playing on the seashore, and diverting myself in now and then finding a smoother pebble or a prettier shell than ordinary, whilst the great ocean of truth lay all undiscovered before me." Among the prettier shells that he discovered were the calculus, three laws of motion, universal gravitation, the refraction of light, besides studies in theology, history, and alchemy. The following excerpts from the Principia illustrate the argument, the methodology, and the laws of motion.

Preface

Since the ancients . . . made great account of the science of mechanics in the investigation of natural things; and the moderns, laying aside substantial forms and occult qualities, have endeavored to subject the phenomena of nature to the laws of mathematics, I have in this treatise cultivated mathematics so far as it regards philosophy. . . .

To practical mechanics all the manual arts belong, from which mechanics took its name. But as artificers do not work with perfect accuracy, it comes to pass that mechanics is so distinguished from geometry, that what is perfectly accurate is called geometrical; what is less so is called mechanical. But the errors are not in the art, but in the artificers. He that works with less accuracy is an imperfect mechanic; and if any could work with perfect accuracy, he would be the most perfect mechanic of all; for the description of right lines and circles, upon which geometry is founded, belongs to mechanics. Geometry does not teach us to draw these lines, but requires them to be drawn; for it requires that the learner should first be taught to describe these accurately before he enters upon geometry; then it shows how by these operations problems may be solved. To describe right lines and circles are problems but not geometrical problems. The solution of these problems is required from mechanics; and by geometry the use of them, when so solved, is shown; and it is the glory of geometry that from those few principles, brought from without, it is able to produce so many things. Therefore geometry is founded in mechanical practice and is nothing but that part of universal mechanics which accurately proposes and demonstrates the art of measuring. But since the manual arts are chiefly conversant in the moving of bodies, it comes to pass that geometry is commonly referred to as their magnitudes, and mechanics to their motion. In this sense rational mechanics will be the science of motions resulting from any forces whatsoever, and of the forces required to produce any motions, accurately proposed and demonstrated. . . .

Our design not respecting arts but philosophy, and our subject not manual but natural powers, we consider chiefly those things which relate to gravity, levity, elastic force, the resistance of fluids, and the like forces, whether attractive or impulsive; and therefore we offer this work as the mathematical principles of philosophy; for all the difficulty of philosophy seems to consist in this—from the phenomena of motions to investigate the forces of nature, and then from these forces to demonstrate the other phenomena; and to this end the general propositions in the first and second book are directed. In the third book we give an example of this in the explication of the System of the World; for by the propositions mathematically demonstrated in the former books, we in the third derive from the celestial phenomena the forces of gravity with which bodies tend to the sun and the several planets. Then from these forces, by other propositions which are also mathematical, we deduce the motions of the planets, the comets, the moon, and the sea. I wish we could derive the rest of the phenomena of nature by the same kind of reasoning from mechanical principles; for I am induced by many reasons to suspect that they may all depend upon certain forces by which the particles of bodies, by some causes hitherto unknown, are either mutually impelled towards each other, and cohere in regular figures, or are repelled and recede from each other; which forces being unknown, philosophers have hitherto attempted the search of nature in vain; but I hope the principles here laid down will afford some light either to this or some truer method of philosophy. . . .

Rules of Reasoning in Philosophy

Rule 1. *We are to admit no more causes of natural things than such as are both true and sufficient to explain their appearances.*

To this purpose the philosophers say that Nature does nothing in vain, and more is in vain when less will serve; for Nature is pleased with simplicity and affects not the pomp of superfluous causes.

Rule 2. *Therefore to the same natural effects we must, as far as possible, assign the same causes.*

As to respiration in a man and in a beast; the descent of stones in Europe and in America; the light of our culinary fire and of the sun; the reflection of light in the earth and in the planets.

Rule 3. *The qualities of bodies, which admit neither intension nor remission of degrees, and which are found to belong to all bodies within the reach of our experiments, are to be esteemed the universal qualities of all bodies whatsoever.*

For since the qualities of bodies are only known to us by experiments, we are to hold for universal all such as universally agree with experiments and such as are not liable to diminution can never be quite taken away. We are certainly not to relinquish the evidence of experiments for the sake of dreams and vain fictions of our own devising; nor are we to recede from the analogy of Nature, which uses to be simple, and always consonant to itself. We no other way know the extension of bodies than by our senses, nor do these reach it in all bodies; but because we perceive extension in all that are sensible, therefore we ascribe it universally to all others also. That abundance of bodies are hard, we learn by experience; and because the hardness of the whole arises from the hardness of the parts, we therefore justly infer the hardness of the undivided particles not only of the bodies we feel but of all others. That all bodies are impenetrable, we gather not from reason, but from sensation. The bodies which we handle we find impenetrable, and thence conclude impenetrability to be a universal property of all bodies whatsoever. That all bodies are moveable, and endowed with certain powers . . . of persevering in their motion or in their rest, we only infer the like properties observed in the bodies which we have seen. The extension, hardness, impenetrability, mobility, and [inertia] of the whole, result from the extension, hardness, impenetrability, mobility and [inertia] of the parts; and thence we conclude the least particles of all bodies to be also all extended, and hard, and impenetrable, and moveable, and endowed with their proper [inertia]. . . .

Lastly, if it universally appears by experiments and astronomical observations, that all bodies about the earth gravitate towards the earth, and that in proportion to the quantity of matter which they severally contain; that the moon likewise, according to the quantity of its matter, gravitates towards the earth; that, on the other hand, our sea gravitates towards the moon; and all the planets mutually one towards another; and the comets in like manner towards the sun; we must in consequence of this rule, universally allow that all bodies whatsoever are endowed with a principle of mutual gravitation. For the argument from appearances concludes with more force for the universal gravitation of all bodies than for their impenetrability; of which, among those in the celestial region, we have no experiments, nor any manner of observation. . . .

Rule 4. *In experimental philosophy we are to look upon propositions collected by general induction from phenomena as accurately or very nearly true, notwithstanding any contrary hypotheses that may be imagined, till such time as other phenomena occur, by which they may either be made more accurate, or liable to exceptions.*

This rule must follow, that the argument of induction may not be evaded by hypotheses.

The Laws of Motion

Law 1: Every body continues in its state of rest, or of uniform motion, in a right line, unless it is compelled to change that state by forces impressed upon it.

Projectiles continue in their motions, so far as they are not retarded by the resistance of the air, or impelled downwards by the force of gravity. A top, whose parts by their cohesion are continually drawn aside from rectilinear motions, does not cease its rotation, otherwise than as it is retarded by the air. The greater bodies of the planets and comets, meeting with less resistance in freer spaces, preserve their motions both progressive and circular for a much longer time.

Law 2: The change of motion is proportional to the motive force impressed, and is made in the direction of the right line in which that force is impressed.

If any force generates a motion, a double force will generate double the motion, a triple force triple the motion, whether that force be impressed altogether and at once or gradually and successively. And this motion (being always directed the same way with the generating force), if the body moved before, is added to or subtracted from the former motion, according as they directly conspire with or are directly contrary to each other; or obliquely joined, when they are oblique, so as to produce a new motion compounded from the determination of both.

Law 3: To every action there is always opposed an equal reaction: or the mutual actions of two bodies upon each other are always equal and directed to contrary parts.

Whatever draws or presses another is as much drawn or pressed by that other. If you press a stone with your finger, the finger is also pressed by the stone. If a horse draws a stone tied to a rope, the horse (if I may say so) will be equally drawn back towards the stone; for the distended rope, by the same endeavor to relax or unbend itself, will draw the horse as much towards the stone as it does the stone towards the horse, and will obstruct the progress of the one as much as it advances that of the other. If a body impinge upon another, and by its force change the motion of the other, that body also (because of the equality of the mutual pressure) will undergo an equal change, in its own motion, towards the contrary part. The changes made by these actions are equal, not in the velocities but in the motions of the bodies; that is to say, if the bodies are not hindered by any other impediments. For, because the motions are equally changed, the changes of the velocities made towards contrary parts are inversely proportional to the bodies.

CHAPTER 12

THE REFORMATION OF THE SIXTEENTH CENTURY

The sixteenth-century Reformation affected the daily lives and the social fabric of the people in Western Europe more profoundly than any of the developments in the arts and letters of the so-called Renaissance. While the roots of the reform movement go deep into the previous centuries, the spark that touched it off was quite modern—money.

The revolution that began in Germany in October 1517 cannot be said to be the work of any one man or even any one country. It was the result of a Church-State conflict that was endemic before Gregory VII; it was a result of the "Babylonian Captivity" of the papacy during the Hundred Years' War, when England refused to recognize the authority of "the French popes"; it was the inevitable result of the Great Schism (1378ff.), when rival popes anathematized each other for forty years, thereby "rending the seamless robe of Christ" as effectively as it would later be rent by the Protestants; it was the result of all sorts of clerical abuses, from simony to nepotism, that were probably inevitable, but now more effectively attacked by the use of the new printing presses.

In the days of Martin Luther, however, a new low was reached in clerical abuse: the sale of one of the sacraments—penance—to pay for an archbishopric bought by a prince of the Hohenzollerns. Now, the sacrament of penance is at the heart of almost every Christian faith. In the Middle Ages it involved oral confession of sins to a priest, coupled with a true spirit of repentance and a final absolution, which was usually dependent on something quite drastic, such as going on a Crusade or a pilgrimage.

Imagine the shock, then, to a devout Augustianian monk like Luther when he found penance being offered for sale in the form of "indulgences," not only for the individual's own sins but also for those of his relatives in purgatory! What did Luther do? He offered to debate the question theologically. Not exactly your Tennis Court Oath, but the start of a revolution nonetheless, a revolution that has changed our lives just as profoundly ever since.

Although the Protestant Reformation was making most of the history at the time, the Catholic Reformation was also going steadily on behind the scenes. Sparked by new religious orders such as the Oratory of Divine Love—initiated a year before Luther's Ninety-five Theses—the Catholic reformers eventually gained a new line of popes with Paul III, who convened the great Council of Trent. That council succeeded, in time, in "reforming the Church in head and members," something the Council of Constance (1414) was supposed to do but did not.

Some questions for thought: How simple or complex are the causes of the Reformation? How do you explain Erasmus's position? Why could not Luther and Calvin agree? Do you see any basic differences between the Protestant Reformation and the Catholic?

SPIRIT OF THE AGE

ERASMUS: JULIUS II EXCLUDED FROM HEAVEN (1517)

From J. Jortin, *The Life of Erasmus* (London, 1808), 3:283–307.

"The prince of Northern Humanists," Erasmus combined wit and sarcasm with classical scholarship to satirize the ignorance and the abuses of the clergy. But he never broke with the Catholic Church and he criticized Luther for doing so. The following dialogue was published anonymously after Julius died.

JULIUS. What's the trouble here? Why won't the gate open? the lock must have been changed, or tampered with.

GUARDIAN SPIRIT. Maybe you brought the wrong key. You can't open this door with the same key you use for your moneybox, you know. Why didn't you bring both keys? That one is the key of power, not knowledge.

JULIUS. It's the only one I've ever used; I don't see the need for any other as long as I have this one.

SPIRIT. Nor do I, but in the meantime we're locked out.

JULIUS. I am getting very angry. I'll beat down these gates. Hey! somebody in there, open up—immediately! What's the matter? Is no one coming? What's keeping the porter? Sleeping, I guess, probably drunk.

SPIRIT. As usual, he judges everybody else by himself.

ST. PETER. It's a good thing we have iron gates here, otherwise this chap would have broken in. He must be some giant, a satrap, or conqueror of cities. But merciful God! What a stench! Before I open the gate, I'll peek out this little window and see what kind of monster this is. Who are you? And what do you want?

JULIUS. If you had done your duty, you would have greeted me with all the choirs of Heaven.

PETER. Rather pretentious, I'd say, but tell me first who you are.

JULIUS. As if you couldn't see for yourself!

Erasmus dictating to his secretary.

PETER. See? Indeed, I see a strange and unprecedented spectacle, some sort of monster, perhaps.

JULIUS. If you're not totally blind, you must recognize this key, even if you don't know the golden oak; and you do see the triple crown of the Papacy gleaming with gems and gold?

PETER. I do see a silver key, but only one, and very different from those keys that Christ gave to me. . . . And how should I recognize that proud crown not even a barbarian tyrant would wear, let alone someone seeking admittance here? Nor does that mantle impress me, who have always despised gold and jewelry as so much trash. But what is this?—on the key, crown, and mantle I see the sign of that rogue and impostor who has my name but not by ways—Simon [Magus], whom I once drove out of the temple of Christ.

JULIUS. Had you any sense at all, you'd stop this joking. If you don't already know, I am Julius the Ligurian. Assuming you learned your letters, you must recognize this *P.M*.

PETER. That's for *Pestis Maxima* [Great Plague], no doubt.

SPIRIT. Ha, ha! This soothsayer has scored a bull's eye.

PETER. If you were thrice *maximus* and greater than Mercury Trismegistus [thrice great], you wouldn't be admitted here unless you were also *sanctus* [holy].

JULIUS. What difference does it make to be called sanctus? After all, you, who impudently delay opening the door for me, you have been called only sanctus all these centuries, while nobody has ever called me anything but *sanctissimus* [holiest of holies] . . .

SPIRIT. [*Aside.*] And *drunkissimus,* too.

PETER. Then go ask admission from those flatterers who made you sanctissimus. You seem to find no difference between being *called* holy and being *in fact* holy.

JULIUS. I am exasperated! If I could only live again, I'd teach you about being holy or unholy, saved or not saved.

PETER. What a picture of a most holy mind! I have been studying you for some time now, and I see no signs of holiness, but many of impiety. And what is this unpapal gang you've brought with you. In all 20,000 of them, I don't see one with the face or countenance of a Christian. Only a horde of loathsome soldiers smelling of brothels, wine, and gunpowder. Also, the more I look at yourself, the less I see of an apostle. To begin with, what kind of monster wears the garment of a priest over the bristle and clink of bloody armor. What savage eyes you have, what a fierce mouth, how threatening a brow, how arrogant and haughty your glances! . . . Your whole body seems withered, wasted, and broken not so much from age and disease as from dissipation and drunkenness.

SPIRIT. How graphically he paints him in his true colors! . . .

ARCHBISHOP ALBERT OF MAINZ: INSTRUCTIONS TO COMMISSIONERS

From Gerdesii, *Introductio in historiam evangelii saeculo XVI renovati,* 1 (supp.):90–93.

In order to meet the debts incurred by his election as archbishop, Prince Albert of Hohenzollern arranged with Pope Leo X to sell indulgences for the remission of sins in his diocese, half the proceeds to go to Albert's debtors and half to the building of St. Peter's.

. . . After having explained to those making confession the importance of this kind of plenary remission, the confessors shall ask them how large a contribution . . . they would like to make, in good conscience. . . .

[Then follows a table of suggested rates for various categories: kings, bishops, etc., 25 guilders; abbots, counts, barons, 10; citizens with incomes of 500, 6; those with private incomes, 1; no income, prayer and fasting.]

For souls in purgatory, the pope brings about the complete remission of their sins in this way: that someone put the same contribution in the box as for himself. . . . It is not necessary that the persons putting the contributions into the chest for the dead be themselves contrite in heart . . . since this grace is based simply on the state of grace in which the dead departed this life. Preachers shall advertise this grace particularly, since it will not only help the departed, but also greatly promote the construction of St. Peter's. . . .

JOHN TETZEL: SERMON ON INDULGENCES

From *Translations and Reprints,* ed. J.H. Robinson, 2:6.

One of Albert's more ambitious salesmen was a Dominican frair named John Tetzel. He is reputed to have said, "As soon as the money clinks in the chest, the soul springs out of purgatory." Excerpts from one of his sermons, below, indicate his dedication. It was in response to Tetzel that Martin Luther posted his Ninety-five Theses in 1517.

. . . You may obtain letters of safe conduct from the vicar of our Lord Jesus Christ by means of which you are able to liberate your soul from the hands of the enemy and convey it by means of contrition and confession, safe and secure from all pain of purgatory, into the happy kingdom. For we know that in these letters are stamped and engraved all the merits of Christ's passion there laid bare. Consider that for each and every mortal sin it is necessary to undergo seven years of penitence after confession and contrition, either in this life or in purgatory.

How many mortal sins are committed in a day, how many in a week, how many in a month, how many in a year, how many in the whole course of life! . . . But with these confessional letters you will be able at any time in life to obtain full indulgence for all penalties imposed upon you, in all cases except the four reserved to the Apostolic See. Throughout your whole life you may receive the same remission, . . . and afterwards, at the hour of death, a full indulgence as to all penalties and sins, and your share of all spiritual blessings that exist in the church militant and all its members. . . .

Wherefore I counsel, order, and by virtue of my authority as shepherd, I command that they shall receive together with me and other priests, this precious treasure, especially those who were not confessed at the time of the holy Jubilee, that they may be able to obtain the same forever. [And] to all who profit by this present brief opportunity and who shall have lent a helping hand to the construction of the aforesaid house of the Prince of the Apostles, they shall all be participants and sharers in all prayers, suffrages, alms, supplications, masses, canonical hours, disciplines, pilgrimages, papal stations, benedictions, and all other spiritual goods . . . in the church militant, and . . . not only they themselves but their relatives, kindred and benefactors who have passed away; and as they were moved by charity, so God, and SS. Peter and Paul, and all the saints whose bodies rest in Rome, shall guard them in peace . . . and conduct them to the heavenly kingdon. . . .

Portrait of Martin Luther by Lucas Cranach the Elder in 1521, *near the beginning of Luther's career as a reformer. Later he settled down to become the recognized leader of a successful religious movement and the proud father of a large family. (By Lucas Cranach/Uffizi Gallery, Florence.)*

MARTIN LUTHER (1483–1546)

Probably nothing more clearly indicates the affinity between the Northern Renaissance and the Reformation than the fact that the leaders of both movements were humanist scholars—which is not surprising, perhaps, when one remembers that Leo X (pope, 1513–1521) was himself a leading humanist.

One difference between Northern humanists and those in Italy, however, is that the North tended to focus on the Christian sources (the Bible and Church Fathers such as St. Augustine), whereas the Italians studied pagan sources, such as Vergil and Cicero.

The unexpected spark that touched off the Reformation in Germany was the quite ordinary action of a university professor: Martin Luther posting a list of propositions for debate in the usual place, the church door, in Wittenberg. Apparently, Luther even expected the pope to support him for exposing the evils of the indulgence business!

THE NINETY-FIVE THESES

From *First Principles of the Reformation*, ed. Wace and Buchheim (Philadelphia, 1885), pp. 6–14.

6. The pope has no power to remit any guilt except by declaring it . . . remitted by God.

26. Preachers of indulgences are in error who say that by the pope's indulgence a man may be loosed and saved from all punishment.

27. They preach mad who say that the soul flies out of purgatory as soon as the money clinks in the moneybox.

28. It is certain that when the money clinks in the box, greed and avarice may be increased, but the church's intercession depends on God's will alone.

35. Those who preach that contrition is unnecessary for those who buy souls out of purgatory . . . preach no Christian doctrine.

36. Every Christian who feels true compunction has of right plenary remission of pain and guilt, even without letters of pardon.

37. Every true Christian, living or dead, has a share in all the benefits of Christ and of the church given him by God, even without letters of pardon.

62. The true treasure of the church is the holy Gospel of the glory and grace of God.

65. Hence the treasures of the Gospel are nets with which of old they fished for the men of riches.

66. The treasures of indulgences are nets with which they now fish for the riches of men.

81. This license in the preaching of pardons makes it difficult, even for learned men, to protect the reverence due to the pope against the calumnies, or at all events, the keen questioning of the laity.

82. As for instance: Why does not the pope empty purgatory for the sake of most holy charity and the supreme necessity of souls, . . . if he redeems an infinite number of souls for . . . money, to be spent on building a basilica? . . .

86. Again, why does not the pope, whose riches are at this day more ample than those of the wealthiest of the wealthy, build the single basilica of St. Peter with his own money rather than with that of poor believers?

94. Christians should be exhorted to strive to follow Christ their head through pains, death, and hells.

95. And thus to trust to enter heaven through many tribulations rather than in the security of peace.

ON CHRISTIAN LIBERTY (1520)

From *Luther's Primary Works,* ed. Wace and Buchheim (London, 1896), pp. 81–86.

Because of the recent invention of the printing press, Luther's works and ideas were soon distributed throughout Germany and Europe. Under pressure from the Church to recant his errors or face excommunication, Luther instead published three famous pamphlets spelling out his mature philosophy: *An Address to the Christian Nobility of the German Nation,* appealing to the secular rulers against the Church; *The Babylonian Captivity of the Church,* attacking the efficacy of the sacraments; and the third, *On Christian Liberty,* from which excerpts are given below, setting forth the doctine of justification by faith.

I first lay down two propositions concerning spiritual liberty and servitude: A Christian man is the most free lord of all and subject to none; a Christian man is the most dutiful servant of all and subject to everyone.

Although these statements appear contradictory, yet when they are found to agree together, they will do excellently for my purpose. They are both statements of Paul himself, who says, "Though I be free from all men, yet have I made myself a servant unto all" (I Cor. 9:19), and "Owe no man anything but to love one another" (Rom. 8:8). Now love is by its own nature dutiful and obedient to the beloved object. Thus even Christ, though Lord of all things, was yet made of a woman; made under the law, at once free and a servant, at once in the form of God and of a servant.

Let us examine the subject on a deeper, less simple principle. Man is composed of a twofold nature, a spiritual and a bodily. As regards the spiritual nature, which they name the soul, he is called the spiritual, inward, new man; as regards the bodily nature, which they name the flesh, he is called the fleshly, outward, old man. . . .

We first approach the subject of the inward man, that we may see by what means a man becomes justified, free, and a true Christian; that is, a spiritual, new, and inward man. It is certain that absolutely none among outward things, under whatever name they may be reckoned, has any influence in producing Christian righteousness or liberty, nor on the other hand, unrighteousness or slavery. . . . What harm can ill-health, bondage, hunger, thirst, or any other outward evil do to the soul, when even the most pious of men and the freest in the purity of their conscience are harassed by these things? . . .

And so it will profit nothing that the body be adorned with sacred vestments, or dwell in holy places, or be occupied in sacred offices, or pray or fast or abstain from certain foods or do whatever works can be done through the body and in the body. Something widely different will be necessary for the justification and liberty of the soul, since the things I have spoken of can be done by an impious person and only hypocrites are produced by devotion to these things. On the other hand, it will not at all injure the soul that the body should be clothed in a profane manner, should dwell in profane places, should eat and drink in the ordinary fashion, should not pray aloud, and should leave undone all the things above-mentioned, which may be done by hypocrites. . . .

Let us therefore hold for certain that the soul can do without everything except the word of God, without which none of its wants are provided for. But having the word, it is rich and wants for nothing. . . .

Hence all we who believe on Christ are kings and priests in Christ, as it is said, "Ye are a chosen generation, a royal priesthood, a holy nation, a peculiar people, that ye should show forth the praises of Him who hath called you out of darkness into His marvellous light" (I Peter 2:9). . . .

Not that . . . any one among the Christians has been appointed to possess and rule all things, [for] that is the office of kings, princes, and men upon earth. In the experience of life we see that we are subjected to all things, . . . even death. Yea, the more of a Christian a man is, to so many more evils, sufferings, and deaths is he subject. . . . This is a spiritual power which rules in the midst of enemies . . . and is nothing else than that strength is made perfect in my weakness, . . . so that even the cross and death are made to serve me and work together for my salvation. . . . There is nothing of which I have need, for faith alone suffices for my salvation. . . .

BEFORE THE DIET OF WORMS (1521)

From *Library of the World's Best Literature*, ed. C.D. Warner (Boston, 1896), 23:9328–9332.

After Luther's excommunication on January 3, 1521, the newly elected Holy Roman Emperor Charles V convened the imperial diet at Worms and gave Luther a safe conduct to come and express his views. Faced with serious problems in his far-flung holdings—the communeros revolt in Spain, the siege of Vienna by the Turks, and the centrifugal forces within the empire itself—Charles wanted to end this "squabble among monks," as he called it.

It was a dramatic moment. Luther, appearing before the princes of all the states in the empire, was asked to recant his views. Hesitant, he asked for time to think it over. They gave him twenty-four hours. We rejoin Luther, speaking after full consideration.

Most Serene Emperor and Most Illustrious Princes:

As to the two articles yesterday presented to me by Your Most Serene Majesty—namely, whether I would acknowledge the books edited and published in my name as mine, and whether I wished to persevere in their defense or to revoke them—I have given my ready and clear response to the first: in that I still persist and shall persist forever; to wit, that those books are mine. . . .

Nevertheless, because I am a man and not God, I cannot offer any other defense than that with which my Lord Jesus Christ vindicated his teaching. For when he was asked about his doctrine before Annas and had been smitten by a servant, he said, "If I have spoken evil, bear witness of the evil." If our Lord, who was always conscious of his inability to err, yet did not decline to hear any evidence against his doctrine even from the most contemptible menial—how much more ought I, who am of the dregs of the people, and powerless in everything save sin, to desire and expect the introduction of testimony against my teaching?

Therefore, Your Most Serene Majesty, Your Most Illustrious Lordships, I beseech you by the mercy of God, that whoever can, whether high or low, let him bring forward the proof, let him convince me of errors; let the Scriptures of Prophecy and Gospels triumph, for I will be wholly ready to revoke any error, if I can be persuasively taught; yes, I will be the first to cast my books into the fire.

[At this point the imperial spokesman interrupted and said that subjects already condemned by church councils were not to be called in question. He therefore demanded that Luther give a simple answer, without horns: Would he revoke or not? To which Luther replied:]

Therefore, Your Most Serene Majesty and Your Lordships, since they seek a simple reply, I will give one that is without horns or teeth, and in this fashion: I believe in neither pope nor councils alone; for it is perfectly well established that they have frequently erred as well as contradicted themselves. Unless then I be convinced by the testimony of the Scriptures or by clear reason, I must be bound by those Scriptures which have been brought forward by me; yes, my conscience has been taken captive by these words of God. I cannot revoke anything, nor do I wish to, since to go against one's conscience is neither safe nor right: Here I stand, I can do no other. So help me God. Amen.

DIET OF WORMS: EDICT ON LUTHER

From Robinson, *Readings in European History,* 2:83–84.

Therefore we [the Emperor] hold that if it was the duty of any of our ancestors to defend the Christian name, much greater is the obligation on us, inasmuch as the unparalleled goodness of Almighty God has, for the protection and increase of his holy faith, endowed us with more kingdoms and lands and greater power in the Empire than any of our ancestors for many years. . . .

Since now it is plain to you all how far these errors and heresies depart from the Christian way, which a certain Martin Luther, of the Augustinian order, has sought violently to introduce and disseminate within the Christian religion and its established order, especially in the German nation, which is renowned as a perpetual destroyer of all unbelief and heresy; so that, unless it is speedily prevented, the whole German nation, and later all other nations, will be infected by this same disorder and mighty dissolution and pitiable downfall of good mortals, and of the peace and the Christian faith will result. . . .

[Luther] has collected many heresies of the worst heretics, long since condemned and forgotten, together with some newly invented ones, in one stinking pool, under pretext of preaching *faith,* which he extols with so great industry in order that he may ruin the true and genuine faith, and under the name and appearance of evangelical doctrine overturn and destroy all evangelical peace and love, as well as all righteous order and the most excellent hierarchy of the church. . . .

Accordingly, . . . we have declared and made known that the said Martin Luther shall hereafter be held and esteemed by each and all of us as a limb cut off from the Church of God, an obstinate schismatic and manifest heretic. . . .

And we publicly attest by these letters that we order and command each and all of you, as you owe fidelity to us and the Holy Empire, . . . we strictly order that immediately after the expiration of the appointed 20 days . . . on 14 May, you shall refuse to give the aforesaid Martin Luther hospitality, lodging, food, or drink; neither shall anyone by word or deed, secretly or openly, succor or assist him by counsel or help; but in whatever place you meet him, you shall proceed against him; if you have sufficient force, you shall take him prisoner and keep him in close custody; you shall deliver him, or cause him to be delivered, to us or at least let us know where he may be captured. . . .

THE PEASANTS' REVOLT

THE GERMAN PEASANTS: TWELVE ARTICLES (1524)

From Robinson, *Readings in European History,* 2:94–99, revised.

Luther's revolt had some surprising side effects. Peasants in the south of Germany took him at his word when he spoke of Christian Liberty and threw off the bonds of feudal serfdom. Their carefully worded manifesto makes their position crystal clear.

Peace to the Christian reader and the grace of God through Christ: . . .
Article 1. It is our humble petition and desire . . . that in the future we should have the power and authority [to] choose and appoint a pastor . . . and to depose him if he conduct himself improperly. . . .

2. According as the just tithe is established by the Old and New Testaments, we are ready and willing to pay the fair tithe of grain. . . . But those whose tithes were appropriated by their ancestors should not be paid anything more by the village. . . .

3. It has been the custom hitherto for men to hold us as their property, which is pitiable enough considering that Christ has delivered and redeemed us all by shedding his precious blood, the lowly as well as the great. Hence it is consistent with Scripture that we should be free. . . . We therefore take it for granted that you will free us from serfdom as true Christians, unless it be shown from the Gospel that we are serfs.

4. It has been the custom heretofore that no poor man be allowed to touch venison or wild fowl or fish in flowing water, which seems . . . not conformable to the word of God. In some places the authorities preserve the game and recklessly allow the mindless beasts to destroy our crops to no purpose. . . . This is neither Christian nor neighborly, for when God created man, he gave him dominion over all the animals, the birds of the air, and the fish in the water. . . .

7. We will not hereafter allow ourselves to be oppressed by our lords, but will recognize only what is just and proper according to the word of the agreement between lord and peasant. . . . The peasant, however, should help the lord when necessary and at appropriate times, when not disadvantageous to the peasant, and for suitable recompense. . . .

10. We are aggrieved by the individual appropriation of meadows and fields which were once part of the commons. These we will take again into our own hands. . . .

Conclusion: If any of the articles here set forth should not be in accordance with the word of God, . . . such article we will willingly reject, if it be clearly proved against the word of God in the Scripture. . . . For this we shall pray to God, since he alone can grant our demands. The peace of Christ abide with us all.

LUTHER'S RESPONSE

Ibid., 99–108 passim.

Luther replied to the Twelve Articles in May 1525. He was shocked that the serfs would not stay in their appointed places, as God and the Bible intended. Instead, they were robbers and blasphemers against Jesus Christ. But then, he said, the lords were not behaving as Christians either: they were "tyrants, enemies of God, and persecutors of men."

But when the peasant revolt spread and became more violent, Luther issued a second pamphlet "Against the Murdering and Robbing Bands of the Peasants."

With three horrible sins against God and men have [they] loaded themselves: . . .

First, they have sworn to their true and gracious rulers to be obedient, in accord with God's command. . . . But since they have . . . abandoned their obedience and have dared oppose their lords, they have thereby forfeited body and soul. . . . "And they that resist shall receive to themselves damnation" (Rom. 13:2). . . .

Second, . . . they rob and pillage monasteries and castles that do not belong to them, for which, like highwaymen and murderers, they deserve the twofold death of body and soul. . . . Therefore, whosoever can, should smite, strangle, and stab, . . . and remember that there is nothing more poisonous, pernicious, and devilish than a rebellious man. Just as one must slay a mad dog, so, if you do not fight the rebels, they will fight you, and the whole country with you.

Third, they cloak their frightful and revolting sins with the Gospel, call themselves Christian brethren, swear allegiance, and compel people to join them in such abominations. Thereby they . . . serve and honor the devil under the semblance of the Gospel, so that they have ten times deserved death of body and soul, for never have I heard of uglier sins. . . . Lo, how mighty a prince the devil is, how he holds the world in his hands and can put it to confusion: who else could so soon capture so many thousands of peasants, lead them astray, blind and deceive them, stir them to revolt, and make them the willing executioners of this malice. . . .

JOHN CALVIN

INSTITUTES OF THE CHRISTIAN RELIGION (1536)

From Robinson, *Readings in European History*, 2:123–128 passim.

Unlike Luther in almost every respect except dedication, John Calvin (1509–1564) was a lawyer, classicist, Hebraic scholar, and French rationalist of the highest order. Whereas Luther, once his movement was successful, settled down, raised a big family, and became fat, Calvin remained always lean, hungry, and unrelenting. He finished his classic *Institutes of the Christian Religion* at age twenty-seven, but continued revising it

Portrait of John Calvin. *Note the contrasting personalities of Luther and Calvin. As Calvin grew older, instead of mellowing, he became more ascetic and more stern. (Francois Martin Photographe/Musée Historique de la Réformation.)*

for the rest of his life; today it is recognized as one of the great theological works of all time. In exile from his native France, Calvin's first edition included a preface to Francis I, in hopes that he might relent in his persecution of the "Huguenots," as the Calvinists were called.

John Calvin, to the most mighty and noble monarch, Francis [I], the most Christian king of the French: . . .

. . . When I perceived that the furious rage of certain wicked men hath so far prevailed in your realm that in it there is no room for sound doctrine, I thought I should . . . give both instruction for them whom I proposed to instruct and send forth an apology to you, whereby you may learn what manner of doctrine that is against which these furious men burn in so great rage, who at this day trouble your realm with sword and fire. . . .

[They] call our teaching new and lately forged, . . . doubtful and uncertain; they demand by what miracle it is confirmed; they ask whether it be meet that it should prevail against the consent of so many holy fathers and most ancient customs; they press upon us to confess it to be schismatical, which moveth war against the Church. . . . Lastly, they say, they need no arguments, for it may be judged by its fruits, . . . which hath bred so big a heap of sects, so many turmoils of sedition, so great licentiousness of vices. . . .

First, whereas they call it new, they do great wrong to God, whose holy word deserves not to be accused of newness. . . . They that know the preaching of Paul to be old, and that Jesus Christ died for our sins and rose again for our justification, shall find nothing new among us. Secondly, that it hath long lain hidden, unknown, and buried,—that is the fault of the ungodliness of men. . . .

They may mock at the uncertainty of our teachings, but if they were driven to seal their own doctrine with their own blood,...men might see how much they set by it.

Far other is our faith, which dreadeth neither the terrors of death nor yet the very judgment seat of God. . . .

They err not a little from the truth when they acknowledge no church but that which they see with the present eye; . . . for they set the true form of the Church in the see of Rome and in the order of their prelates. We, on the contrary, affirm both that the Church may consist of no visible form and that the form itself is not contained in that outward splendor which they foolishly admire, but hath a far other indication, namely, the pure teaching of the word of God and the right ministration of the sacraments. . . .

On Predestination

After the heavenly image of [Adam] was defaced he did not alone suffer this punishment, that in place of wisdom, strength, holinesss, truth, and justice—with which ornaments he had been adorned—there came in the most horrible pestilences, blindness, weakness, filthiness, emptiness, and injustice,—but also he entangled and drowned his whole offspring in the same misery. This is the corruption that comes by inheritance, which the old writers called *original sin,* meaning by this word the corruption of nature, which before was good and pure. . . .

Predestination we call the eternal decree of God, whereby he has determined with himself what he wills to become of every man. For all are not created to like estate; but to some eternal life, to some eternal damnation is foreordained. Therefore as every man is created to the one or the other end, so we may say that he is predestinate either to [eternal] life or death. . . . Foolish men do quarrel with God, as though they had him subject to their accusations. First, they ask by what right is the Lord angry with his creatures by whom he hath not first been provoked by any offense; for to condemn to destruction whom he will agreeth rather with the willfulness of a tyrant than with the lawful sentence of a judge. Therefore they say that there is no cause why men should accuse God if by his forewill, without their own deserving, they be predestinate to eternal death. If such thoughts do at any time come into the mind of the godly, this shall suffice to break their violent assaults, although they have nothing more, if they consider how great wickedness it is even to so much as to inquire of the causes of the will of God. . . . For the will of God is the highest rule of righteousness, that whatsoever he willeth, even for this that he willeth it, ought to be taken for righteousness.

THE CATHOLIC REFORMATION

Ever since the Great Schism (1378–1417) and Saint Catherine of Siena, the Catholic Church had been valiantly trying to reform itself. In fact, the third item on the agenda of the Council of Constance (1414) had been "the reform of the Church in head and members," but the first two items—heresy and schism—took so much time that they never got around to the third item. Two other elements of resistance made reform difficult: such Renaissance popes as the Borgias and Medicis and powerful prelates as Prince Albert Hohenzollern, archbishop of Mainz.

But just when the Protestants seemed on the verge of taking over, three major forces came to the rescue: a series of great reforming popes, beginning with Paul III (1534–1549); new religious orders dedicated to reform, such as the Theatines and the Jesuits; and the Church Council of Trent (1545–1563).

IGNATIUS LOYOLA: SPIRITUAL EXERCISES

Biblioteca dels Exercisis espirituals (Barcelona, 1930), 2:250–255.

The Society of Jesus (Jesuits), approved by the pope in 1540, was not originally established to combat heresy: its original aims were the education of youth and the formation of overseas missions. Ignatius of Loyola was of noble birth, left court life in 1517 to become a soldier, was seriously wounded, and became converted to Christ. More spiritual than scholarly, he wrote a classic of Christian mysticism, from which these excerpts are taken.

Rules for Thinking with the Church

For the true thoughts we ought to hold in the church militant, the following:

1. Laying aside all criticism, we ought to keep our minds ready and prompt to obey in all things the true Spouse of Christ our Lord, which is our Holy Mother the Hierarchical Church.

2. Second: To praise confession made to a priest, and the reception of the Most Holy Sacrament once a year, and what is much better once a month, and much better still every eight days. . . .

3. To praise the frequent hearing of Mass, also chants, psalms, and long prayers, both in and out of church, and likewise the hours ordained at fixed times for all Divine Office for prayers of any kind and all canonical Hours.

4. To praise Religious Orders, virginity, and continence, and matrimony not so much as any of the above.

5. To praise vows of religion, obedience, poverty, and chastity. . . .

6. To praise relics of the saints and to praise likewise stations, pilgrimages, indulgences, jubilees, . . . and the lighting of candles in churches.

7. To praise precepts regarding fasts and abstinence, as those of Lent, Ember Days, Vigils, Fridays, and Saturdays; likewise penances, not only internal but external also.

8. To praise the building and ornamentation of churches; also images, and to venerate them according to what they represent.

9. To praise all precepts of the church, keeping our minds ready to find reasons to defend and never to impugn them.

10. We ought to be very ready to approve and praise the constitutions, recommendations, and habits of life of our superiors; because, although they may not be or may not have been praiseworthy, still to speak against them in public, or before the lower

classes, would give rise to talk and scandal, rather than be of any use, and thus the people would be angry with their temporal or spiritual rulers. Nevertheless, just as it is harmful to speak ill before the people concerning superiors in their absence, so it may be useful to speak of their shortcomings to those who can remedy the wrong.

11. To praise positive and scholastic theology; for as it belongs to the positive doctors—St. Jerome, St. Augustine, St. Gregory, etc.—to arouse the emotions to the love and service of God our Lord in all things, so it belongs to the scholastic doctors—St. Thomas, St. Bonaventure, and the Masters of the Sentences—to define and explain for our times what is necessary for salvation, and further to attack and expose all errors and fallacies. . . .

13. To attain the truth in all things, we ought always to believe that what seems white is black if the Hierarchical Church so defines it. . . .

COUNCIL OF TRENT: PROCEEDINGS

Canons and Decrees of the Council of Trent, ed. J. Wentworth (London, 1848).

It would be difficult to understand the modern Catholic Church without understanding the role of the Council of Trent, held over nearly two decades (1545–1563). It issued three types of decrees: (a) those defining the doctrines of the Church and defending them against the objections of the Protestants; (b) those anathematizing the various heretical beliefs; and (c) the largest number, abolishing the various abuses within the Church and establishing a more rigid discipline among secular and regular clergy alike. The following excerpts illustrate some of the decrees and the clarity of the language in which they were couched.

On Scripture and Tradition

The sacred and holy, ecumenical, and general Synod of Trent, lawfully assembled in the Holy Ghost, . . . keeping this always in view, that errors being removed, the purity of the Gospel be preserved in the Church; which our Lord Jesus Christ . . . first promulgated with His own mouth and then commanded to be preached . . . as the fountain of all, both saving truth and moral discipline are contained in the written books and the unwritten traditions which, received by the Apostles from the mouth of Christ Himself . . . have come down to us, transmitted as it were from hand to hand; the [Synod] venerates with an equal affection of piety and reverence all the books of both the Old and New Testaments—seeing that one God is the author of both—as also the said traditions [both] of faith and of morals, as dictated by Christ . . . or by the Holy Ghost and preserved in the Catholic Church by continuous succession. . . .

On Justification

Canon 1. If anyone saith that man may be justified before God by his own works, whether done through the teaching of human nature or that of the law, without the grace of God through Jesus Christ; let him be anathema.

2. If anyone saith that the grace of God through Jesus is given only for this, that man may be able more easily to live justly and to merit eternal life, as if by free will, without grace, he were able to do both, though hardly indeed and with difficulty; let him be anathema.

3. If anyone saith that with the prevenient inspiration of the Holy Ghost, and with His help, man can believe, hope, love, or be penitent as he ought, so as that the grace of Justification may be bestowed upon him; let him be anathema.

5. If anyone saith that since Adam's sin, the free will of a man is lost and extinguished; or that it is a thing with only a name, . . . introduced into the Church by Satan; let him be anathema.

6. If anyone saith that it is not in man's power to make his ways evil, but that the works that are evil God worketh as well as those that are good, . . . in such wise that the treason of Judas is no less His own proper work than the vocation of Paul; let him be anathema.

8. If anyone saith that the fear of hell—whereby by grieving for our sins, we flee unto the mercy of God, or refrain from sinning—is a sin, or makes sinners worse; let him be anathema.

9. If anyone saith that by faith alone the impious is justified, in such wise as to mean that nothing else is required to cooperate in order to obtain the grace of Justification, and that it is not necessary that he be prepared and disposed by the movement of his own will; let him be anathema.

15. If anyone saith that a man who is born again and justified is bound of faith to believe that he is assuredly in the number of the predestined; let him be anathema.

23. If anyone saith that a man once justified can sin no more, nor lose grace, and that . . . he is able, during his whole life, to avoid all sins, even venial—except by a special privilege from God, as the Church holds in regard to the Blessed Virgin; let him be anathema.

CHAPTER 13

LOUIS XIV: HOW GREAT WAS HE?

Voltaire, the darling of the Enlightenment, claimed that Louis XIV did more for France "than any twenty of his predecessors combined." But an archbishop and tutor to the Dauphin declared that the king destroyed half the power of the state for the sake of useless conquests abroad; even worse, he said, the people came to believe that their king loved nothing but power and glory. A third critic, from the Court of Versailles, believed that, although the king was not very intelligent, he did apply himself well and might have been a great monarch were it not for the troubles that came from his environment.

Each person reading the following documents will form his own conclusion; but first, *un peu d'histoire*. The religious wars of the sixteenth century had been terminated by Louis XIV's grandfather, Henry IV, who found a compromise solution in his Edict of Nantes, providing freedom of worship for the Huguenots (French Calvinists) and allowing them to fortify certain towns against all and sundry.

In the next reign Louis XIII's great minister, Cardinal Richelieu, revoked the privilege of all groups—Protestants, nobles, or other—to fortify any areas against the State, but left intact the purely religious provisions of Henry IV's edict.

Richelieu also effected other changes in the domestic scene to strengthen the central government, but his greatest achievement was in making France the leading nation in Europe after a protracted struggle in the Thirty Years' War (1618–1648). Without the international prestige which France enjoyed under Louis XIV and his minister Mazarin (d. 1661), Louis would have been a king like any other. Mazarin deserves credit not only for his role in the Regency (Louis was only five years old when he inherited the throne), but Mazarin also succeeded in defeating the nobles in the *Fronde* (1648–1653), when they revolted against his centralizing tendencies that were to provide more bases for Louis XIV's absolutism.

Although the question of arts and letters is not dealt with in the following documents, it should be pointed out that the Age of Louis XIV is to French culture what the Augustan Age is to Classical, or the Elizabethan to English, culture. When Voltaire called to mind the Age of Louis XIV, he must immediately have thought of dramatists such as Corneille, Racine, and Molière; poets such as La Fontaine and Boileau; musicians such as Lully and Couperin; and Pascal, Poussin, Mansart, and Lenôtre, in other areas.

BISHOP BOSSUET

POLITICS DRAWN FROM HOLY WRIT

From Robinson, *Readings,* 2:273-277.

French orator and writer, Bishop Bossuet was the Dauphin's tutor (1670–1681) and wrote this treatise for his use.

The four basic qualities of royalty are: It is sacred, it is paternal, it is absolute, and it is subject to reason. . . . God establishes kings as His ministers and through them reigns over the peoples of the earth. . . . Hence the royal throne is not that of a man but the throne of God Himself. "God hath chosen Solomon my son to sit upon the throne of the kingdom of the Lord over Israel [1 Chron. 28:5]." . . .

It appears from all this that the person of the king is sacred and that to attack him in any way is sacrilege. . . . Kings are sacred by their very office, as representatives of the divine Majesty delegated by Providence for the execution of His purposes. . . .

Royal authority is paternal and its fundamental quality is benevolence. . . . Kings hold power from God, who is the Father of the human race; also the first idea of power among men was paternal power and kings have been molded in the image of fathers. . . .

Royal power is absolute. . . . The prince need render account of his acts to no one. "The word of the king is law and none may say, What doest thou? Whoso keepeth his commandment shall feel no evil [Eccles. 8:2-5]." . . .

Government is a work of reason and intelligence. . . . All men are created capable of understanding. But especially you, the king, upon whom rests the entire nation, you have to be the mind and soul of the State; . . . the less you have to justify yourself to others, the more you must seek justification and reason within yourself. . . .

The ruler, as ruler, is not regarded as a private person; he is a public figure: the entire State is in him. The will of the people is included in his will. Just as all perfection and all strength are united in God, so all the power of the individuals is united in the person of the king. . . .

Behold an immense people united in a single person; behold this holy power, paternal and absolute; behold the secret cause that governs the whole body of the State, contained in a single head: you see the image of God in the king and you have the idea of royal majesty. . . .

So great is this majesty that its source cannot reside in the king; rather, it is borrowed from God, who bestows it on him for the good of the people, which has to be restrained by a higher power. Something of divinity itself, surrounding the prince, inspires awe in the people. The king should never forget this: "I have said"—this is God speaking—"I have said, Ye are gods, and all of you are children of the Most High. But ye shall die like men and fall like one of the princes [Ps.82]."

"Ye are gods," meaning you bear a divine imprint. . . . "Children of the Most High"—He gives you power for man's good. But O gods of flesh and blood. "Ye shall die like men and fall like princes." A common fall makes all men equal in the end.

DECLARATION OF THE GALLICAN CHURCH (1682)

From *Recueil général des anciennes lois françaises,* ed. F.A. Isambert (Paris, 1821–1823), 19:384-385.

Drafted by Bossuet, the following statement was approved by an assembly of the French (Gallican) Church and issued as a royal edict.

Many people are attempting to overturn the decrees of the Gallican Church and undermine the foundations of its liberties, which are based on the sacred canons and traditions of the Fathers. Others, claiming to defend it, dare to attack the supremacy of St. Peter and his successors, the popes of Rome, . . . while heretics, for their part, are doing all they can to make that power intolerable to kings and people alike.

Seeking to remedy these improprieties, we archbishops and bishops, assembled at Paris by order of the King, with other ecclesiastical representatives of the Gallican Church, have deemed it necessary to make the following declaration:

1. That St. Peter and his successors, Vicars of Jesus Christ, and the whole Church herself, have received power from God only in things spiritual, pertaining to eternal salvation; and not in things civil or temporal, the Lord Himself having said, "My kingdom is not of this world," and: "Render unto Caesar the things that are Caesar's, and unto God the things that are God's," as also declareth the Apostle, "Let every soul be subject unto the higher powers, for there is no power but of God; the powers that be are ordained of God; whosoever therefore resisteth the power, resisteth the ordinances of God."

Therefore, in temporal affairs, kings and princes, appointed by God, are in no way subject to any ecclesiastical power; neither can the authority of the Keys of the Church depose them, either directly or indirectly; nor their subjects be dispensed from their oaths of fidelity and obedience to them. We affirm this doctrine to be essential for public peace and order, no less profitable to the Church than to the State, and to be everywhere observed as agreeable to the word of God, to the tradition of the Fathers, and the example of the saints. . . .

4. And that, although the pope has a preeminent voice in matters of faith and his decrees concern all churches, nevertheless his judgment is not unalterable, except with the consent of the Church. . . .

LOUIS XIV

ON THE FUNCTIONS OF A KING (1661)

Mémoires de Louis XIV, écrits par lui-même, adressés à son fils, ed. Gain-Montagnac (Paris, 1808), passim.

Louis began compiling instructions and advice for his son the year the boy was born (1661) and kept at it for twenty more years. Do not imagine, however, that the king wrote this work unaided: he had very capable help from his minister Colbert and later from a certain President de Périgny. But Louis supplied notes and ideas and, typically, insisted on overseeing the results.

Two things are absolutely essential: hard work on my part and careful selection of people capable of supporting me in it. As for work, my son, it may be that you will read these memoirs at an age when you will be more apt to dread it than to enjoy it—delighted, perhaps, to have escaped from your tutor, strict discipline, and endless required studies.

[But] one reigns only by dint of hard work and it is *for* that that one reigns also. I made it a rule to work regularly twice a day, each time for two or three hours and each time with different people, not counting the hours I spent alone or spent on certain affairs that came up [unexpectedly]. I never prevented people from speaking to me about particular questions if they were urgent. . . .

I cannot tell you how much I profited from this decision. I felt uplifted, as it were, in mind and heart. I was a different person and reproached myself for having waited so long. My initial timidity, which came from self-criticism, bothered me for a while, especially when I had to speak in public, but it soon disappeared. Then my only feeling was that I was the King and born to be one. Next I was overcome with such indescribable delight that you will have to experience it to understand it.

For you must not imagine, my son, that affairs of State are like some dark, difficult path of learning of the kind that may already have worn you out—a path on which the mind seeks in vain to find meaning and direction. . . .

The function of king consists principally in allowing good sense to act, which it always does naturally and without effort. What we do for work is sometimes less difficult than what we do for amusement. Its usefulness is always apparent. However skillful and enlightened his ministers, the king's efforts added to theirs is immediately visible. Success, agreeable in even the smallest matters, is especially gratifying in the largest; and no satisfaction equals that of seeing daily progress in lofty and glorious enterprises—and in the happiness of the people when that happiness has been planned and thought out by yourself.

Everything that is necessary in this work is at the same time most agreeable. It consists essentially, my son, in keeping your eye on the whole world and learning the news every hour concerning each province and nation, the secrets of every court, the moods and weaknesses of each prince and foreign minister; to be informed on an infinite number of questions about which we are not supposed to know anything; to elicit from our subjects things they try diligently to keep from us; and to discover the motives of those who come to us with quite contrary expectations. I know of no other pleasure that we would exchange for this one.

TO THE MERCHANTS OF MARSEILLES (1664)

From Robinson, *Readings in European History,* 2:279–280.

The following letter, written shortly after Colbert became Minister of Finance, indicates the kind of assistance that an able minister might provide even an "absolute" monarch.

Very dear and well beloved:
Considering how advantageous it would be to this realm to reestablish its foreign and domestic trade, . . . we have decided to form a council devoted particularly to commerce, to meet fortnightly in our presence, and in which the interests of merchants will be considered and all means conducive to the revival of trade explored and decided upon.

This is to tell you also that we are setting aside a million livres a year in State funds for the encouragement of manufactures and the improvement of navigation, not to mention the sizable sums we have raised to supply the East and West India Companies; and

That we are working continually to abolish the tolls being collected on the navigable rivers;

That more than a million livres has already been spent for the repair of public highways, to which we are giving our constant attention;

That we will assist all those who wish to reestablish old manufactures or undertake new ones with money from our royal treasury;

That we are giving orders to all our ambassadors and residents at the courts of the princes, our allies, to make all appropriate efforts, in our name, to cause justice to be done in all cases involving our merchants and to secure for them entire commercial freedom;

That we will comfortably lodge at our court each and every merchant having business there during all the time he is obliged to remain there. . . .

SAINT-SIMON: MEMOIRS OF THE COURT OF LOUIS XIV

From *Mémoires complets et authentiques du Duc de Saint-Simon sur le siècle de Louis XIV et la Régence,* vol. 28 passim.

Louis de Rouvroy, duc de Saint-Simon (1675–1755), although bitterly disappointed at not being chosen for office by Louis XIV, and even more disturbed at the rise of the middle classes to power and influence, nevertheless managed to keep a diary (running to over forty volumes) of his personal observations and analyses of life at Court. His memoirs are valuable both as literature and as history. The excerpts below offer portraits of the king in the various functions of his office, not the least of which was getting out of bed!

The King's Day

At 8 o'clock the chief *valet de chambre,* who alone slept in the royal chamber [with the king], woke him up. Then the head physician, the chief surgeon, and the nurse entered the room together. The latter kissed the king while the others massaged him and usually changed his shirt, for he had a habit of perspiring rather heavily. At 8:15 the chamberlain was called, . . . as well as those who were privileged to share the *grandes entrées.* The chamberlain drew back the bed-curtains and offered the king holy water from the vase at the head of the bed. After these gentlemen left, it was time for anyone who wanted to ask a favor or to speak to the king; usually nobody had anything to say and they all left rather shortly. . . .

As soon as he was dressed, the king prayed to God by the side of his bed; the clergy also knelt beside him, the cardinals without cushions and the laity all standing. The captain of the guards came to the balustrade during the prayer, after which the king went into his cabinet. There he found . . . a very numerous company. To each of them he gave his orders for the day and it was therefore soon known what he planned to do; then the crowd left and only the royal bastards, some favorites, and the valets remained. . . . That was a good opportunity to talk with the king about, say, plans for new buildings or the gardens. Such conversations might be more or less protracted, depending on the personage involved.

Meanwhile the court were all awaiting the king in the gallery, the captain of the guard remaining alone in the chamber, seated by the door to the cabinet. . . . During this interval the king granted audiences to whom he pleased, spoke privately with others, and gave "secret" interviews to foreign ministers—called *secret* simply to distinguish them from the informal ones by his bedside after prayers.

Next the king went to mass, where his musicians always sang a motet. . . . On his way to and from the chapel anyone who wished might speak to him, provided he had alerted the captain of the guard, if he was not a celebrity. . . . During the mass the royal ministers assembled in the king's chamber, where distinguished people might talk to them. After mass, the king amused himself for a bit and shortly called for the council. Then the morning was over. . . .

Dinner was always *au petit couvert,* meaning that the king ate by himself on a square table in front of the middle window. Every morning he would order either "a little" or "a very little" service, but it was always ample, with many dishes and three courses, not counting the fruit. . . .

On leaving the table the king immediately entered his cabinet; that was a time for distinguished people to speak to him. He stopped at the door a moment to listen, then entered; rarely did anyone follow him and never without asking permission, but few had the courage for that. If followed, he would stand in the embrasure nearest the door, which closed of itself and which you yourself had to open on leaving the king. This was also the time for the bastards and valets. . . .

The king amused himself by feeding his dogs and spent considerable time with them. Then he asked for his valet and changed his clothes, before the first gentleman of the chamber admitted the few distinguished people he had selected for this honor. Immediately afterwards, he left for the court of marble by the back stairs and entered his coach. Between the foot of the stairs and the coach, anyone who wished might speak to him. . . .

After supper, the king stood for a while with his back to the balustrade at the foot of his bed, surrounded by his court. Then, bowing to the ladies, he went into his cabinet and gave his orders. There he would spend a little less than an hour, seated in an armchair, with his legitimate children, his bastards, his grandchildren—legitimate and other—and their wives and husbands. Monsieur (the king's eldest brother) was in another armchair, while Monseigneur (the king's son, *le Dauphin)* and the other princes remained standing. . . .

When he wanted to retire, the king went and fed his dogs. Then he said good-night and entered his chamber, where he said his prayers again by the side of the bed and got undressed. He nodded good-night as the people left. Standing by the corner of the chimneypiece, he next gave his orders to the head of the guards alone.

Then began what was called the *petit coucher,* to which only the especially privileged were admitted. It was short. But they did not leave until he got into bed. It was a moment to speak to him. . . .

Louis's Character

The king was not very intelligent, but he applied himself well. He wanted everything to be in proper form and in good order. He was by nature sensible, moderate, reserved, and deliberate, in speech and behavior. . . . Endowed with enough goodness and justice to have been a good king, he might even have been a great one, but his troubles came from without. . . .

He had barely been taught to read and write and was so ignorant that most of the famous events in history and well-known deeds . . . and laws were unknown to him. Consequently, he sometimes made serious mistakes in public. . . .

Now, one might have thought the king would be fond of the higher nobility, but he feared them as much as he feared intelligence, and if those two characteristics happened to be combined in the same person, the jig was up.

Louis's ministers, generals, courtiers, mistresses, all having discovered his weakness, they outdid each other in praising and spoiling him. Praise, or rather flattery, pleased him so much that even the grossest sort was well received and the basest even more. . . . That is how his ministers gained so much authority—from having repeated opportunities to flatter him, especially by giving him credit for everything. . . .

Naturally inclined toward pettiness, Louis took pleasure in details of all sorts. He was constantly occupied with those involving his troops, their uniforms, arms, discipline—in short with the lowest concerns. He was no less occupied with the details of his buildings. . . . In these matters, he always figured he had something to teach the experts, who for their part accepted like novices the lessons they had long since learned by heart. Such a waste of time was a pleasure for the king because he thought this kind of concern on his part was a virtue. It was also a boon to his ministers, . . . because it enabled them to lead the king by the nose, while letting him bury himself in nonessentials. . . .

[Nevertheless,] Louis was made for a brilliant court. In the midst of other men, his figure, his courage, his grace, his beauty, his grand mien, even the tone of his voice, the majestic and natural charm of his whole being, distinguished him all his life as the King Bee. They indicated that even if he had been born a simple nobleman, he would equally have excelled at parties, pleasures, and gallantry; he would have had the greatest success in love. The intrigues and adventures in which he engaged early in life . . . had an unfortunate influence on him. . . . From that time on, intellect, education, nobility of sentiment, and high principle in others became for him objects of suspicion and soon, hatred. The older he got, the more this feeling was confirmed in him.

He wanted to reign all by himself. His sensitivity on this point became increasingly a weakness. He reigned in little things, the larger escaped him; but even in the former he was more often led than leading. The superior ability of his early ministers and generals soon became an annoyance to him; he disliked anyone who was distinguished in any way. Thus he chose his ministers not for their knowledge but for their ignorance, not for their ability but for their lack of it. He liked to *form* them, he said, to teach them even the most trifling things; the same with his generals: he took credit himself for instructing them and wanted people to think he commanded and directed all his armies from his office. . . .

After he became master on the death of Mazarin, he followed two maxims. One, which was very sound, was to have no first minister and never include in his cabinet any cardinal, bishop, or other ecclesiastic, who . . . might try to make themselves masters of all. . . .

The other maxim, which was far from good, was to include in his council only men of mediocre ability and influence; anything more would have eclipsed him; most of all, he feared the nobles, who, he thought would try to impose themselves on him or try to improve their status and take too much. . . . He wanted men to owe everything to their position as ministers, men he could treat as he pleased, fire whenever and however he chose, men who, being nothing in and of themselves, would disappear into the obscurity from which he had plucked them. Realizing this, they would make every effort to serve him well and please him. So completely did he pursue this policy that from his coming of age until his death fifty years later, he included only one person of noble birth in the council. . . .

Gradually he reduced everyone to serving him and increasing the size of his court, even those for whom he had the least consideration. . . . Not only was he alert to the . . . attendance of the great nobles, but also to those of the lower ranks. He would look to left and right, at his *levers,* at his *couchers,* at his meals, while walking through the palace or in the gardens at Versailles, he saw everyone, no one escaped. . . . He carefully noted down the absentees . . . and investigated the reasons therefor. And he never missed an occasion to treat those people accordingly. When it became a question of doing something for such a person, the king would say, "I don't know him at all." . . . He was particularly annoyed at those who found their pleasure in Paris. . . .

Louis took great pains to keep himself informed of what was going on. . . . He had all kinds of spies, but his cruelest source of information was . . . the opening of private letters. The speed and efficiency of this system was incredible. The king got to see excerpts from every letter that the heads of the postal service . . . deemed important. A word of criticism, a little sarcasm . . . could ruin a person [and he never knew why].

ON THE REVOCATION OF THE EDICT OF NANTES (1685)

LOUIS XIV

From Robinson, *Readings in European History,* 2:287–289, revised.

Louis, after having pursued a policy of repression against the Protestants for twenty years, finally decided to seek the ultimate goal of absolutism, "one King, one State, one

Church," by completely revoking Henry IV's edict of toleration. Some of the results of this action are given in Saint-Simon's comments, following the revocation.

Louis, by the grace of God king of France and Navarre, to all present and to come, greeting:

King Henry the Great, our grandfather of glorious memory, desirous that the peace he had procured for his subjects, after the grievous losses they had suffered in the domestic and foreign wars, should not be disturbed because of the R.P.R. [Protestant religion], . . . by his edict granted at Nantes in 1598, regulated the procedures regarding those of the said religion, determined the places where they could hold public worship, . . . and provided whatever might be thought necessary for the tranquillity of the kingdom, . . . in order to be in a better position to work . . . for the reunion to the Church of those who had so lightly withdrawn from it. . . .

Now that God has willed our people perfect peace, we . . . are able to profit from this peace (which we ourselves have facilitated) to devote ourselves to the means of achieving the ends of our father and grandfather, which we haye kept continually before us since our accession. . . .

And now we perceive that our efforts, with God's help thankfully acknowledged, have borne fruit inasmuch as the better and greater part of our subjects of the R.P.R. have embraced the Catholic faith. Since by that fact the execution of the Edict of Nantes . . . has been rendered nugatory, we have determined that we can do nothing better to obliterate the memory of the troubles, confusions, and evils caused by this false religion in our kingdom . . . than to completely revoke the said edict. . . .

1. In consequence we desire and it is our pleasure that all temples of the said R.P.R. situate in our kingdom, regions, territories, and lordships under our crown, be demolished without delay.

2. We forbid our subjects of the R.P.R. to meet any more for the exercise of the said religion in any public place or private home, under any pretext whatever. . . .

4. We enjoin all ministers of the said R.P.R., who do not choose to become converts to . . . the Catholic . . . religion, to leave our kingdom . . . within a fortnight of the publication of our present edict. . . .

8. Children . . . born of persons of the said R.P.R. [shall] henceforth be baptized by the parish priests. . . .

10. All our subjects of the said R.P.R. are [prohibited] from leaving our kingdom, lands, and territories . . . under penalty of being sent to the galleys, and as respects women, of imprisonment and confiscation. . . .

SAINT-SIMON

Mémoires, 28:227–230.

Without the slightest pretext or necessity, the revocation of the Edict of Nantes and the various proscriptions that followed it were the result of a frightful plot in which the new spouse [Mme. de Maintenon] was one of the chief conspirators. It depopulated a quarter of the realm, ruined its commerce, weakened it in every sense, gave it over for a long period to the open and avowed pillage of the dragoons, authorized punishments and tortures which killed thousands of innocent men and women. It ruined a numerous class, tore families apart, armed relative against relative, encouraging them to seize their property and leave them to die of hunger.

The decree banished our manufactures to foreign lands, made those lands flourish at France's expense and enabled them to build new cities. It gave the world the spectacle of a prodigious population proscribed, stripped, fugitive, wandering, guilty of no crime, and seeking shelter far from its own country.

All kinds of people it sent to the galleys: nobles, once-wealthy old men, people esteemed for their piety, learning, and virtue; strong, weak, delicate people—all on account of religion. In fact, to overload the measure of horror, it filled the realm with perjury and sacrilege, amidst the echoing cries of these unfortunate victims of human folly, as others sacrificed their conscience to their property and security and purchased them both by simulated abjuration, after which they were immediately dragged to adore what they did not believe in and to receive the divine body of the Saint of Saints, while remaining convinced that they were eating only bread which they ought to abhor! . . .

From all sides the king received the news and details of all these persecutions and conversions. Those who had abjured and taken communion were counted in the thousands: 12,000 in one place, 6,000 in another—instantaneously. The king congratulated himself on his power and his piety. Believing himself to have recreated the times of the Apostles, . . . he took all the credit to himself. Bishops wrote panegyrics of him, and Jesuits made the pulpit resound with his praises. While the whole of France was filled with horror and confusion, [the monarchy] was filled with triumphant joy and glorification.

The king never doubted the sincerity of these mass conversions and the converters were careful to demonstrate it and beatify him beforehand. He swallowed their poison in long draughts. Never before had he believed himself so great! . . .

CRITIQUES OF THE REIGN

ARCHBISHOP FENELON: TO LOUIS XIV (1694)

Oeuvres de Fénelon, ed. A. Martin, (3 vols., Paris, 1870), 3:425ff.

One of the bitterest critics of the Sun King turned out to be an archbishop and former tutor to Louis's grandson. Fénelon wrote the following letter anonymously, and it probably never reached the king.

Sire,

. . . For some thirty years your ministers have overturned all the ancient maxims of the State so as to augment your authority beyond all bounds, it having become theirs by being in their hands. They no longer speak of the State and its Constitution but only of the king and his royal pleasure. They have increased your revenues and expenses to unheard-of heights. They have exalted you to the heavens in order, they say, to make your grandeur outshine that of your predecessors; which is to say, that the whole of France is impoverished to provide monstrous . . . luxuries at the Court. They have sought to establish you on the ruin of the State, as if you could be great by ruining all your subjects on whom your greatness depends.

It is true that you have been jealous of your authority, . . . but in fact, each minister is the master of his own administration. Because you regulated the limits of those who govern, you thought you were in control. But they have demonstrated their power to the people—and that, only too well. They have been harsh, overbearing, unfair, violent, and dishonest. Recognizing no rule . . . but to threaten, crush, and destroy all who opposed them, . . . they have made your name hateful and the whole nation intolerable to all our neighbors. Wanting only slaves, they have discarded all our traditional allies. . . . and caused twenty years of bloodshed. . . .

Your people, meanwhile, whom you should love as your children and who have supported you so eagerly in the past, are dying of hunger. Agriculture is almost abandoned; the villages and the countryside are depopulated; business is stagnant and unable to offer people any work. Commerce is ruined. Consequently, you have destroyed half the power of your state in order to make useless conquests abroad. Instead of taking money and taxes from the poor, you should be giving them alms—and food. All France is one great poorhouse. . . . The people, who have loved you and trusted you up to now, are losing that love and trust—and even respect. Instead of bringing them joy, your victories now bring bitterness and despair. A spirit of sedition is growing, little by little, all over. The people believe you love nothing but power and glory.

VOLTAIRE: AGE OF LOUIS XIV (1751)

Siècle de Louis XIV (Paris, 1854), pp. 68–69, 336–346.

Having been born and raised to maturity under the reign of Louis XIV, Voltaire then went on to write a pioneer history of that regime. Instead of attacking it, however—as might have been expected from that eighteenth-century censor—Voltaire found much to praise and little to blame.

Never, in any court anywhere, were so many intrigues and hopes spawned as when Cardinal Mazarin lay dying. Beautiful women felt sure they could handle a 22-year-old prince whom love had already beguiled into offering the crown to his mistress. The younger courtiers were expecting a new reign of favorites, while every minister was hoping to be named the next head of government. Nobody expected that a king raised so far from the affairs of state would have the audacity to take on the burdens of government himself. Mazarin had prolonged Louis's childhood as much as he could and had only recently, at the king's request, begun to teach him matters of state. All those who had served under Mazarin were so far from expecting to be ruled by the king that they had never thought of going to him to ask when he would require their services. Instead, they asked, "To whom shall we report?" And Louis replied, "To me!" . . .

At that time, King Charles II of England was said to rule all by himself, which is supposed to have put Louis XIV on his mettle. If that is true, then he went far beyond his rival, for he achieved throughout his life what could be said of Charles only in the beginning.

Louis began by putting his finances in order, after long neglect; he introduced discipline into the armed forces; and he embellished his court to the point of magnificence. Pleasure itself took on brilliance and grandeur. All forms of art were supported and dedicated to the glory of Louis XIV and France. . . .

From 1661 on, the king was building constantly: the Louvre, Saint-German-en-Laye, Versailles. . . . He took a special delight in architecture, landscape gardening, and sculpture, always tending toward the grand and the stately. From 1664 Controller-general Colbert. . . . set about carrying out his master's plans. First the Louvre: François Mansard, one of the greatest French architects, was chosen to build the enormous structures that were being projected. [But] when he cast doubts on the scheme, his services were terminated. . . . Bernini, famous for St. Peter's colonnade, was brought from Rome. . . . But no Roman palace has an entrance to compare with the Louvre's, for which we are indebted to Perrault. . . . Bernini's plans were well rewarded . . . and never used.

After building the Louvre, the town of Versailles near the Château (that cost so many millions), the Trianon, Marly, and . . . so many other buildings, the king built the Observatory, which had been started in 1666, the same year in which he founded the Academy of Science. But his achievement that is most remarkable for its utility, magnitude, and difficulty is the Languedoc Canal, linking the two seas [Atlantic and Mediterranean]. . . . The work was begun in 1664 and continued without interruption until 1681.

The founding of the *Invalides* with its chapel, the most beautiful in Paris, and the building of Saint-Cyr, the last of the king's constructions, would alone suffice to make his memory blessed. Four thousand soldiers and many officers find comfort in their old age and relief for their wounds in the Invalides; and at Saint-Cyr 250 girls of noble birth receive an education befitting their station. . .

Louis XIV was determined to do even greater things—things with wider utility if also more difficulty. One of these was to reform the laws. . . . An initial statute appeared in 1667, the year of his first conquest. After the civil ordinance came the code for the waterways and forests, followed by those for manufacturers, for criminals, for commerce, for maritime law, and all adopted in rapid succession. . . .

The suppression of duelling was one of the greatest services to his country. Formerly, such contests had been permitted by the *parlements* [sovereign courts] and the Church. Even though legally outlawed since the time of Henry IV, the pernicious custom was more prevalent than ever. The notorious La Frette duels in 1663, involving eight combattants, convinced Louis not to condone any more of them. His fortunate decision led to the gradual reform of our country and even neighboring countries. . . . There are a hundred times fewer duels in Europe today than in Louis XIII's time.

Legislator for his people, he was a Solon for his armies. It is amazing to think that, before this time, troops had no uniform dress. At the beginning of his regime he ordered each regiment to be distinguished by the colors of their uniforms or by different badges—a rule that was soon adopted by other nations as well. . . .

He abolished the posts of High Constable and . . . of Colonels-general of infantry, because they were too much the master. He himself resolved to be the only master, and deservedly so. . . .

The bayonet fixed at the end of the musket was also his innovation. Before this they were sometimes used [but] there was no standard practice, no drills, and it was all left to the particular commanding officer. Pikes were the favored weapon, as being more formidable. The first regiment to be trained in the use of bayonets was that of the Fusillers, founded in 1671.

And the present use of artillery is due to him entirely. He founded schools at Douai and later at Metz and Strasbourg, and the regiments of artillery were almost all staffed by officers capable of conducting an effective siege. . . .

In order to maintain military discipline he created inspectors-general and, later, superintendents who reported on the condition of the troops and the extent to which the commissaries had fulfilled their duties. He also founded the Order of St. Louis—an honor more sought after than wealth. . . .

By 1762, as a result of all such means, he had 180,000 regular troops, and by increasing his forces in proportion to his enemies', he eventually had 450,000 men under arms, including those in the navy. Before this, no such powerful armies had been seen. His enemies opposed him with forces almost as large, but only by combining them. He showed what France could do by herself, and, if he did not have great success, he did have great resources. . . .

The same zeal used to form numerous and well-trained armies he also applied to achieve control of the seas. . . . Ship-building commissions, to provide the best possible designs, were set up in the ports. Naval arsenals were built at five of these: Brest, Rochefort, Toulon, Dunkirk, and Le Havre. By 1672 there were 60 ships of the line and 40 frigates; by 1681, 198 men-of-war, including auxiliaries, and 30 galleys in Toulon; . . . 11,000 regular soldiers served on board the ships, and 3,000 more on the galleys. The total of all classes of men serving in the navy was 166,000. . . .

The French fleet held the advantage in every naval engagement up to the battle of La Hogue in 1692, when the [admiral], following orders from the court, attacked a combined English-Dutch fleet of 90 ships with a French fleet of 44. . . .

Hence, from this cursory glance, one can see what changes Louis XIV effected in the nation and how useful those changes were, since they are still with us. His ministers vied with one another in supporting him, and they deserve credit both for the detail and the execution, but the over-all organization was certainly his. The magistrates would never have reformed the laws, the country's finances would not have been regulated, discipline would not have been introduced into the army, nor a regular police force instituted throughout the realm; there would have been no navy and no encouragement given to the arts; all those things would never have been accomplished, surely in such a short time under so many different ministers, if there had not been a ruler to conceive of such great plans and with the will to carry them out.

He never separated his own glory from that of France, never looked upon his kingdom the way a noble looks upon his lands—as a means for him to live in luxury. Every king who loves glory loves the public weal. Around 1698, when he no longer had a Colbert or a Louvois, he ordered each intendant to prepare a detailed inventory of his province for the Duke of Burgundy [the heir apparent]. By such means we would have had an exact record of the whole kingdom and a correct census of the population. The project was useful, even though not all the intendants gave it the care and attention . . . as was done in the case of Languedoc, . . . [including] the number of inhabitants in each district, broken down by nobles, citizens, farmers, artisans, and unskilled workers; also numbers and kinds of livestock, types of land, whether fertile, mediocre, or poor; all clergy, regular and secular, and their incomes, both for those living in towns and in monasteries. . . .

And so I have given you what Louis XIV did or tried to do to make his country more flourishing. It seems to me that one can scarcely look at all his works and efforts without some feeling of gratitude or feeling for the public spirit behind them. One has only to imagine the condition of the country during the Fronde [insurrections of 1648–1652] and compare it with today. Louis XIV did more for his nation than any twenty of his predecessors combined, and he could have done more than he did. The war that ended with the Treaty of Ryswick [1697] began the ruin of that flourishing trade started by Colbert, and the war of the [Spanish] Succession [1701–1714] ended it. . . .

It is a good thing to have reformed the laws, but crime has not yet been eliminated. It was intended to make the administration of justice uniform, and so it was in criminal cases, in commercial cases, and in court procedures; but it should be in civil suits also. It is highly undesirable that the same court should have to rule on the basis of a hundred different customary laws; Various territorial rights and privileges—ambiguous, onerous, and socially detrimental—still survive, from the age of Feudalism, as the rubbish of a Gothic ruin.

We do not say that the different classes in the nation should all be subject to the same law. The customs of the nobles, the clergy, the magistrates, the farmers are all different of necessity, but it is surely desirable that each class be subject to the same law throughout the kingdom. . . . Uniformity is a virtue in all branches of administration, but the obstacles to its achievement are formidable. . . .

If Louis had not believed that his mere wish would force a million men to change their religion, France would not have lost so many citizens. Despite such shocks, however, this country is still one of the most prosperous on earth, since all the good Louis XIV did for her remains, whereas the evil, which is hard to avoid in bad times, he has remedied. Posterity, the judge of kings, . . . in weighing his greatness and his defects, will find that, although he was over-praised in his lifetime, he deserved it, and that he merits the statue erected to him at Montpelier, with the Latin inscription: *To Louis the Great after His Death.*

CHAPTER 14

THE GLORIOUS REVOLUTION OF 1688

I stood in the Strand and beheld . . . His Majesty Charles II come to London after a sad and long exile. . . . Such a restoration was never mentioned in any history, ancient or modern, since the return of the Jews from the Babylonian captivity, nor so joyful a day and so bright ever seen in this nation. . . .

—John Evelyn, Diary, *May 29, 1660*

The Stuart Restoration, after the bloody civil war and the collapse of England's experiment with republicanism, was a period of great rejoicing. It was also a period of continuous jockeying for power by both sides of the uneasy partnership—king and Parliament, since the basic questions raised by the first two Stuarts, James I and Charles I, were still being raised by Charles II and James II.

Could Parliament prevent the rule of an absolute king?

In the "partnership," if such it was, who had the final authority—king or commons?

Would the king be allowed to appoint men opposed to the laws and customs of the nation and assign them to such sensitive areas as the courts, the universities, the armed forces, the local administrations, and the Parliament itself?

Finally, could a Protestant country be ruled by a Catholic king—or dynasty—after the birth of James's son in 1688?

CHARLES II

BISHOP BURNET: ON CHARLES II AND JAMES II

History of My Own Times (London, 1723–1724), 1:611–613, 168–170.

A leading personage of the period as well as historian, Burnet offers a character study of the last two Stuart kings. He began his History in 1683, when Charles was still ruling.

Charles II Stuart, *portrait by an unknown artist. (National Portrait Gallery, London. Art Reference Bureau.)*

Charles II

The king was then 30 years of age and, as might have been supposed, past the levities of youth and the extravagance of pleasure. He had a very good understanding. He knew well the state of affairs both at home and abroad. He had a softness of temper that charmed all who came near him, till they found how little they could depend on good looks, kind words, and fair promises; in which he was liberal to excess, because he intended nothing by them, but to get rid of importunities and to silence all further pressing upon him. He seemed to have no sense of religion: Both at prayers and sacrament he, as it were, took care to satisfy people that he was in no sort concerned in that about which he was employed. So that he was very far from being a hypocrite, unless his assisting at those performances was a sort of hypocrisy (as no doubt it was).

But he was sure not to increase that by any the least appearance of religion. He said once to myself, he was no atheist, but he could not think God would make a man miserable only for taking a little pleasure out of the way. He disguised his Popery to the last. But when he talked freely, he could not help letting himself out against the liberty that under the Reformation all men took of inquiring into matters of religion: For from their inquiring into matters of religion they carried the humor further, to inquire into matters of state. He said often, he thought government was a much safer and easier thing where the authority was believed infallible, and the faith and submission of the people was implicit: About which I had once much discourse with him.

He was affable and easy, and loved to be made so by all about him. The great art of keeping him long was, the being easy, and the making everything easy to him. He had made such observation on the French Government, that he thought a king who might be checked, or have his ministers called into account by a parliament, was but a king in name. He had a great compass of knowledge, tho' he was never capable of much application or study. He understood the Mechanics and Physics; and was a good chemist, and much set on several preparations of mercury, chiefly the fixing it. He understood navigation well: But above all he knew the architecture of ships so perfectly that in that respect he was exact rather more than became a prince. His apprehension was quick, and his memory good.

He was an everlasting talker. He told his stories with a good grace: But they came in his way too often. He had a very ill opinion of men and women; and did not think that there was either sincerity or chastity in the world out of principle, but that some had either the one or the other out of humor or vanity. He thought that nobody did serve him out of love: And so he was quits with all the world, and loved others as little as he thought they loved him. He hated business, and could not be easily brought to mind any: But when it was necessary, and he was set to it, he would stay as long as his ministers had work for him. The ruin of his reign, and of all his affairs, was occasioned chiefly by his delivering up at his first coming over to a mad range of pleasure. . . .

In the state his affairs were . . . in [during his exile] he accustomed himself to say to every person, and upon all occasions, that which he thought would please most: So that words or promises went very easily from him. And he had so ill an opinion of mankind that he thought the great art of living and governing was to manage all things and all persons with a depth of craft and dissimulation. And in that few men in the world could put on the appearance of sincerity better than he could: Under which so much artifice was usually hid, that in conclusion he could deceive none, for all were become mistrustful of him. He had great vices, but scarce any virtues to correct them: He had in him some vices that were less hurtful, which corrected his more hurtful ones.

He was during the active part of life given up to sloth and lewdness to such a degree that he hated business and could not bear the engaging in any thing that gave him much trouble, or put him under any constraint. And, tho' he desired to become absolute and to overturn both our religion and our laws, yet he would neither run the risk, nor give himself the trouble, which so great a design required. He had an appearance of gentleness in his outward deportment: But he seemed to have no bowels nor tenderness in his nature: And in the end of his life he became cruel. He was apt to forgive all crimes, even blood itself: Yet he never forgave any thing that was done against himself, after his first and general act of indemnity, which was to be reckoned as done rather upon maxims of state than inclinations of mercy.

James II

I will digress a little to give an account of the Duke's character, whom I knew for some years so particularly that I can say much upon my own knowledge. He was very brave in his youth, and so much magnified by Monsieur Turenne, that till his marriage lessened him he really clouded the King, and passed for the superior genius. He was naturally candid and sincere, and a firm friend, till affairs and his religion wore out all his first principles and inclinations. He had a great desire to understand affairs: And in order to do that he kept a constant journal of all that pass'd of which he showed me a great deal.

The Duke of Buckingham gave me once a short but severe character[ization] of the two brothers. It was the more severe because it was true: The King (he said) could see things if he would, and the Duke would see things if he could. He had no true judgment and was soon determined by those whom he trusted: But he was obstinate against all other advices. He was bred with high notions of kingly authority and laid it down for a maxim that all who opposed the King were rebels in their hearts. He was perpetually in one amour or another, without being very nice in his choice: Upon which the King said once, he believed his brother had his mistresses given him by his priests for penance. . . .

THE SECRET TREATY OF DOVER (22 MAY 1670)

From F. Mignet, *Négotiations relatives à la succession d'Espagne sous Louis XIV* (Paris, 1835–1842), 3:187–197.

Shortly after England had formed the Triple Alliance with Sweden and Holland against the French in 1668, Charles II secretly negotiated the following treaty with Louis XIV. Only a few of Charles's ministers were privy to it, and the text was not known till 1830.

For the perpetual union and friendship between the two kings and their states, articles so secret and so advantageous to both sovereigns have been agreed upon that a treaty of such importance can scarcely be found in history.

The king of England, convinced of the truth of the Roman Catholic religion, is determined to announce it and to reconcile himself with the Church of Rome as soon as the state of affairs in his country allows. He is so confident of his subjects' allegiance and affection that none of them, not even those who have (so far) been denied the full measure of divine grace, will be wanting in obedience to their sovereign. But because there are always restless spirits who conceal their intentions under a religious disguise, the King of England will accept the assistance of the King of France, who, for his part, is eager to contribute to a design that is not only glorious for the King of England but for the whole of Catholic Christendom, promises to pay the king of England the sum of 2,000,000 francs, one half payable three months after the ratification of the present treaty and the other half three months later. Further, the King of France agrees to provide, at his own expense, 6,000 troops for the execution of this plan, if they should be needed. The timing of the declaration of Catholicism is left to the discretion of the King of England. . . .

Each of the contracting monarchs has a sufficiently large population to warrant their joint resolution to humble the pride of the [Dutch] States General, and destroy the power of a nation that has not only shown itself ungrateful to those who helped create its republic, but has had the arrogance to offer itself as an arbiter among other states. Accordingly, both monarchs will jointly declare war on the States General and neither will make a truce or treaty without the other. . . .

In the agreed-upon hostilities, the King of France will pay for the campaign on land and the King of England will supply 6,000 foot soldiers at his expense. For the war at sea, the King of England will arm a minimum of 60 men-of-war and ten fireships, joined by a French auxiliary fleet of at least 30 good ships, the whole to be under command of the Duke of York. To help the King of England defray the costs of the campaign, the King of France agrees to pay him 3,000,000 francs each year for as long as the war shall last. The English share in the Dutch conquest shall be Walcheren, Sluys, and Cadsand. . . .

DECLARATION OF INDULGENCE (1672)

From *The Stuart Constitution,* ed. J.P. Kenyon (Cambridge, 1966), p. 407.

Charles's new policy is reflected in the following declaration, issued at a time when Parliament was not in session.

Charles Rex.

Our care and endeavors for the preservation of the rights and interests of the Church, have been sufficiently manifested to the world, by the whole course of our government since our happy restoration, and by the many and frequent ways of coercion that we have used for reducing all erring of dissenting persons, and for composing the unhappy differences in matters of religion, which we found among our subjects upon our return; but it being evident by the sad experience of 12 years, that there is very little fruit of all these forcible courses, we think ourselves obliged to make use of that supreme power in ecclesiastical matters, which is not only inherent in us, but hath been declared and recognized to be so, by several statutes and acts of Parliament; and therefore we do now accordingly issue this our declaration, as well for the quieting of our good subjects in these points, as for inviting strangers in this conjecture to come and live under us; and for the better encouragement of all to a cheerful following of their trades and callings, from whence we hope, by the blessing of God, to have many good and happy advantages to our government; as also for preventing for the future the danger that might otherwise arise from private meetings and seditious conventicles.

And in the first place, we declare our express resolution . . . that the Church of England be preserved, and remain entire in its doctrine, discipline, and government, as it now stands established by law; and that this be taken to be, as it is, the basis . . . of the public worship of God, and that the . . . clergy receive and enjoy the revenues belonging thereunto, and that no person . . . be exempt from paying his tithes or dues whatsoever. . . .

We do in the next place declare our will and pleasure to be, that the execution of all, and all manner of penal laws in matters ecclesiastical, against . . . nonconformists or recusants, be immediately suspended. . . .

And that there may be no pretense for any of our subjects to continue their illegal meetings and conventicles, we do declare, that we shall from time to time allow a sufficient number of places as they shall be desired, in all parts of this our kingdom, for the use of such as do not conform to the Church of England, to meet and assemble in order to their public worship and devotion, which places shall be open and free to all persons.

. . . But our express will and pleasure is, that none of our subjects do presume to meet in any place, until such places be allowed, and the teacher of that congregation be approved by us.

And lest any should apprehend that this restriction should make our said allowance and approbation difficult to be obtained, we do further declare, that this our indulgence . . . shall extend to all sorts of nonconformists and recusants, except the recusants of the Roman Catholic religion, to whom we shall in no wise allow public places of worship, but only indulge them their share in the common exemption from the penal laws, and the exercise of their worship in their private houses only.

And if after this our clemency and indulgence any of our subjects shall pretend to abuse this liberty, and shall preach seditiously, or to the derogation of the doctrine, discipline or government of the established church, or shall meet in places not allowed by us, we do hereby give them warning, and declare we will proceed against them with all imaginable severity. And we will let them see, we can be as severe to punish such offenders when so justly provoked, as we are indulgent to truly tender consciences.

Given at our court at Whitehall this 15th day of March, in the four and twentieth year of our reign.

DEBATE ON THE DECLARATION OF INDULGENCE (1673)

From *Journals of the House of Commons* (London, 1803–1863), 9:252, 256–257; *Journals of the House of Lords* (London, ?–1887), 12:549.

It was almost a year before Parliament was convened and took up the king's declaration.

February 14, 1673

. . . Mr. Powle reports from the committee appointed to prepare and draw up a petition and address to his majesty, . . . which he read [as follows:]

Most gracious sovereign:

We your majesty's most loyal and faithful subjects, the commons assembled in parliament, do in the first place, as in all duty bound, return your majesty our most humble and hearty thanks for the many gracious promises and assurances, which your majesty hath several times during this present parliament given to us, that your majesty would secure and maintain unto us the true reformed Protestant religion, our liberties, and properties; which most gracious assurances your majesty hath out of your great goodness been pleased to renew unto us more particularly at the opening of this present session of parliament.

And further we crave leave humbly to represent that we have with all duty and expedition taken into our consideration several parts of your majesty's last speech to us, and withal the declaration therein mentioned for indulgence to dissenters, dated the 15th of March last. And we find ourselves bound in duty to inform your majesty that penal statutes in matters ecclesiastical cannot be suspended but by act of parliament. We therefore . . . do most humbly beseech your majesty that the said laws may have their free course until it shall be otherwise provided for by act of parliament; and that your majesty would graciously be pleased to give such directions herein that no apprehensions or jealousies may remain in the hearts of your majesty's good and faithful subjects.

Resolved, etc., that this house doth agree with the committee in the petition and address . . . to be presented to his majesty.

February 24, 1673

. . . Mr. Secretary Conventry reports . . . his majesty['s] answer to the humble petition and address of this house: . . .

Charles R[ex]. His majesty hath received an address from you, and he hath seriously considered of it, and returneth you this answer: that he is very much troubled that that declaration which he put out for ends so necessary to the quiet of his kingdom, and especially in that conjuncture, should have proved the cause of disquiet in this house of commons and give occasion to the questioning of his power in ecclesiastics; which he finds not done in the reigns of any of his ancestors. He is sure he never had thoughts of using it otherwise than as it hath been entrusted to him—to the peace and establishment of the Church of England and the ease of all his subjects in general.

Neither doth he pretend to the right of suspending any laws wherein the properties, rights, or liberties of any of his subjects are concerned, nor to alter anything in the established doctrine or discipline of the Church of England; but his only design was to take off the penalties the statutes inflict on the dissenters, and which he believes, when well considered of, you yourselves would not wish executed according to the rigor and letter of the law. Neither hath he done this with any thought of avoiding or precluding the advice of his parliament; and, if any bill shall be offered him which shall appear more proper to attain the aforesaid ends and secure the peace of the church and kingdom, when tendered in due manner to him, he will show how readily he will concur in all ways that shall appear good for the kingdom. . . .

February 26, 1673

. . . Mr. Powle reports . . . an answer agreed by the committee:

Most gracious sovereign: We, your majesty's most humble and loyal subjects, the knights, citizens, and burgesses in this present parliament assembled, do render to your sacred majesty our most dutiful thanks for that, to our unspeakable comfort, your majesty hath been pleased so often to reiterate unto us those gracious promises and assurances of maintaining the religion now established and the liberties of your people. And we do not in the least measure doubt but that your majesty had the same gracious intentions in giving satisfaction to your subjects by your answer to our last petition and address.

> Yet, upon a serious consideration thereof, we find that the said answer is not sufficient to clear the apprehensions that may justly remain in the minds of your people by your majesty's having claimed a power to suspend penal statutes in matters ecclesiastical, and which your majesty does still seem to assert . . . to be entrusted in the crown and never questioned in the reigns of any of your ancestors—wherein we humbly conceive your majesty hath been very much misinformed; since no such power was ever claimed or exercised by any of your majesty's predecessors, and, if it should be admitted, might tend to the interrupting of the free course of the laws and altering the legislative power, which hath always been acknowledged to reside in your majesty and your two houses of parliament.
>
> We do therefore, with an unanimous consent, become again most humble suitors unto your sacred majesty that you would be pleased to give us a full and satisfactory answer to our said petition and address, and that your majesty would take such effectual order that the proceedings in this matter may not for the future be drawn into consequence or example.

. . . Resolved, etc., that the whole address be agreed to as it was brought in by the committee. . . .

March 8, 1673

. . . His majesty sitting in his royal throne, adorned with his crown and regal ornaments, commanded the gentleman usher of the black rod to give notice to the house of commons that they attend his majesty presently. The commons being come with their speaker, his majesty made this short speech following:

> My lords and gentlemen:
> . . . If there be any scruple remaining with you concerning the suspension of penal laws, I here faithfully promise you that what hath been done in that particular shall not for the future be drawn either into consequence or example. . . .

Next the lord chancellor reported . . . that his majesty had the last night, in pursuance of what he then intended and declared this morning concerning the suspension of penal laws not being for the future drawn either into consequence or example, caused the original declaration under the great seal to be cancelled in his presence; whereof himself and several other lords of the council were witnesses. . . .

THE TEST ACT OF 1673

Statutes of the Realm (London, 1810–1818), 5:782–783.

Not satisfied with the king's having withdrawn the Declaration of Indulgence, the Parliament adopted the following bill, which the king approved on March 29, 1673.

An act for preventing dangers which may happen from popish recusants and quieting the minds of his majesty's good subjects: be it enacted . . .

That all and every person or persons, as well peers as commoners, that shall bear any office or offices civil or military; or shall receive any pay, salary or wages by reason of any grant from his majesty; or shall have command or place of trust from or under his majesty or from any of his majesty's predecessors . . . or shall be of the household or in the service or employment of his majesty or of his royal highness the duke of York, who shall inhabit . . . the city of London or Westminster; . . . the said person or persons shall appear in his majesty's high court of chancery or . . . king's bench, and there in public take the several oaths of supremacy and allegiance. . . . And the said officers shall also receive the sacrament of the Lord's Supper according to the usage of the Church of England. . . .

And be it further enacted . . . that all that refuse to take the said oaths and sacraments . . . shall be *ipso facto* adjudged incapable and disabled in law [to hold] the said offices. . . .

And be it further enacted . . . that at the same time when the persons concerned in this act shall take the aforesaid oaths of supremacy and allegiance, they shall likewise make and subscribe this declaration following: . . . "I, ______, do declare that I do believe that there is not any transubstantiation in the sacrament of the Lord's Supper, or in the elements of bread and wine, at or after the consecration by any person whatsoever."

JAMES II

JOHN EVELYN: ON THE REVOCATION OF THE EDICT OF NANTES

The Diary of John Evelyn, ed. W. Bray (London, 1901), 2:241–242.

John Evelyn was a royalist sympathizer, a civil servant under the Restoration, a writer, and one of the founders of the Royal Society. He is best known today for his lifelong diary, a mine of historical information for the period.

3d November 1685. The French persecution of the Protestants raging with the utmost barbarity, exceeded even what the very heathens used: innumerable persons of the greatest birth and riches leaving all their earthly substance, and hardly escaping with their lives, dispersed through all the countries of Europe. . . . In Holland, Denmark, and all about Germany, were dispersed some hundred thousands; besides those in England, where, though multitudes of all degree sought for shelter and welcome as distressed Christians and confessors, they found least encouragement, by a fatality of the times we were fallen into, and the uncharitable indifference of such as should have embraced them. . . . One thing was much taken notice of, that the "Gazettes" which were still constantly printed twice a week, informing us what was done all over Europe, never spoke of this wonderful proceeding in France, nor was any relation of it published by any, save what private letters and persecuted fugitives brought. Whence this silence, I list not to conjecture; but it appeared extraordinary in a Protestant

James II, *brother of Charles. Portrait by Sir Godfrey Kneller, c. 1685, when James ascended the throne. (National Portrait Gallery, London. Art Reference Bureau.)*

country that we should know nothing of what Protestants suffered, while great collections were made for them in foreign places, more hospitable and Christian to appearance.

SIR WILLIAM PETTY: ON THE POWERS OF THE KING OF ENGLAND (1685)

From *The Economic Writings of Sir William Petty,* ed. C.H. Hull (Cambridge, 1899), 2:630–632.

Physician, statistician, and political economist, Petty was also a founder of the Royal Society; he was knighted by Charles II, who appointed him surveyor-general of Ireland.

2. The king makes peers in Parliament, who are perpetual legislators.

4. The king makes bishops, and they priests and deacons and clerks of the convocation, and has all the power which the pope had formerly. . . .

5. The king makes the chancellors of the universities, makes heads and fellows in the several colleges. . . .

7. The king makes sheriffs and they juries upon life and estate, limb and liberty, and also jailors, bailiffs and executioners of all sorts.

8. The king makes a chancellor, or chief judge in equity, who stops proceedings in other courts of law &c. The Chancellor makes justices of the peace, and they high and petty constables and sessions of peace &c.

9. The king makes judges and . . . can suspend the law, pardon or prosecute.

10. The king can give charters for boroughs to Parliament; appoint electors and judges of elections; prorogue, adjourn and dissolve Parliaments. . . .

11. The king appoints his lieutenants to command the grand standing militia [and] can press any man to serve his allies beyond seas as soldiers. . . .

13. The king has great power over forests and mines, colonies, monopolies.

14. The king can do no wrong, and his coming to the crown clears him from all punishments. . . .

15. The king, by ceasing or forebearing to administer the several powers above-named, can do what harm he pleases to his subjects.

DECLARATION OF INDULGENCE (1687)

From *Documentary Annals of the Reformed Church of England,* ed. E. Cardwell (Oxford, 1839), 2:308–311.

On the death of Charles II in 1685, his brother, the duke of York, became king as James II. A converted Catholic, he began by appointing his correligionists to high positions, despite Parliament's clear position on the question. Using his "dispensing power" to circumvent the penal statutes, James appointed Catholic officials in the armed forces, the courts, the universities, the House of Lords, and local government. In 1687 he issued the following declaration:

. . . We cannot but heartily wish . . . that all the people of our dominions were members of the Catholic Church. Yet we humbly thank Almighty God it is, and hath of long time been our constant sense and opinion . . . that conscience ought not to be constrained, nor people forced in matters of mere religion. . . .

We therefore, out of our princely care and affection unto all our loving subjects, that they may live at ease and quiet, and for the increase of trade and encouragement of strangers, have thought fit by virtue of our royal prerogative to issue forth this our declaration of indulgence, making no doubt of the concurrence of our two Houses of Parliament when we shall think it convenient for them to meet.

In the first place, we do declare that we will protect and maintain our archbishops, bishops and clergy, and all other our subjects of the Church of England in the full exercise of their religion as by law established. . . .

We do likewise declare that it is our royal will and pleasure that from henceforth the execution of all . . . penal laws in matters ecclesiastical, for not coming to Church, or for not receiving the sacrament, or for other nonconformity to the religion established, or for or by reason of the exercise of religion in any manner whatsoever, be immediately suspended; and the further execution of the said penal laws . . . is hereby suspended. . . .

We do hereby further declare that it is our royal will and pleasure that the oaths commonly called the oaths of supremacy and allegiance, and also the several tests and declarations . . . shall not at any time hereafter be required to be taken, declared, or subscribed to by any person . . . whatsoever, who is or shall be employed in any office . . . under us or in our government. . . .

JOHN EVELYN: THE TRIAL OF THE BISHOPS (1688)

Diary, 2:272–273.

June 8, 1688

This day, the Archbishop of Canterbury, with the Bishops of Ely, Chichester, St. Asaph, Bristol, Peterborough and Bath and Wells, were sent from the Privy Council prisoners to the Tower, for refusing to give bail for their appearance, on their not reading the Declaration for liberty of conscience; they refused to give bail, as it would have prejudiced their peerage. The concern of the people for them was wonderful, infinite crowds on their knees begging their blessing, and praying for them, as they passed out of the barge along the Tower wharf. . . .

June 29, 1688

They appeared; the trial lasted from 9 in the morning to past 6 in the evening . . . they were acquitted. When this was heard, there was great rejoicing; and there was a lane of people from King's Bench to the waterside on their knees, as the bishops passed and repassed, to beg their blessing. Bonfires were made that night, and bells rung, which was taken very ill at Court, and an appearance of nearly 60 earls and lords, etc., on the bench, did not a little comfort them; but indeed they were all along full of comfort and cheer.

WILLIAM OF ORANGE

BISHOP BURNET: ON WILLIAM OF ORANGE

History, 4:133–135.

The prince has been much neglected in his education; for all his life long he hated constraint. He spoke little. He put on some appearance of application. . . . The depression of France was the governing passion of his whole life. . . .

He had a way that was affable and obliging to the Dutch. But he could not bring himself to comply enough with the temper of the English, his coldness and slowness being very contrary to the genius of the nation. . . . I asked his sense of the church of England. He said he liked our worship well, and our government in the church. . . . When he found I was in my opinion for toleration, he said, that was all he would ever desire to bring us to, for quieting our contentions at home. He also promised to me, that he should never be prevailed with to set up the Calvinistical notions of the decrees of God, to which I did imagine some might drive him. . . . I thought it necessary to enter with him into all these particulars, that so I might be furnished from his own mouth to give a full account of his sense to some in England, who would expect it of me, and would be disposed to believe what I should assure them of. . . .

INVITATION TO WILLIAM OF ORANGE (30 JUNE 1688)

From Cheyney, *Readings in English History,* pp. 545–547.

We have great satisfaction to find . . . that your Highness is so ready and willing to [assist] us. . . . We have great reason to believe, we shall be every day in a worse condition that we are and less able to defend ourselves. . . . The people are so generally dissatisfied with the present conduct of the government in relation to their religion, liberties, and properties . . . that your Highness may be assured, there are 19 [out of] 20 of the people . . . who would contribute to it, if they had such protection to countenance their rising as would secure them from being destroyed before they could get to be in a position able to defend themselves. . . .

Much the greater part of the gentry are as much dissatisfied . . . many of the officers [are] so discontented that they continue in their services only for a subsistence . . . and very many of the common soldiers do daily show such an aversion to the popish religion, that there is the greatest probability imaginable of great numbers of deserters which would come from them, should there be such an occasion; and amongst the seamen, it is almost certain, there is not one in ten who would do them any service in such a war. . . . If upon a due consideration of all these circumstances, your Highness shall think fit to adventue upon the attempt . . . there must be no time lost, in letting us know your resolution concerning it, and in what time we may depend that all the preparations will be ready.

Signed:	Shrewsbury	[Protestant convert from Catholicism]
	Devonshire	[Whig]
	Danby	[Tory]
	Lumley	[Protestant convert from Catholicism]
	Bishop of London	[Tory]
	Russell	[Whig]
	Sydney	[Whig]

BILL OF RIGHTS (1689)

Statutes of the Realm, 6:142.

Whereas the said late King James II having abdicated the government, and the throne being thereby vacant, his Highness the prince of Orange (whom it hath pleased Almighty God to make the glorious instrument of delivering this kingdom from popery and arbitrary power) did (by the advice of the lords spiritual and temporal, diverse principal persons of the commons) cause letters to be written . . . for the choosing of such persons to represent them, as were of right to be sent to parliament . . . being now assembled in a full and free representative of this nation . . . do in the first place (as their ancestors in like case have usually done) for the vindicating and asserting their ancient rights and liberties, declare:

1. That the pretended power of suspending of laws, or the execution of laws, by regal authority, without the consent of parliament, is illegal.

2. That the pretended power of dispensing with laws, or the execution of laws, by regal authority, as it hath been assumed and exercised of late, is illegal.

3. That the commission for erecting the late court of commissioners for ecclesiastical causes, and all other commissions and courts of like nature are illegal and pernicious.

4. That levying of money for or to the use of the crown, by pretence of prerogative without the grant of parliament for a longer time, or in other manner than the same is or shall be granted, is illegal.

5. That it is the right of the subjects to petition the king, and all commitments and prosecutions for such petitioning are illegal.

6. That the raising or keeping of a standing army within the kingdom in time of peace, unless it be with the consent of parliament, is against the law.

7. That the subjects which are Protestants may have arms for their defense suitable to their conditions, and as allowed by law.

8. That election of members of parliament ought to be free.

9. That the freedom of speech, and debates or proceedings in parliament, ought not to be impeached or questioned in any court or place out of parliament.

10. That excessive bail ought not to be required, nor excessive fines imposed; nor cruel and unusual punishments inflicted.

13. And that for redress of all grievances, and for the amending, strengthening, and preserving of the laws, parliament ought to be held frequently. . . .

THE TOLERATION ACT (1689)

Statutes of the Realm, 6:74–76.

An Act for exempting their Majesties' Protestant Subjects, differing from the Church of England, from the Penalties of certain laws.

Forasmuch as some ease to scrupulous consciences in the exercise of religion may be an effectual means to unite their Majesties' Protestant subjects in interest and affections: . . .

2. Be it enacted . . . That neither the statute made in . . . the reign of the late Queen Elizabeth, entitled An Act to retain the Queen's Majesty's Subjects in their due obedience; . . . nor that branch or clause of a statute made in . . . the reign of the said Queen intituled, An Act for the uniformity of common prayer and service in the Church . . . by all persons, having no lawful or reasonable excuse to be absent, are required to resort to their parish church or chapel, or some usual place where the common prayer shall be used, upon pain of punishment by the censures of the church; . . . and the statute made in the third year of the reign of the late King James I, intituled An Act for the better discovering and repressing popish recusants; . . . nor any other law or statute made against papists or popish recusants; except . . . the statute made in the thirtieth year of . . . King Charles II, intituled An Act for the more effectual preserving the King's person and government by disabling papists from sitting in either house of parliament, shall be construed to extend to any person . . . dissenting from the Church of England, that shall take the oaths mentioned in a statute made by this present parliament . . . which oath and declaration the justices of peace at the general sessions of the peace . . . are hereby required to tender and administer to such persons as shall offer themselves to take . . . the same and thereof keep a register; and likewise none of the persons aforesaid shall give or pay, as any fee or reward, to any officer . . . above the sum of sixpence, nor that more than once, for his entry of [having taken] the said oaths. . . .

3. And be it further enacted . . . That all persons already convicted of recusancy . . . that shall take the said oaths . . . shall be thenceforth exempted from all penalties . . . incurred by force of the aforesaid statutes. . . .

4. And be it further enacted . . . That all persons that shall take the said oaths and . . . declarations shall not be liable to any pains, penalties, or forfeitures [nor] be prosecuted in any ecclesiastical court for . . . their nonconforming to the Church of England.

5. Provided always . . . That if any assembly of persons dissenting from the Church of England shall be had in any place for religious worship with the doors locked . . . during any time of such meeting, [they] shall not receive any benefit from this law, but be liable to all the pains and penalties of all the aforesaid laws recited in this act. . . .

6. Provided always, That nothing herein contained shall . . . exempt any of the persons aforesaid from paying of tithes or other parochial dues. . . .

7. Provided always, . . . That neither this act nor any . . . clause herein [shall] extend to give any ease, benefit, or advantage to any papist or popish recusant whatsoever, or any person that shall deny in his preaching or writing the doctrine of the Blessed Trinity, as it is declared in the aforesaid articles of religion.

CHAPTER 15

DEBATE ON FREEDOM AND AUTHORITY: HOBBES, LOCKE, ROUSSEAU

Freedom vs. Authority—what is the relationship between the individual and the State? That question occupied some of the keenest political minds in the seventeenth and eighteenth centuries.

Thomas Hobbes (1588–1679), one-time tutor to the Prince of Wales and a writer who managed to antagonize some of the most powerful groups in England—Monarchists, Parliamentarians, Churchmen—Hobbes held that man is so selfish that he cannot survive in a "state of nature," but must combine with his fellows to found a monster government, *Leviathan,* to hold him in check against both himself and his neighbors. From such a government, then, there is no effective means of escape, since this would mean returning to the state of nature where life, according to Hobbes, is "nasty, brutish, and short." Even tyranny, he felt, is better than anarchy.

John Locke (1632–1704), Oxford professor and "spiritual father" of the American Declaration of Independence, accepted Hobbes's social-contract theory while disagreeing with his conclusions. Locke felt that the original "state of nature" was more like the Garden of Eden than the "war of every man against every man" that Hobbes had posited. The only things lacking to man in the state of nature, according to Locke, were the legislative, executive, and judicial functions of a sovereign who would be responsible to the people—a sovereign, indeed, like the one England obtained by the Glorious Revolution, which happened at the very time that Locke was writing his *Treatises on Government.*

In the following century, Jean-Jacques Rousseau (1712–1778), the problem child of the Enlightenment, managed to combine the theories of Hobbes and Locke and go beyond them into areas that presaged Robespierre and the French Revolution, Marx and Socialism, Hitler and Nazism. As Norman L. Torrey puts it:

[Rousseau] has exercised a tremendous dual influence on political thinking. His defense of the inalienable rights of man and of the sovereignty of the people were echoed in the American Declaration of Independence and the French Declaration of the Rights of Man and the Citizen. His individualistic tendencies appealed to such writers as John Stuart Mill, Emerson, Thoreau and Whitman. The collectivistic aspects were developed by Kant, Hegel, Fichte and Marx [*Les Philosophes* (New York: Capricorn, 1960), pp. 143–144].

Do all three of these writers have the same views of human nature? Is the concept of the social contract valid today?

THOMAS HOBBES: THE LEVIATHAN (1651)

(London, 1651), pp. 63–65, 82–86.

Of the Natural Condition of Mankind As Concerning Their Felicity, and Misery

Nature hath made men so equal, in the faculties of body and mind, as that though there be found one man sometimes manifestly stronger in body or of quicker mind than another, yet when all is reckoned together, the difference between man and man is not so considerable as that one man can thereupon claim to himself any benefit to which another may not pretend, as well as he. For, as to the strength of body, the weakest has strength enough to kill the strongest, either by secret machination or by confederacy with others, that are in the same danger with himself.

As to the faculties of mind, setting aside the arts grounded upon words, . . . I find yet a greater equality amongst men than that of strength. For prudence is but experience, which equal time equally bestows on all men, in those things they equally apply themselves to. That which makes such equality incredible, is but a vain concept of one's own widsom, which almost all men think they have in greater degree than the vulgar, that is, than all men but themselves. . . . For such is the nature of men, that howsoever they may acknowledge others to be more witty, or more eloquent, or more learned; yet they will hardly believe there be many so wise as themselves; for they see their own wit at hand, and other men's at a distance. But this proveth rather that men are in that point equal. . . . For there is not ordinarily a greater sign of the equal distribution of anything, than that every man is contented with his share.

From this equality of ability ariseth equality of hope in attaining our ends. And therefore if any two men desire the same thing, which nevertheless they cannot both enjoy, they become enemies; and [to achieve] their end, which is principally their own conservation or sometimes their delectation only, endeavor to destroy or subdue one another.

From hence it comes to pass that where an invader hath no more to fear than another man's single power, if one plant, sow, build, or possess a convenient seat, others may probably be expected to come prepared with forces united to dispossess and deprive him not only of the fruit of his labor but also of his life or liberty. And the invader again is in the like danger of another.

And from this diffidence of one another, there is no way for any man to secure himself, so reasonable, as anticipation; that is, by force or wiles to master the persons of all men he can, so long till he see no other power great enough to endanger him: and this is no more than his own conservation requireth, and is generally allowed. Also because there be some, that taking pleasure in contemplating their own power in the acts of conquest, which they pursue farther than their security requires; if others, that otherwise would be glad to be at least within modest bounds, should not by invasion increase their power, they would not be able [for long], by standing only on their defense, to subsist. By consequence, such augmentation of dominion over men being necessary to a man's conservation, it ought to be allowed him.

Again, men have no pleasure, but on the contrary, a great deal of grief, in keeping company where there is no power able to overawe them all. For every man looketh that his companion should value him at the same rate he sets upon himself: and upon all signs of contempt or undervaluing, naturally endeavors, as far as he dares . . . to extort a greater value from his contemners, by damage. . . .

Hereby it is manifest that during the time men live without a common power to keep them all in awe, they are in that condition which is called war; and such a war as is of every man against every man. For "war" consisteth not in battle only, or the act of fighting, but in a tract of time, wherein the will to contend by battle is sufficiently known; and therefore the notion of "time" is to be considered in the nature of war, as it is in the nature of weather. For as the nature of foul weather lieth not in a shower or two of rain, but in an inclination thereto of many days together; so the nature of war consisteth not in actual fighting, but in the known disposition thereto during all the time there is no assurance to the contrary. All other time is "peace."

Whatsoever therefore is consequent of a time of war, where every man is enemy to every man, the same is consequent to the time wherein men live without other security than what their own strength and their own invention shall furnish them withal. In such a condition there is no place for industry, because the fruit thereof is uncertain, and consequently no culture of the earth; no navigation, nor use of the commodities that may be imported by sea; no commodious building; no instrument of moving and removing such things as require much force; no knowledge of the face of the earth; no account of time; no arts; no letters; no society; and, which is the worst of all, continual fear and danger of violent death; and the life of man, solitary, poor, nasty, brutish, and short. . . .

To this war of every man against every man, this also is consequent: that nothing can be unjust. The notions of right and wrong, justice and injustice, have there no place. Where there is no common power, there is no law; where no law, no injustice. Force and fraud are in war the two cardinal virtues. Justice and injustice are none of the faculties neither of the body nor mind. If they were, they might be in a man that were alone in the world, as well as his senses and passions. They are qualities that relate men in society, not in solitude. It is consequent also to the same condition that there be no propriety, no dominion, no "mine" and "thine" distinct; but only that to be every man's, that he can get; and for so long as he can keep it. . . .

Of the Causes, Generation, and Definition of a Commonwealth

The final cause, end, or design of men, who naturally love liberty and dominion over others, in the introduction of that restraint upon themselves in which we see them live in commonwealths, is the foresight of their own preservation, and of a more contented life thereby; that is to say, of getting themselves out from that miserable condition of war, which is necessarily consequent . . . to the natural passions of men, when there is no visible power to keep them in awe, and tie them by fear of punishment to the performance of their covenants, and observation of [the] laws of nature. . . .

For the laws of nature, as *justice, equity, modesty, mercy,* and, in sum, *doing to others, as we would be done to,* of themselves, without the terror of some power to cause them to be observed, are contrary to our natural passions, that carry us to partiality, pride, revenge, and the like. And covenants without the sword are but words, and of no strength to secure a man at all. Therefore notwithstanding the laws of nature, which every one hath then kept, when he has the will to keep them, when he can do it safely, if there be no power erected, or not great enough for our security, every man will, and may lawfully rely on his own strength and art, for caution against all other men. . . .

The only way to erect such a common power as may be able to defend [men] from the invasions of foreigners and the injuries of one another, and thereby secure them in such sort as that by their own industry, and by the fruits of the earth, they may nourish themselves and live contentedly; is, to confer all their power and strength upon one man, or upon one assembly of men, that may reduce all their wills, by plurality of voices, unto one will: which is as much as to say, to appoint one man, or assembly of men, to bear their person; and every one to own and acknowledge himself to be author of whatsoever he that so beareth their person, shall act . . . in those things which concern the common peace and safety; and therein to submit their wills, every one to his will, and their judgment to his judgment. This is more than consent, or concord; it is a real unity of every man with every man, in such manner as if every man should say to every man:

> I authorize and give up my right of governing myself to this man, or to this assembly of men, on this condition: that thou give up thy right to him and authorize all his actions in like manner.

This done, the multitude so united in one person is called a COMMONWEALTH, in Latin CIVITAS. This is the generation of that great LEVIATHAN, or rather, to speak more reverently, or that *mortal god,* to which we owe under the *immortal God,* our peace and defense. For by this authority, given him by every particular man in the commonwealth, he hath the use of so much power and strength conferred on him, that by terror thereof, he is enabled to perform the wills of them all, to peace at home, and mutual aid against their enemies abroad. And in him consisteth the essence of the commonwealth, which, to define it, is ONE PERSON, OF WHOSE ACTS A GREAT MULTITUDE, BY MUTUAL COVENANTS WITH ONE ANOTHER, HAVE MADE THEMSELVES EVERY ONE THE AUTHOR, TO THE END HE MAY USE THE STRENGTH AND MEANS OF THEM ALL, AS HE

SHALL THINK EXPEDIENT, FOR THEIR PEACE AND COMMON DEFENSE. And he that carrieth this person is called *Sovereign* and said to have *sovereign power;* and every one besides, his *subject*. . . .

Of the Rights of Sovereigns by Institution

From the institution of a commonwealth are derived all the *rights* and *faculties* of him, or them, on whom sovereign power is conferred by the consent of the people. . . .

Because they convenanted, it is to be understood, they are not obliged by any former covenants. . . . And consequently, . . . being bound by covenant to own the actions and judgments of a [commonwealth], they cannot lawfully make a new covenant, amongst themselves, to be obedient to any other. . . . And therefore, they that are subjects of a monarch cannot without his leave cast off monarchy and return to the confusion of a disunited multitude. . . .

Secondly, because the right of bearing the person of them all, is given to him they make sovereign, by covenant only of one to another, and not of him to any of them, there can happen no breach of covenant on the part of the sovereign: and consequently none of his subjects, by any pretense of forfeiture, can be freed from his subjection. . . .

Thirdly, because the major part hath by consenting voices declared a sovereign, he that dissented must now consent with the rest; that is, be contented to avow all the actions he shall do, or else be justly destroyed by the rest. For if he voluntarily entered into the congregation of them that were assembled, he sufficiently declared thereby his will, and therefore tacitly covenanted to stand to what the major part should ordain. . . .

Fourthly, because every subject is by this institution author of all the actions and judgments of the sovereign, . . . it follows that whatsoever he doth it can be no injury to any of his subjects, nor ought he to be by any of them accused of injustice. For . . . by this institution of a commonwealth every particular man is author of all the sovereign doth. . . .

Fifthly, and consequently, . . . no man that hath sovereign power can justly be put to death, or otherwise punished . . . by his subjects in any manner. For seeing every subject is author of the actions of his sovereign, he punisheth another for the actions committed by himself. . . .

Sixthly, it is annexed to the sovereignty to be judge of what opinions and doctrines are averse and what conducive to peace; and consequently, on what occasions, how far, and what men are to be trusted withal, in speaking to multitudes of people, and who shall examine the doctrines of all books before they are published. . . .

Seventhly, is annexed to the sovereignty, the whole power of prescribing the rules whereby every man may know what goods he may enjoy, and what actions he may do, without being molested by any of his fellow subjects; this is [called] *propriety*. For before constitution of sovereign power . . . all men had a right to all things, which necessarily causeth war; therefore this propriety, being necessary to peace, and depending on sovereign power, is the act of that power, [for] the public peace. . . .

Eighthly, is annexed to the sovereignty, the right of judicature, of hearing and deciding all controversies, which may arise concerning law . . . or fact. . . .

Ninthly, is annexed to the sovereignty, the right of making war and peace with other nations, . . . of judging when it is for the public good, and how great forces are to be assembled, armed, and paid for that end. . . .

JOHN LOCKE: SECOND TREATISE ON GOVERNMENT (1690)

From *Works* (London, 1823), 5:339–347, 378–396, 426–427, 464–471.

On the State of Nature

To understand political power aright, and derive it from its original, we must consider what estate all men are naturally in, and that is, a state of perfect freedom to order their actions, and dispose of their possessions and persons as they think fit, within the bounds of the law of nature, without asking leave or depending upon the will of any other man.

A state also of equality, wherein all the power and jurisdiction is reciprocal, no one having more than another, there being nothing more evident than that creatures of the same species and rank, promiscuously born to all the same advantages of nature, should also be equal one amongst another without subordination or subjection, unless the lord and master of them all should, by any manifest declaration of his will, set one above another, and confer on him, by an evident and clear appointment, an undoubted right to dominion and sovereignty. . . .

The state of nature has a law of nature to govern it, which obliges everyone, and reason, which is that law, teaches all mankind who will but consult it, that being all equal and independent, no one ought to harm another in his life, health, liberty, or possessions. For men being all the workmanship of one omnipotent and infinitely wise Master; all the servants of one sovereign Master, sent into the world by His order and about His business, they are His property, whose workmanship they are, made to last during His, not one another's pleasure. And, being furnished with like faculties, sharing all in one community of nature, there cannot be supposed any such subordination among us that may authorize us to destroy one another, as if we were made for one another's uses, as the inferior ranks of creatures are for ours. Everyone, as he is bound to preserve himself, and not to quit his station willfully, so by the like reason, when his own preservation comes not in competition, ought he as much as he can, to preserve the rest of mankind, and not unless it be to do justice on an offender, take away, or impair the life or what tends to be the preservation of the life, liberty, health, limb, or goods of another. . . .

Of the Beginnings of Political Societies

Men being, as has been said, by nature all free, equal, and independent, no one can be put out of this estate and subjected to the political power of another without his own consent. The only way whereby anyone divests himself of his natural liberty and puts on the bonds of civil society, is by agreeing with other men, to join and unite into a community for their comfortable, safe, and peaceable living one amongst another, in a secure enjoyment of their properties, and a greater security against any that are not of it. This any number of men may do, because it injures not the freedom of the rest; they are left, as they were, in the liberty of the state of nature. When any number of men have so consented to make one community or government, they are thereby presently incorporated, and make one body politic, wherein the majority have a right to act and conclude the rest. . . .

Thus every man, by consenting with others to make one body politic under one government, puts himself under an obligation to everyone of that society to submit to the determination of the majority, and to be concluded by it. . . .

Of the Ends of Political Society and Government

If man in the state of nature be so free as has been said, if he be absolute lord of his own person and possessions, equal to the greatest and subject to nobody, why will he part with his freedom? why will he give up this empire and subject himself to the domination and control of any other power? To which it is obvious to answer, that though in the state of nature he hath such a right, yet the enjoyment of it is very uncertain, . . . for all being kings as much as he, every man his equal, and the greater part no strict observers of equity and justice, the enjoyment of [his] property is very unsafe, very insecure. This makes him willing to quit this condition . . . and join in society with others who are already united . . . for the mutual preservation of their lives, liberties and estates, which I call by the general name, *property*.

The great and chief end, therefore, of men uniting into commonwealths . . . is the preservation of their property; to which in the state of nature there are many things wanting.

First, there wants an established, settled, known law, received and allowed by common consent to be the standard of right and wrong, and the common measure to decide all controversies between them. For though the law of nature be plain and intelligible to all rational creatures, yet men, being biased by their interest, as well as ignorant for want of study of it, are not apt to allow of it as a law binding to them in the application of it to their particular cases.

Secondly, in the state of nature there wants a known and indifferent judge with authority to determine all differences according to the established law. For everyone in that state, being both judge and executioner of the law of nature, men being partial to themselves, passion and revenge is very apt to carry them too far, and with too much heat in their own cases, as well as negligence and unconcernedness, make them too remiss in other men's.

Thirdly, in the state of nature there often wants power to back and support the sentence when right, and to give it due execution. [Those] who offend will seldom fail where they are able by force to make good their injustice. Such resistance many times makes the punishment dangerous, and frequently destructive to those who attempt it.

Thus mankind, notwithstanding all the privileges of the state of nature, . . . are quickly driven into society. Hence it comes to pass that we seldom find any number of men live any time together in this state. The inconveniences that they are therein exposed to by the irregular and uncertain exercise of the power every man has of punishing the transgressions of others, makes them take sanctuary under the established laws of government, and therein seek the preservation of their property. It is this makes them so willingly give up every one his single power of punishing to be exercised by such alone as shall be appointed to it amongst them and by such rules as the community . . . shall agree on. And in this we have the original right and rise of both the legislative and executive power as well as of the governments themselves. . . .

But though men when they enter into society give up the equality, liberty, and executive power they had in the state of nature into the hands of the society, to be so far disposed of by the legislative as the good of society shall require, yet it being only with an intention in everyone the better to preserve himself, his liberty and property, . . . the power of the society . . . can never be supposed to extend farther than the common good, but is obliged to secure everyone's property by providing against those three defects above mentioned that made the state of nature so unsafe and uneasy. So whoever has the legislative or supreme power of any commonwealth is bound to govern by established standing laws, promulgated and known to the people, and not by extemporary decrees. . . . [and] directed to no other end but the peace, safety, and public good of the people. . . .

Of the Subordination of the Powers of the Commonwealth

Though in a constituted commonwealth . . . there can be but one supreme power, which is the legislative, to which all the rest are and must be subordinate, yet the legislative being only a fiduciary power to act for certain ends, there remains still in the people a supreme power to remove or alter the legislative, when they find the legislative act contrary to the trust reposed in them. For all power given with trust for the attaining an end being limited by that end, whenever that end is manifestly neglected or opposed, the trust must necessarily be forfeited, and the power devolve into the hands of those that gave it, who may place it anew where they shall think best for their safety and security. And thus the community perpetually retains a supreme power of saving themselves from the attempts and designs of anybody, even of their legislators, whenever they shall be so foolish or so wicked as to lay and carry on designs against the liberties and properties of the subject. For no man or society of men having a power to deliver up their preservation, or consequently the means of it, to the absolute will and arbitrary dominion of another, whenever anyone shall go about to bring them into such a slavish condition, they will always have a right to preserve what they have not a power to part with, and to rid themselves of those who invade this fundamental, sacred, and unalterable law of self-preservation. . . .

Of Tyranny

. . . It is a mistake to think this fault is proper only to monarchies. Other forms of government are liable to it as well, . . . for whenever the power . . . put in any hands for the government of the people and the preservation of their properties is applied to other ends, and made use of to impoverish, harass, or subdue them to the arbitrary and irregular commands of those that have it, there it presently becomes tyranny, whether those that thus use it are one or many. Thus we read of the thirty tyrants at Athens, as well as one at Syracuse. . . .

Whenever law ends, tyranny begins, if the law be transgressed to another's harm; and whosoever in authority exceeds the power given him by the law, and makes use of the force he has under his command to compass that upon the subject which the law allows not, ceases in that to be a magistrate, and acting without authority may be opposed, as any other man who by force invades the right of another. . . .

May the commands, then, of a prince be opposed? . . . May he be resisted, as often as anyone shall find himself aggrieved, and but imagine he has not right done him? This will unhinge and overturn all politics, and instead of government and order, leave nothing but anarchy and confusion. . . . Force is to be opposed to nothing but to unjust and unlawful force. . . . Any other opposition . . . draws . . . a just condemnation, both from God and man.

JEAN JACQUES ROUSSEAU: THE SOCIAL CONTRACT (1762)

Contrat social (Paris, 1762), pp. 236–238, 243–247, 252–253, 294–297.

Subject of the First Book

Man is born free; and everywhere he is in chains. One thinks himself the master of others, but remains a greater slave than they. How did this change come about? I don't know. What can make it legitimate? That question I think I can answer.

Were I to consider force alone and the effects derived from it, I should say: "As long as a people is compelled to obey and does so, it does well; as soon as it can shake off the yoke, and does so, it does even better. For, in recovering its liberty by the same right by which it was removed, either it is justified in regaining it, or there was no justification for those who took it away." The social order is a sacred right, which is the basis of all the others. This right, however, does not come from nature; it must therefore be founded on conventions. We must then find out what those conventions are. . . .

The Right of the Strongest

The strongest is never strong enough to be always the master, unless he converts strength into right, and obedience into duty. Hence the right of the strongest, which sounds ironical, is really established as a principle. But can we not explain this phrase? Might is physical power, but I myself fail to see that it has any moral effect. To yield to force is an act of necessity, not will, an act of prudence, at most. In what sense can it become a duty?

Let us suppose for a moment that this so-called right exists. In my opinion, the only result is pure nonsense; for if might makes right, the effect changes with the cause, and every force that is greater than the original succeeds to its right. As soon as it becomes possible to disobey with impunity, one disobeys legitimately. If the strongest is always in the right, then the only thing to do is to work to become the strongest. But what kind of a right is it that disappears when might fails? . . . Clearly, the word *right* adds nothing to force and has no meaning here.

Obey the powers that be. If this means: Yield to superior force, the precept is good, but unnecessary. I dare say it will never be violated. I admit that all power comes from God, but so does sickness. Does that mean we should not call the doctor? A robber surprises me on the edge of a wood: Am I compelled not only to give up my money, but am I also in conscience obliged to hand it over even if I could keep it? Certainly the gun he holds is also a force.

Let us therefore admit that might does not make right, and that we are obliged to obey only those powers that are legitimate. In which case, my original question stands. . . .

The Social Compact

Let us suppose mankind arrived at a point where obstacles which threaten his preservation in the state of nature outweigh the force of each individual to maintain himself in that state. That primitive condition can then no longer continue and man would perish if he did not change his way of life.

Now, since men cannot create new forces but only combine existing ones, they have no other means of preservation than to form, by congregating together, a sum of forces great enough to overcome the resistance; then bring them into play by a single motive power and make them act in concert.

This sum of forces can arise only by the concurrence of many people. But since the strength and freedom of each man constitute the chief instruments of his self-preservation, how can he pledge them without harming his own interests and neglecting the care he owes himself? This difficulty . . . may be stated as follows: To find a form of association that will defend and protect with the common force the person and property of each associate, and in which each, while uniting with the others, shall still obey himself alone and remain as free as before—this is the fundamental problem for which the Social Contract provides the solution.

The clauses of this contract are so determined by the nature of the act that the slightest modification would make them null and void; so that, although they may never have been formally enunciated, they are everywhere the same, everywhere tacitly admitted and recognized, until, upon the violation of the social compact, each regains his original rights and resumes his natural liberty, in favor of which he had renounced it.

Properly understood, these clauses may be reduced to one: The total alienation of each associate, with all his rights, to the entire community. For, in the first place, as each person gives himself absolutely, the conditions are the same for all; and this being so, no one has any interest in making it onerous for the others. . . .

In giving himself to all, each man gives himself to no one; and since there is no associate over whom he does not acquire the same right as he ceded, an equivalent is gained for all that is lost, plus increased force to keep what is his. If we then discard from the social compact what is nonessential, we find it reduced to the following:

EACH OF US PUTS HIS PERSON AND ALL HIS POWER IN COMMON UNDER THE SUPREME DIRECTION OF THE GENERAL WILL, AND IN OUR CORPORATE CAPACITY WE RECEIVE EACH MEMBER AS AN INDIVISIBLE PART OF THE WHOLE.

Immediately, in place of the individual personalities of each of the contracting parties, this act of association creates a moral and collective body, composed of as many members as the assembly has voters; from this act it receives its unity, its identity, its life, and its will. This public person, formed of the union of all the other persons, formerly took the name *city,* and now *republic* or *body politic;* by its members it is known as the *State* when passive, the *Sovereign* when active, and a *Power* when compared to others like itself. Those associated in it take collectively the name of *people,* individually the name of *citizen,* as sharing the sovereign power; or *subject,* as being under the laws of the state. . . .

The Sovereign

. . . The body politic or Sovereign, deriving its existence wholly from the sanctity of the contract, can never bind itself . . . to do anything derogatory to this first act: for instance, to alienate any part of itself or submit to another sovereign. Violation of the act by which it exists would be self-annihilation; and that which is nothing can create nothing. . . .

As soon as the multitude is thus united in one body, it is not possible to offend one of its members without attacking the body, or to offend against the body without the members resenting it. . . . Further, the Sovereign, being wholly formed of the members comprising it, has not and cannot have any interest contrary to theirs. . . .

But the same is not true of subjects toward the Sovereign. . . . Nothing binds them to their promise unless measures are taken to assure their fidelity. Each individual, in fact, may have a particular will contrary to . . . the general will which he has as a citizen; . . . his naturally independent existence may make him look upon his debt to the common cause as a gratuitous contribution . . . or look upon the moral entity of the State as a legal fiction. . . . He would enjoy his rights of a citizen and not fulfill his duties as a subject. The spread of such iniquity would destroy the body politic.

In order not to be an empty formula, therefore, the social compact tacitly includes the following engagement, which alone gives force to the rest: *Whosoever refuses to obey the general will shall be compelled to do so by the whole body:* if this means anything, it means that he will be forced to be free. This is the condition which, by giving each citizen to his country, secures him against all personal dependence; this is the key to the working of the political machine; this alone legitimizes civil undertakings, which would otherwise be absurd, tyrannical, and liable to great abuse.

The Civil State

The passage from the state of nature to the civil state produces a remarkable change in man, substituting justice for interest in his conduct and giving his actions a moral dimension they previously lacked. Only when the voice of duty replaces physical impulse, and mere appetite, does man . . . find himself forced to act on other principles and consult his reason before yielding to desire. Although he gives up some of the advantages he had in nature, his gains are so great, his faculties so stimulated and enhanced, his ideas so expanded, his sentiments so ennobled, and his whole spirit so elevated that—if the abuses of his new situation did not often degrade him below his previous condition—he would continually bless the happy moment when he left it once and for all to become, instead of a dull, stupid animal, an intelligent being—a man.

Drawing up the ledger in simple terms: What man loses by the social contract is his natural freedom and an unlimited right to whatever tempts him or whatever he can get; what he gains is civil liberty and the ownership of all his possessions. In order not to be deceived in these calculations, we must distinguish between *natural* liberty, limited only by the individual's strength, and *civil* liberty, which is limited by the general will; also, *possession,* which results from brute force or the first-come principle, and *property,* which is based on a positive title.

Over and above all this, on the credit side of the civil state, we might add *moral* freedom, which alone makes man truly his own master: for the impulse of appetite by itself is slavery, but obedience to self-imposed law is freedom. . . .

Whether the General Will Is Fallible

From the above it follows that the general will is always right and tends to the public good; but it does not follow that the people's deliberations are also infallible. Our will is always for our own good, but we do not always see what that is. Although never corrupted, the people is often deceived: only then does it seem to will what is bad.

There is a big difference between the will of everybody and the general will; the latter considers the common interest only, whereas the former takes private interests into account; it is merely the sum of the particular wills. But take away from these wills the plusses and minuses that cancel each other out and the general will is what remains.

If the people are sufficiently informed before holding their deliberations and if the citizens have not been in contact with each other, the general will will result from the total number of small differences and the decisions will always be good. But when factions and partial associations arise at the expense of the whole, then the will of each of these groups becomes general with respect to its members, but individual with respect to the state; and instead of having as many votes as men, there are only as many votes as there are groups or associations. . . . In order to have an expression of the general will, therefore, there should be no partial societies within the state and each citizen should vote only in accordance with his own views. . . .

The Abuse of Government and Its Tendency to Degenerate

Since the particular will always acts in opposition to the general will, the government continually exerts itself against the Sovereignty. The greater this exertion, the more the constitution changes, and since there is no other corporate will to create an equilibrium by resisting the will of the prince, he must sooner or later suppress the Sovereign and break the social compact. This is the inevitable defect which, from the very birth of the body politic, tends ceaselessly to destroy it, just as aging and death destroy the human body. . . .

The dissolution of the state may come about in one of two ways: first, when the prince, ceasing to administer it in accord with the laws, usurps the Sovereign power. Then . . . the great State is dissolved and another formed within it, composed solely of the members of the government, which then becomes a simple master or tyrant over the rest of the people. As soon as the government usurps the Sovereignty, the social compact is broken and the citizens, by right, recover their natural liberty, being now forced—but not obliged—to obey.

The same thing happens when the members of the government severally usurp the power they should exercise only as a body. . . . Then there are as many princes as magistrates, and the State . . . either perishes or changes its form.

When the State is dissolved, the abuse of government, whatever it is, is known as *anarchy;* democracy degenerates into *mobocracy,* aristocracy into *oligarchy,* and I would add royalty into *tyranny,* except that this word is ambiguous and needs explanation: In popular language, a tyrant is a king who governs by violence, without regard for law or justice. To be more exact, a tyrant is one who arrogates to himself the royal authority without having any right to it. . . . To make a finer distinction, therefore, I call him who usurps the royal authority a tyrant, and him who usurps the Sovereign power a *despot*. The former thrusts himself in, contrary to the laws, to govern in accordance with the laws, whereas the despot sets himself *above* the laws. Thus a tyrant cannot be a despot, but a despot is always a tyrant.

BIBLIOGRAPHY OF SOURCES
(by chapters)

Chapter 1. THE ANCIENT NEAR EAST.

Instructions of the Vizier Ptah-Hotep to His Son, in A. Erman, *Die Literatur der Aegypter* (Leipzig, 1923).

The Epic of Gilgamesh, in M. Jastrow, *Religion of Babylonia and Assyria* (Boston, 1898).

Hammurabi's Law Code, in C.H.W. Johns, *Babylonian and Assyrian Laws, Contracts, and Letters* (New York, 1904).

The Bible, King James Version, Genesis 1–3; Deuteronomy 5–7; Isaiah 65.

Chapter 2. THE CLASSICAL AGE OF GREECE.

Sophocles, *Antigone,* in *Tragedies,* ed. E. Coleridge (London, 1905).

Thucydides, *The Peloponnesian War,* trans. Jowett (London, 1881).

Plato, *Dialogues,* trans. Jowett (London, 1892).

———. *The Republic,* trans. Jowett (London, 1888).

Aristotle, *Politics,* Trans. Jowett (2 vols., Oxford, 1885).

Plutarch, "Life of Lycurgus," in *Ideal Commonwealths,* ed. H. Morley (London, 1889).

Chapter 3. ROME: THE AUGUSTAN AGE.

Cicero, *Treatises,* trans. C.D. Yonge (London, 1853).

Augustus, *Res gestae divi Augusti,* ed. Mommsen (Berlin, 1883).

Tacitus, *Annals,* trans. Church and Bodribb (London, 1877).

Suetonius, *History of the Twelve Caesars,* trans. P. Holland (London, 1899).

Pliny, *Correspondence with Trajan,* ed. E.G. Hardy (London, 1889).

Lucretius, *On the Nature of Things,* trans. H. Munro (Cambridge, 1891).

Epictetus, *Discourses,* in J.H. Robinson, ed., *Readings in European History* (New York, 1904).

Marcus Aurelius, *Meditations,* trans. G. Long (New York, 1900).

Chapter 4. ROME: THE CHALLENGE OF CHRISTIANITY.

The Bible: Luke 3, 5–6; Mark 15, 16; Acts 7–9; Romans 3–13; Timothy I, 1–6.

Pliny, *Epistolae,* 10:96–97.

Augustine, *The City of God,* in *Fathers of the Christian Church,* ed. P. Schaff and H. Wace (New York, 1888).

Chapter 5. EASTERN ROMAN EMPIRE.

Justinian, *Institutes,* trans. T. Sandars (London, 1874).

Procopius, *Ανεκδοτα, ou histoire secrète de Justinien,* ed. M. Isambert (Paris, 1856).

J. Nicole, *Le livre du préfet* (Paris, 1894).

Liudprand von Cremona, *Werke*, ed. J. Becker (3d ed., Leipzig and Hanover, 1915).
John of Damascus, *Exposition of the Orthodox Faith*, trans. S. Salmond, in P. Schaff and H. Wace, ed., *A Select Library of Nicene and Post-Nicene Fathers of the Christian Church* (2d ser., 1899).
The Russian Primary Chronicle, trans. S.H. Cross, in *Harvard Studies and Notes in Philology and Literature*, 1930.

Chapter 6. MEDIEVAL FEUDALISM.

Einhard, *Life of Charlemagne*, trans. A.J. Grant (London, 1907).
Charlemagne to Fulrad, in *Monumenta Germaniae Historica, Leges*, vol. 1, No. 75, cited in F.A. Ogg, ed., *Source Book of Medieval History* (New York, 1907), pp. 142–143.
———. *General Capitulary on the Missi Domenici*, in Thatcher and McNeal, eds., *A Source Book for Medieval History* (New York, 1905), pp. 49–51.
John of Toul, *Oath of Fealty*, in E.P. Cheyney, ed., *Translations and Reprints from the Original Sources of European History* (Philadelphia, 1898), 4: pt. 3:12–13.
Louis IX, *Definition of Knight Service*, in ibid., 30.
The Truce of God, in Thatcher and McNeal, pp. 417–418.
Mathilda, *Oath of Fealty*, in Cheyney, 4: Pt. 3: 24–25.
Société de l'Histoire de France, *Les miracles de Saint-Benoît* (Paris, 1858).
The Song of Roland, trans, I. Butler (Boston, 1904).
Fulcher of Chartres, *Histoire des Croisades*, in F. Guizot, ed., *Collection des mémoires relatifs à l'histoire de France* (Paris, 1825), 24:3–9, 70–74.
Guibert de Nogent, in ibid., 9:47–49.
Le Koran, trans. M. Kasimirski (Paris, 1859).

Chapter 7. THE MEDIEVAL CHURCH.

Leo the Great, "Sermons," trans. C.L. Feltoe, in *The Library of Nicene and Post-Nicene Fathers* (New York, 1895), 12:117.
The Rule of St. Benedict, in E.F. Henderson, ed., *Select Historical Documents of the Middle Ages* (London, 1905), pp. 274–296.
Cluny Monastery Charter, in A. Bernard, *Recueil des chartes de l'Abbaye de Cluny* (6 vols., Paris, 1876–1903), 1:124–128.
Papal Election of 1046, in C. Mirbt, *Quellen zur Geschichte des Papstums* (Freiburg, 1895), p. 107.
Decree on Papal Elections, 1095, in Henderson, pp. 361–362.
Decrees against Simony, Clerical Marriage, and Lay Investiture, in Thatcher and McNeal, pp. 134–135; Robinson, 1:276.
Gregory VII versus Henry IV, in Thatcher and McNeal, pp. 147–156.
Innocent III, On Papal Authority, in ibid., p. 208.
Frankfort Diet, On Imperial Authority, in Henderson, pp. 437–438.
St. Francis, Rule, in Henderson, pp. 344–349.
———, *Speculum perfectionis* (Paris, 1898).

Chapter 8. THE MEDIEVAL UNIVERSITY.

P. Abelard, *Historia suarum calamitatum*, in *Patrologiae*, ed. J. Migne (Paris, 1855), 178:115–136.

———, *Yea and Nay,* in Robinson, 1:450–452.

Philip Augustus, Charter to the University of Paris, in D. Munro, *Translations and Reprints,* 2:3:4–6.

Aquinas, *Summa Theologica,* in *Opera omnia* (16 vols., Rome, 1882–1906).

———, *Summa contra Gentiles,* in ibid., vol. 14.

Jacques de Vitry, *Student Life at Paris,* in Munro, 2:3:19–21.

J.A. Symonds, *Wine, Women, and Song* (London, 1884).

Chapter 9. OF TOWNS AND BURGESSES.

King John, Charter to Burgesses of Gloucester, in Ballard, ed., *British Borough Chapters* (2 vols., Cambridge Univ. Press, 1913–1923).

The Guild Merchant of Southampton, *Ordinances,* University of Pennsylvania, *Translations and Reprints* (Philadelphia, 1895), 2:1:12–17.

The Guild of London Hatters, *Articles,* in H.T. Riley, *Memorials of London and London Life, 1276–1419* (London, 1868), pp. 239–240.

St. Godric, *De vita S. Godrici,* ed. Reginaldo (London, 1847).

Annals of Lambert, in Thatcher and McNeal, pp. 585–586.

Hanseatic League, Documents, in ibid., pp. 610–612.

Statute of Laborers, 1349, in *Statutes of the Realm,* 1:307.

Chapter 10. THE ITALIAN RENAISSANCE.

Petrarch, *Epistolae,* trans. Robinson and Rolfe, in *Petrarch, the First Modern Scholar and Man of Letters* (New York, 1898).

Cellini, *Autobiography,* trans. J.A. Symonds (2 vols., London, 1888).

Machiavelli, *Il principe* (Florence, 1927).

Ciompi, *Petition,* in L.A. Muratori, *Rerum italicarum scriptores* (Bologna, 1902), 3:146–147.

Chapter 11. AGE OF DISCOVERY.

Columbus, *Journal,* trans. C. Markham, in *Works Issued by the Hakluyt Society,* vol. 56 (London, 1893).

Copernicus, *De revolutionibus orbium coelestium* (1543).

Galileo, *The Sidereal Messenger,* trans. E.S. Carlos (London, 1880).

F. Bacon, *Novum organum,* in *The Philosophical Works of Francis Bacon* (London, 1905).

René Descartes, *Discourse on Method,* in *Oeuvres et lettres* (Paris, 1953).

Isaac Newton, *Principia mathematica philosophiae naturalis* (London, 1687).

Chapter 12. THE REFORMATION.

Erasmus, *Julius II Excluded from Heaven,* in J. Jortin, *The Life of Erasmus* (London, 1808), 3:283–307.

Albert of Mainz, *Instructions to Commissioners,* in Gerdesii, *Introductio in historiam evangelii saeculo XVI renovati,* 1 (supp.), 90–93.

Martin Luther, *Ninety-five Theses,* in *First Principles of the Reformation,* ed. Wace and Buchheim (Philadelphia, 1885), pp. 6–14.

———. *On Christian Liberty,* in *Luther's Primary Works,* ed. Wace and Buchheim (London, 1896).

Luther before the Diet of Worms, in *Library of the World's Best Literature,* ed. C.D. Warner (Boston, 1896), 23:9328–9332.
Diet of Worms, *Edict on Luther,* in Robinson, 2:83–84.
German Peasants, *Twelve Articles,* in ibid., 94–99.
Luther's Response to the Peasants, in ibid., 99–108.
John Calvin, *Institutes of the Christian Religion,* in ibid., 123–128.
Ignatius Loyola, *Spiritual Exercises,* in *Biblioteca dels Exercisis espirituals* (Barcelona, 1930).
Council of Trent, *Canons and Decrees,* ed. J. Wentworth (London, 1848).

Chapter 13. LOUIS XIV.
Bossuet, *Politics Drawn from Holy Writ,* in Robinson, 2:273–277.
Declaration of the Gallican Church, in *Recueil général des anciennes lois françaises,* ed. F.A. Isambert (Paris, 1821), 19:384.
Louis XIV, *Mémoires écrits par lui-même, adressés à son fils,* ed. Gain-Montagnac (Paris, 1808).
———. *To the Merchants of Marseilles,* in Robinson, 2:279–280.
Saint-Simon, Duc de, *Mémoires complets et authentiques du Duc de Saint-Simon sur le siècle de Louis XIV et la Régence* (41 vols., Paris, 1916), vol. 28.
Louis XIV. *Revocation of the Edict of Nantes,* in Robinson, 2:287ff.
Fénelon, Archbishop, *Oeuvres,* ed. A. Martin (3 vols., Paris, 1870).
Voltaire, *Siècle de Louis XIV* (Paris, 1854).

Chapter 14. THE GLORIOUS REVOLUTION OF 1688.
Burnet, Bishop, *History of My Own Times* (London, 1723–1724).
Secret Treaty of Dover, in F. Mignet, *Négotiations relatives à la succession d'Espagne sous Louis XIV* (Paris, 1835–1842), 3:187–197.
Kenyon, J.P., ed., *The Stuart Constitution* (Cambridge, 1966).
Journals of the House of Commons (London, 1803–1863).
Journals of the House of Lords (London, ?–1887).
Statutes of the Realm (London, 1810–1818).
Evelyn, John, *Diary,* ed. W. Bray (London, 1901).
Petty, William, *Economic Writings,* C.H. Hull (Cambridge, 1899).
Cardwell, E., ed., *Documentary Annals of the Reformed Church of England* (Oxford, 1839).

Chapter 15. DEBATE ON FREEDOM AND AUTHORITY.
Thomas Hobbes, *The Leviathan* (London, 1651).
John Locke, *Second Treatise on Government,* in *Works* (London, 1823), vol. 5.
Jean-Jacques Rousseau, *Contrat Social* (Paris, 1762).